SERIALS MANAGEMENT AND MICROFORMS
A Reader

Microform Review Series in
Library Micrographics Management

1. Microforms in Libraries: A Reader
Albert Diaz, editor
(Weston, CT 1975)
Cloth   CIP   ISBN 0-913672-03-3

2. Studies in Micropublishing: A Reader
Allen B. Veaner, editor
(Weston, CT 1977)
Cloth   Index   CIP   ISBN 0-913672-07-6

3. Microforms and Library Catalogs: A Reader
Albert Diaz, editor
(Westport, CT 1977)
Cloth   Index   CIP   ISBN 0-913672-16-5

4. Serials Management and Microforms: A Reader
Patricia M. Walsh, editor
(Westport, CT 1979)
Cloth   Index   CIP   ISBN 0-913672-11-4

5. Microforms Management in Special Libraries: A Reader
Judy Fair, editor
(Westport, CT 1979)
Cloth   Index   CIP   ISBN 0-913672-15-7

6. Government Documents and Microforms: A Reader
Robert Grey Cole, editor
Cloth   Index   CIP   ISBN 0-913672-12-2

7. Developing Microform Reading Facilities
Francis Spreitzer
Cloth   Index   Illustrated   CIP   ISBN 0-913672-09-2

8. Microform Research Collections: A Guide
Suzanne Dodson, editor
(Westport, CT 1978)
Cloth   Index   CIP   ISBN 0-913672-21-1

SERIALS MANAGEMENT AND MICROFORMS

A Reader

Edited by
Patricia M. Walsh

MICROFORM REVIEW INC.
520 Riverside Avenue ■ Box 405 Saugatuck Station
Westport, Connecticut 06880

Z
692
M5
S46

Library of Congress Cataloging in Publication Data
Main entry under title:

Serials management and microforms.

(Microform review series in library micrographics
management; 4)
Bibliography: p.
Includes index.
1. Periodicals in microform—Addresses, essays,
lectures. 2. Libraries—Special collections—Microforms—
Addresses, essays, lectures. 3. Serials control systems—
Addresses, essays, lectures. I. Walsh, Patricia M., 1947-
II. Series.
Z692.M5S46   686.4'3   78-13179
ISBN 0-913672-11-4

Microform Review Inc.
520 Riverside Avenue
P.O. Box 405 Saugatuck Station
Westport, CT 06880
Printed in the United States of America

Published outside North and South America by
Mansell Publishing
3 Bloomsbury Place
London WC1A 2QA, England

To Harry and Solomon

CONTENTS

III ■ Specific Microform Applications: Case Studies

IV ■ The Impact of Microforms Upon Journal Format

V ■ Extended Applications of Microforms for Serials

Appendix

Index

INTRODUCTION

"If you have more shelf space than you can fill, more budget dollars than you need, and every subscription (with complete backfile runs) you're ever going to want - then you don't need microforms." So begins one advertising flyer. What serials librarian could muster up the courage (if one were in such an enviable position!) to say, "Yes, that is exactly my library's situation." But approaching reality, the serials librarian is forced *by necessity* to consider microforms both seriously and soon (immediately). The following is an attempt to analyze factors that would affect the efficient functioning of the microform serials collection, both from a management point of view and from the point of view of the user. The user resistance that is so often cited in the literature is in many cases a product of poor management decisions in regard to facilitating the use of microforms for the reader.

Microform requires a commitment, whether it be in the physical facilities designed for its use or in the policy decisions regarding what is to be acquired on film. It is significant that one become familiarized with microform technology and micropublishing resources before embarking on a microform acquisition program. Pamela Darling, in "Developing a Preservation Microfilming Program,"[1] presents a detailed description of the form this commitment should take in the preservation area. However, her excellent summary and outline of procedures to follow should be required reading for anyone involved with microforms. Especially important is her delineation of adopting policies, developing guidelines and implementing strategies for specific categories of materials. Examples of policies pertinent to the serials field would be:

a) maintaining back files in microform and current files in hardcopy;

b) maintaining both hardcopy and microformats for high demand titles;
c) using microformat for infrequently consulted items.

Whatever policy decisions are made, procedural guidelines must be created for their enforcement. In policy "a," a cut-off date would be required, together with a system for microform replacement at regular intervals. In policies "b" and "c," user statistics would provide the base for decisions.

The fundamental commitment to microforms is far more than the mere assignment of an account number in a budget. The entire program requires planning and forethought. Every detail of the microform information system must be subjected to rigorous analysis through flowcharting techniques. The total impact of the microform system upon the user must be studied, and guidelines and policy decisions formulated according to this. The most suitable equipment and optimum location should be found. The maintenance requirements should be analyzed, as well as the additional personnel required. The decision to implement a microform acquisitions program for serials should be the work of a committee established for this purpose and should include librarians from reader services, technical processing, library administration and the serials librarian. The latter should be prepared to present well researched data at the initial meeting. This procedure should not be interpreted as solely applicable to those who wish to initiate a microform serials acquisition program. It is also intended for those who have already an established microform collection, but without a clearly defined rationale.

The essential starting point should be the collection of data regarding insufficiencies that can be corrected or improvements that can be made in terms of user access. It is only then that the objectives of a microform serials collection can be defined. This would attempt to avoid what the majority of serials librarians presently face, i.e. the microform hydra, out of bibliographical, technical and physical control. (This statement is not intended to underrate the role of the micropublishing industry and equipment dealers in contributing to this condition of a lack of standardization.) Once defined, these objectives would have a retroactive, as well as present, application.

Where to start? A good place to begin would be by defining why microform in certain instances would be a more suitable purchase than hardcopy. The following conditions are thus offered:

a) Is the physical state of the collection one of deterioration?
b) Is there a preponderance of incomplete volumes in the collection?
c) Are there wide gaps in the holdings of individual titles? Are there many years missing from the collection of titles on the whole?
d) Are the volumes mutilated to a point beyond repair?
e) Are copies of heavily used material lacking?

f) What is the hardcopy versus microform cost factor in regard to storage space, binding, replacement, closing gaps, additional copies and the adding of new titles?

g) What are the patterns of use for the entire collection? This, of course, is related to "e," but "g" would more clearly define patterns of non-use (not necessarily a result of "e").

h) What is the availability factor for microform versus hardcopy in terms of collection needs?

The above is only a small sampling of the questions to be asked. Some of these are of general significance, while others are based upon the unique situation within an individual library. The answer at times is only solved by microforms. This, of necessity, severely delimits debate on the issue! One element appears throughout: the need for a thorough examination of the collection and the subsequent compilation of data. Such a study demands time and qualified clerical assistance. The data collected would also aid in the formulation of the collection policies in general.

The underlying implication of positive findings in relation to the preferability of microforms is that through the use of this medium, the user obtains service benefits. Microform should not be looked upon primarily as a means of keeping the serials collection tidy. Its object is use, and means must be found once the collection has been acquired to promote usage and provide an environment that encourages this.

A correlation can be seen between user problems with microforms and the specific microformat (fiche, roll film, etc.) chosen to service a particular need. However, before format problems arise, one must first grapple with the issue of deciding what *journal formats* in the collection would be most suitable for conversion. This is an interesting problem, as journal content and style analysis can prove an invaluable means of choosing the *right* journals to be acquired on microform as suited to the user's point of view. Although suitability in terms of use remains the basic tenet which enables one to make proper decisions, this is essentially a ground level decision, based on the concept of provision — materials are being provided for use in some form. There must be an active attempt to overcome user resistance, stemming from an analysis of the types of material found within a given journal. Through proper choice, an attempt would thus be made to transform provision into active encouragement.

The crux of the suitability problem is the debate concerning microform as an appropriate medium for sustained reading. Even if this is answered in the negative, periodical articles would still easily lend themselves to microformat. However, the page quota in terms of human tolerance is yet to be determined. In a recent *Library Journal* article, William R. Hawken presented an excellent summary of the current state of micrographics and its dilemmas.[2] According to this article, the problem of producing microforms has been solved, but not that of successfully utilizing them. The article proceeds to outline and analyze the problem areas: inadequate reading equipment *vis-a-vis* the nature of the printed page; user needs for print on paper; the lack of simultaneous service to readers due to cost of reading equipment; and the resulting demand for paper reproductions of microform materials. Hawken sees microform as an expensive intermediate stage in the information transfer process. However, he does not deny the value of microform as a valuable means for the preservation of information. An extended field of possibility, he contends, lies in the realm of data application. Sustained reading should not be required of microforms, and in data retrieval, this is not demanded.[3] It is this last point that is particularly relevant to the problem of content analysis. Following Hawken's emphasis on data application, the following might be considered prime candidates for microform: a) journals which contain summaries of scientific and technical data, b) journals containing short, informational articles, such as news publications, and c) indexing and abstracting services.

The benefits derived from scrutinizing journal content according to the "data premise" extends to both the user and library alike. For the library, there is a major saving in terms of equipment. As extensive use is not required, the number of reading stations necessary for simultaneous use would decrease, as would also the need for the extensive reproduction of periodical articles via the reader/printer. These are two strong selling points to anyone who is forced to hear the constant drone of the reader/printer when it is in use, or the constant groan of the user when it is nonfunctional. For the user, time at the microform reading station is reduced; fatigue is minimized; and a positive attitude toward microforms is created. Of course, any library desires these goals. However, the overall benefits of a microform acquisitions program would be vitiated if any of these guidelines were interpreted as letters of law. They are all factors which should be considered in the listing of priorities.

The concept of microform editions of indexing and abstracting services is entirely a problem in itself. These are sets of tools which are used to locate information on a specific topic. By all definitions, they are collections of *data*. However, extensive research on a topic requires extensive searching. The question remains: How many more reading stations would be necessary for this purpose? Such searching would essentially represent a doubled load on the presently available equipment and, as such, would be unfeasible in the usual library situation. Based on experience, it is recommended to retain after conversion heavily used research tools in hardcopy, unless there is a situation where they are fully integrated into the COM subject index of a particular library's main catalog. This, of course, would imply a total cooperation between the COM service organization and the commercial abstracting and indexing services. At this time, such a service does not appear to be readily available, but a consolidated subject index for both monographs and serials would certainly solve a major problem in bibliographic access. For that matter, a consolidated microform index of abstracting and indexing services might work quite well if enough access points were provided. As it now stands, with such an abundance of tools to use for access to periodical and serial information, microform conversion of this type of heavily used item would most assuredly add to user frustration since this would necessitate the user to consult a microform in order to find another microform.

A key issue in the organization of a microform serials collection is whether or not there is a suitable area for reading and storage. One can reach a theoretical decision based on the preceding points that a microform serials collection would be ideal. However, though microforms can save a library 90 percent of the space required by the equivalent amount of bound hardcopy volumes, do not be misled. Microforms do save shelving space, but additional space is needed for a reading area, equipment and allied storage. A preliminary study must be conducted to first determine if such an area would prove feasible within the context of an individual library case.

Once an area has been decided upon (hopefully larger than a closet on the "lower level"), perhaps even adjacent to the serials section, one can then consider the possibilities which the area can offer in terms of units needed, floorspace, etc. According to one's choice of microforms, the room should include space for fiche and film readers, a reader/printer, storage cabinets, a repair and servicing area, and a fiche duplicator. This is not meant to be an accurate listing of individual equipment needs but only meant to reasonably show the amount of space needed, equipment necessitated and personnel required. A microform collection demands constant maintenance. The price of a piece of fiche or reel of film is now quite reasonable; however, one must examine the hidden costs of equipment and ancillary services needed. Yet a properly maintained microform collection in an environment conducive to its use provides information to the user that might not be available otherwise.

Consideration of microform facilities for serials collections must take into account a problem particularly endemic to the nature of serials and periodicals, that of bibliographic control and shelf integrity. A monograph can well afford to be shelved in its own niche in the microform storage area since it is a bibliographic unit unto itself, with its own set of cataloging data to be found in the public catalog. Whether the serial collection is cataloged or not is not the question here. How does one explain to the reader that only odd volumes of a journal he is seeking are in the microform reading room, while others are kept in the main collection in hardcopy? An answer could be found in adequate cross-references and superior bibliographic instruction. Does this, however, overcome the frustration of using an index in the Reference Room, checking the periodicals holding list, requesting the journal in the Periodicals Room, only to be informed that some issues of the periodical are to be found in the Microform Reading Room? The file integrity of periodicals is difficult enough in hardcopy, with the customary separate shelving facilities for current issues, bound volumes, newsletters, newspapers, etc. Indeed, one might ask if microforms would not be a further complication? Benefits to be derived, however, do outweigh drawbacks. The main problem remains one of treatment.

There are a few ways of coping with this difficulty, with each solution exhibiting a varying degree of efficacy. However, whichever way collection integrity is strengthened, a positive attitude on the part of the librarian can only aid the attempt. A total conversion of the periodical collection (where economically feasible) solves the access problem nicely. However, with today's ever increasing subscription costs, it is a hard decision to choose to purchase in microformat what is already held in hardcopy. Hence, the bound volume and microform ''bind'' that most periodical collections are currently experiencing.

The physical and bibliographic control of serial publications has, to say the least, always been a problem area. In most instances the definition of a serial is a law unto itself in each library, ISSN notwithstanding. Over and above this, the physical nature of serial publications lend them to being shelved separately according to format. If not given the proper treatment, microforms will definitely add their share to any existing amount of user frustration. A preventative is needed prior to any bibliographic instruction program that takes place. Several remedies are available, all valid in terms of encouraging use by providing proper information; however, their effectiveness is directly related to the proper choice for the individual library situation.

The integration of microforms into the periodicals collection can take either of two shapes, the bibliographical or physical. A choice is to be made between a microform reading room that functions for both serials and monographs in the library, or a microform serials reading area directly adjacent to the serials collection.

The microtext reading room has obvious advantages in terms of library administration. It is a centralized unit with its own maintenance staff, equipment budget and distinct cataloging. In terms of maintenance and assistance to readers that can be provided, as well as the physical facilities designed for microreading, this situation is decidedly advantageous. One questions, however, its efficacy for serial publications. Would the potential reader dismiss that one citation discovered in an index in the reference room in favor of others to be found more easily available in the bound collection? This happens all too frequently! If it is necessary that a reader be totally dependent on the use of a microtext reading room, the six or seven page article on microform has a low priority in comparison to other articles available in hardcopy.

If the microtext reading room is a necessary evil, ways must be found to encourage the use of serials located there. Much depends, of course, on maintaining a working relationship with the microform librarian whose aid is needed in devising a "bibliographic alert." The integration of hardcopy and microform serial records is a necessity. There must be one central source which indicates the entirety of whatever is available, regardless of format distinctions. This locating device should be preferably situated near the reference tools and the collection. In many instances, serial records are placed in proximity to the main catalog. What purpose can this serve, if these titles are listed in it as well?

Another possibility would be to house the microform periodicals within the collection itself. This can be accomplished by either a partial or total physical integration with the hardcopy collection. The equipment could either be housed in a microtext reading area in proximity to the serials collection or in a special serials microform viewing locale. Partial integration of the collection would entail the housing of microforms in storage facilities within adjacent shelving distance of the bound volumes. Proper relative humidity and temperature have to be maintained here. These conditions notwithstanding, the microfilm/-fiche cabinets would be placed so that ease of cross-reference would be possible to ascertain the sequence of volumes of a journal that are actually totally available. From cross-reference within the bound collection, the user would be referred to the location and obtain the microform (either independently or with assistance) and then proceed to the reading area (either centralized or within the serials service area itself).

A more radical approach would be to house the microforms directly upon the shelf, in proper sequence with their hardcopy counterparts. This method has the advantage of solving the access problem. Using fiche binders, problems of file integrity, so often touted as being an exceptional problem of file microfiche, are avoided by designating separate binders for each title. Microfilm, unfortunately, does not easily lend itself to this process of integration; however, shelf-size storage units are available for microfilm as well.

The principle problems to be encountered in this procedure are the physical storage conditions of the microforms and the maintenance of film quality. The very basis of the above consideration is the assumption that silver halide fiche/film would be stored elsewhere, in conditions conducive to its preservation as an "archival" unit, be it a film master or otherwise. The microforms integrated totally with the hardcopy would be either diazo or vesicular (as being less expensive and easier to replace), and would be expected to deteriorate under usage. Yet this, in its own way, would be a measure of the success of the program: microforms are being *used*. With the necessary provision for systematic and immediate replacement of worn microforms (generated from silver halide masters or produced from fiche duplicators), this procedure implies a thorough-going double standard: separate approaches to silver halide film and to diazo and vesicular. One is attended to for preservation; the others are intended for heavy usage *and replacement*. All microforms need not necessarily be intended as archival; to suit this demand, certain stringent conditions must be met—and heavy usage does not further this condition.

The shelving conditions of most libraries do not meet the requirements for the archival storage of silver halide microforms. However, one must ask if this is needed for a heavily-used collection of serials on microform. Archival storage conditions are of the utmost importance for the maintenance of master negatives and the preservation of rare collections. In the case of periodicals, one could argue for *usage* over preservation. Ideally, the problem would be solved by having one archival copy and producing many duplicate fiches from this. Also, as most micropublishers retain a master negative, it is quite possible to replace damaged film/fiche, since microforms do not so usually go "out of print."

To demand that all microforms meet silver halide standards might not be either realistic or necessary. Given the stricture emphasized above regarding the preservation of silver halide microforms to provide replacement copies on demand, one can justify the utilization of diazo or vesicular microforms for periodicals and serials; rather than indicate a lapse in library standards, this would constitute a recognition of the use factor and the realization that certain types of microforms have their own worthwhile frame of usage. Certainly, one must assure the preservation of the contents of journals and serials; however, one must also be aware of their value in *current awareness,* a condition which in turn might promote their physical deterioration through heavy usage.

A duplicating process for microforms eliminates such problems, as it permits the retention and preservation of an archival microform, while providing duplicates for usage. The present cost of a fiche duplicator is not prohibitive and generally runs less than the price of the average reader/printer. None of the above should be misconstrued as in any way going against the library's rightful insistence upon maintaining the highest standards to insure the physical conditions of its collection. Rather, it is meant to point to the need to understand the nature of individual materials and formats. If current and multiple use is the mandate, then a way must be found to provide many copies in an inexpensive manner. If a library is not able to purchase every microform title it acquires in the twin forms of silver halide and diazo or vesicular, then usage studies should be made to ascertain which microforms are to be purchased in both types (the assumption being that *a single purchase must be, without saying, in silver halide*). It has been estimated that from the time a journal appears in the abstracting and indexing services, it has a normal lifespan of approximately six years. Such a statistic goes far in aiding a library in determining archival and heavy-usage titles, but this determination must also take into account the individual nature of a specific library and its users. Both factors interact in designating heavy-usage items.

As each type of microform has its uses, advantages and disadvantages, so also do both microfiche and microfilm have their individual assets and detriments. It appears that microfiche lends itself more easily to being the format for current materials. Microfiche is less intimidating—being in sheet, or card, form, it resembles a reduced printed page. The reading equipment required for fiche is less expensive, easier to operate and virtually maintenance free. Since each issue of a periodical is contained in a separate envelope, user access is potentially higher. (An analogy exists here between a single issue of a journal and a bound volume.) While presenting less of a problem in terms of file integrity and collection maintenance, the bound volume permits use on a one-at-a-time basis. The storage capacity of a roll of microfilm is, however, much greater, since more than one volume can be fit upon one reel. Microfilm is advantageous for archival preservation, volume runs prior to present use materials and current items of low usage. Perhaps current materials would again profit by being acquired in both reel microfilm and microfiche: the past five years on fiche, and prior years on microfilm. At a given interval determined by the librarian, permanent microfilm copies would then be acquired to replace the hopefully worn fiche.

To return to an earlier set of polarities, hardcopy and microform, it is also to be determined whether current materials are to be obtained exclusively in microform. If journals have art illustrations, maps, etc., the latter question must be carefully scrutinized from the point of view of the nature of the material involved. In any case, upon conversion to microformat, one becomes involved with the question as to the disposing of the hardcopy issues. Unfortunately, most micropublishers are not too concerned with helping libraries dispose of their hardcopy collections. The advantages of converting to microform at one time are apparent as one can offer the entire backfile collection for sale as a unit. Certainly less time is spent, thereafter, in disposing of bits and pieces. Unfortunately, better monetary value is usually obtained by offering individual titles for sale; in balance, the market for hardcopy backfiles is currently a "chancy" one, and with a set price for the entire collection, one makes considerable savings in time. It is up to the librarian to explore the options and decide upon a feasible method, after which it is only a matter of outlining a regular clerical routine.

The acquisition of microforms does not provide any additional solutions to the perennial problem of the disposition of duplicates; rather, it complicates the issue. In general, micropublishers would rather avoid this consideration. The librarian is usually placated at this point in the "sales pitch" with promises of a listing of addresses and names of "interested" back issue dealers. In a time of constrained budgets, micropublishers would be wiser to accept hardcopy credit for microform purchases. Currently, a few publishers do maintain a trade-in subscription rate when the hardcopy is returned upon receipt of the microfilm. This is only a partial solution as it usually covers only journals that they publish. Microforms International Marketing Company does offer exchange programs of microforms for hard copy sets, as well as other variations on the theme, including custom microfilming. One must remember that with dealers, only those titles that are commercially viable are usually accepted for credit or exchange of a hard copy set for one on microform. In terms of dollar value, the hardcopy set is certainly the more costly of the two—should this be exchanged on an equal basis? Again it is up to the librarian to weigh other factors, such as storage costs. One can reiterate by stating that the relationship between hardcopy disposition and micropublishers is at best ''primitive''!

Since 1940, the Duplicates Exchange Union of the Resources and Technical Services Division of the American Library Association has provided a much needed service to serials librarians. An annual directory of participating libraries is sent to each member. Member libraries are then required to send out to all other members at least two duplicate lists per year. Requests are then filled in the order of receipt at each institution. Shipping is by parcel post ''Library Rate'' and if the postage tops 50 cents, the full amount must be returned to the shipping library. The benefits of the system are obvious, especially if one has a growing collection of duplicates primarily caused by microform replacement. The Duplicates Exchange Union provides a viable way of disposing of the duplicates of items supplanted by microform at volume completion intervals as well as of regular duplicates, with the added advantage of being able to secure other items missing from the collection. Unfortunately, the procedures do involve a considerable amount of clerical correspondence. The issues one might need might not necessarily appear on the availability listings. Duplicates that are received are free of charge. One must keep in mind that the DEU functions in terms of what its member libraries have to offer, and encourages participation on the part of other libraries in order to increase the pool of its available materials.

The Universal Serials and Book Exchange is a non-profit agency whose policies are formulated by its constituent member libraries. For a membership fee of $25.00, the library can dispose of all unwanted material and have access to an enormous store of periodicals. One must pay an average price of around $2.00 (quoted catalog price as of April 1977), plus any shipping or mailing costs for materials received. Of special interest to someone with large runs of back volumes for sale is its periodical brokerage service. As a special service, this agency will list as sale items runs of ten volumes or more in return for 10 percent of the sale price and a $5.00 filing charge. This service provides an ideal solution for the disposition of those hardcopy runs replaced by microform and should be considered as a viable alternative to the back issue vendor with specialized interests and particular needs.

The following is a partial listing of micropublishers who deal in periodical and serial titles in microform:

Academic Press, Inc.
A.C.R.P.P.
American Association for the Advancement of Science
American Astronautical Society
American Chemical Society Publications
American Institute of Aeronautics & Astronautics, Inc.
American Institute of Physics
American Jewish Periodical Center
American Psychological Association, Journal Supplement Abstract Service
AMS Press, Inc.
Andronicus Publishing Co., Inc.
Asia Library Services
Association for Computational Linguistics
ATLA (American Theological Library Association)
Bay Microfilm, Inc.
Bell & Howell, Microphoto Division
Biblioteca Nacional, Brazil
Bibliothèque Nationale du Québec
Biosciences Information Service of Biological Abstracts
Brookhaven Press
Butterworths
J.S. Canner & Company
Center for Chinese Research Materials
Central Asian Research Centre
The Centre for East Asian Cultural Studies
Le Centre National de la Recherche
Chadwyck-Healey, Ltd.
Chapman & Hall, Ltd.
Chemical Abstracts Service
The Chemical Society
Clearwater Publishing Co., Inc.
Commerce Clearing House, Inc.
Congressional Digest
Congressional Information Service, Inc.
Congressional Quarterly, Inc.
Consultants Bureau
Consumer's Association Library
Consumer's Research Magazine
Datamics, Inc.
Wm. Dawson & Sons Ltd.
Walter de Gruyter, Inc.
Disclosure Inc.

Editions de l'Avant-Scène
Educational Information Services, Inc.
Elsevier Sequoia S.A.
Engineering Index, Inc.
EP Microform Ltd.
Excerpta Medica
Financial Times
General Microfilm Co.
Gordon & Breach Science Publishers
Greenwood Press
Harvester Press, Ltd.
Heyden & Son Ltd.
ILO Publications
Information Handling Services
INSPEC Marketing Dept.
Institute of Electrical & Electronics Engineers
Institute of Paper Chemistry
The Institute of Physics
Inter Documentation Co.
Irish Microforms Ltd.
Jewish Chronicle Newspapers Ltd.
Johnson Associates, Inc.
Journal of Commerce
Juta and Co., Ltd.
KTO Microform
Library Microfilms
Library of Congress Photoduplication Service
The Frederic Luther Company
McLaren Micropublishing
Maclean-Hunter Microfilm Services
Microfilm Center, Inc.
Microfilming Corporation of America
Microform Review Inc.
Microforms International Marketing Corp.
Micrographics II
Micromedia Ltd.
Micro Publishers Australasia
Mikrofilmarchiv der deutschsprachigen Presse e.V.
Mikropress GMBH
Minerva Mikrofilm A/S
National Library of Canada
National Micrographics Association
National Reprographic Centre for documentation
New York Law Journal
New York Public Library

NewsBank, Inc.
Newspaper Archive Development Ltd.
Georg Olms Verlag GMBH
Oxford Microform Publications Ltd.
Oxford University Press
W. & F. Pascoe Pty. Ltd.
Pergamon Press
Plenum Publishing Corp.
Princeton Microfilm Corporation
Psychological Reports/Perceptual and Motor Skills
Research Publications, Inc.
The Rockefeller University Press
Fred B. Rothman and Co.
Scheffel'sche Verlagsbuchhandlung
Schnase Microfilm Systems
Service International de Microfilms
Society of Automotive Engineers, Inc.

Society of Exploration Geophysicists
Society for Industrial and Applied Mathematics
Somerset House
Southern Baptist Convention
Springer-Verlag New York
Swets & Zeitlinger B.V.
Taylor and Francis Ltd.
TV Guide Microfilm Library
Univelt Inc.
University Microfilms International
Updata Publications, Inc.
J. Whitaker and Sons Ltd.
Wildlife Disease Association
John Wiley & Sons, Inc.
Williams and Wilkins Co.
World Microfilm Publications
Yushodo Microfilm Publications

References

1. Pamela W. Darling, "Developing a Preservation Microfilming Program," *Library Journal*, vol. 99 (November 1, 1974), pp. 2803-2809.

2. William R. Hawken, "Making Big Ones out of Little Ones: Current Trends in Micrographics," *Library Journal*, vol. 102 (October 15, 1977), pp. 2127-2131.

3. Ibid, p. 2129.

General Note

Certain illustrations, which were not deemed as intrinsically crucial to the contents of the pertinent articles, were not reproduced. Correspondingly, all mention to these figures has been excised from the text. Also, the use of the term "microfiche" with regard to considerations of regular and plural meaning has adhered to the authors' original usage.

Note: Since the area of newspapers and microforms is a complete topic in itself, needing a thorough analysis from a multiplicity of perspectives, i.e., preservation, file integrity, acquisition and disposal, usage, etc., it has been deemed as lying outside of the intended scope of the present work. The following articles are intended as introductory material to the topic:

Association of Research Libraries. Committee on Cooperative Access to Newspapers and Other Serials. *Current Foreign Newspapers Recommended for Cooperative Microfilming: A Preliminary List*. Washington, DC: Library of Congress, 1954.

Bryant, Charles R. "Survey of Selected Current and Recent Research Materials on Southeast Asia. " *Microform Review*, vol. 2, no. 1, January 1973, pp. 14-22.

Cole, John Y. "Developing a National Foreign Newspaper Microfilming Program." *Library Resources and Technical Services*, vol. 18, no. 1, Winter 1974, pp. 5-17

"Comment and News." *Microform Review*, vol. 7, no. 3, May/June 1978, pp. 137-138.

Crate, Barbara. "Yesterday's Headlines—Today's History." *Canadian Library Journal*, vol. 31, 1974, pp. 436-438.

Fussler, Herman H. "A New Pattern for Library Cooperation." *Library Journal*, vol. 81, January 15, 1956, pp. 126-133.

Grulioro, Leo. "Soviet Serials on Microform." *Microform Review*, vol. 1, no.3, July 1972, pp. 203-205.

Henderson, James W. "The Acquisition and Preservation of Foreign Official Gazettes." *Farmington Plan Newsletter*, no. 31, May 1970, pp. 1-24.

Marley, S. Branson. "Newspapers and the Library of Congress." *Library of Congress Quarterly Journal*, July 1975, pp. 207-237.

Microform Review, [Serials Issue] vol. 7, no. 2, March/April 1978.

Das Mikrofilmarchiv der deutschsprachigen Presse. *Ten Years Microfilm Archives of the German Language Press.* (Brochure.) Dortmund, 1975.

Montague, P. McC. "Technological Changes That May Affect Newspaper Libraries in the Future." *ASLIB Proceedings*, vol. 25, 1973, pp. 216-219.

National Micrographics Association. *Recommended Practice: Microfilming Newspapers.* Silver Spring, MD: NMA, 1978. ANSI/NMA MS111-1977.

Newspaper and Gazette Report. v. 1—, 1973—.

Newspapers in Microform. Washington, DC: Library of Congress, 1973—.

Rider, Freemont. "A Proposed Standard for the Micrographic Reproduction of Newspapers." *American Documentation*, vol. 1, 1950, pp. 46-50.

Shaffer, Norman J. "Study to Develop Recommendations for a National Foreign Newspaper Microfilm Program." In U.S. Library of Congress. *Foreign Newspaper Report*, vol. 1, 1973, pp. 3-5.

Shoemaker, R.J. "Remarks on Microcards and Microfilm for Newspapers." *American Documentation*, vol. 1, 1950, pp. 207-208.

UNESCO. *Statistics of Newspapers and Other Periodicals.* Paris, 1959.

U.S. Library of Congress. *Specifications for the Microfilming of Newspapers in the Library of Congress.* Washington, DC: Library of Congress, 1972.

U.S. Library of Congress. Union Catalog Division. *Selected List of United States Newspapers Recommended for Preservation by the ALA Committee on Cooperative Microfilm Projects.* Washington, DC: Library of Congress, 1953.

Weber, D.C. "The Foreign Newspaper Microfilm Project." *Harvard Library Bulletin*, vol. 10, pp. 275-281.

Bibliographic Control

Essential for the control of serials titles proliferating on microform are:

Guide to Microforms in Print: Author/Title, and *Guide to Microforms in Print: Subject.* Both are annuals. Westport, CT: Microform Review Inc.

National Register of Microform Masters. Washington, DC: Library of Congress.

Serials in Microform. Annual. Ann Arbor, MI: University Microfilms International.

Additional Readings

Avedon, Don M., ed. *Glossary of Terms for Microphotography and Reproductions Made from Micro Images*. 4th ed. Annapolis: National Microfilm Association, 1966.

Avedon, Don M. "Microfilm Generation and Polarity Terminology." *Special Libraries*, April 1977, pp. 141-144.

Avedon, Don M. "Microfilm Permanence and Archival Quality." *Special Libraries*, December 1972, pp. 586-588.

Avedon, Don M. "The Technology of Micrographics." *IEEE Transactions on Professional Communication*, vol. PC-18, September 1975, pp. 154-159.

Ballou, Hubbard, ed. *Guide to Microreproduction Equipment*. 3rd ed. Annapolis: National Microfilm Association, 1965.

Cluff, E. Dale. "Development in Copying, Micrographics, and Graphic Communications, 1977." *Library Resources and Technical Services*, vol. 22, no. 3, Summer 1978, pp. 263-293

Crawford, Franklin D. *The Microfilm Technology Primer on Scholarly Journals*. Princeton: Princeton Microfilm Corp, 1969.

Dranov, Paula. *Microfilm: The Librarian's View*. White Plains, NY: Knowledge Industry Publications, 1976.

Fair, Judy. "The Microtext Reading Room: A Practical Approach." *Microform Review*, 1; 199-202 (July 1972); 1: 269-273 (October 1972); 2: 9-13 (January 1973); 2: 168-171 (July 1973); 3:11-14 (January 1974).

Gaddy, Dale. *A Microform Handbook*. Silver Spring, MD: National Micrographics Association, 1974.

Guilfoyle, Marvin C. *Guidelines for the Acquisitions, Control, and Handling of Microform...* 1977. ERIC Document 144 578.

Hawken, William R. *Copying Methods Manual*. Chicago: American Library Association, 1966. (LTP Publication No. 11).

Holmes, Donald C. *Determination of User Needs and Future Requirements for a Systems Approach to Microform Technology*. ERIC Document 029 168, July 19, 1969.

James, John R. "Development in Serials: 1977." *Library Resources and Technical Services*, vol. 22, no. 3, Summer 1978, pp. 294-309.

James, John R. "Serials '75- Review and Trends." *Library Resources and Technical Services*, vol. 20, no. 3, Summer 1976, pp. 259-269.

"Microfiche or Roll Film?: A Chart of Comparisons." [Flyer.] Ann Arbor, MI: University Microfilm International, n.d.

Microform Review ("Serials Issue"), vol. 7, no. 2, March/April 1978.

Microforms for Libraries. Elmsford, N.Y.: Pergamon Press, n.d.

Napier, Paul A. "Developments in Copying, Micrographics and Graphic Communications, 1975." *Library Resources and Technical Services*, vol. 20, no. 3, Summer 1976, pp. 236-258.

Nitecki, Joseph Z. "Simplified Classification and Cataloging of Microforms." *Library Resources and Technical Services*, vol. 13, no. 1, Winter 1969, pp. 79-85.

Rice, E. Stevens. *Fiche and Reel*. Rev. 3rd ed. Ann Arbor, MI: University Microfilms Intl., 1977.

Spaulding, Carl M. "The Fifty Dollar Reading Machine... and Other Micromarvels." *Library Journal*, October 15, 1976, pp. 2133-2138.

Spaulding, Carl M. "Kicking the Silver Habit: Confessions of a Former Addict." *American Libraries*, December 1978, pp. 653-669.

Spigai, Frances G. *The Invisible Medium: The State of the Art of Microform and a Guide to the Literature.* Stamford, CA: ERIC Clearinghouse on Media and Technology, 1973.

Veaner, Allen B. *The Evaluation of Micropublications: A Handbook for Librarians.* Chicago: American Library Association, 1971. (LTP Publication No. 17).

Veaner, Allen B. "Microfilm and the Library: A Retrospective." *Drexel Library Quarterly*, vol. 11, no. 4, October 1975, pp. 3-16.

Veaner, Allen B. "Microreproduction and Micropublication Technical Standards: What They Mean to You, the User." *Microform Review*, 3:80-84 (April 1974).

Veit, Fritz. "Microforms, Microform Equipment and Microform Use in the Educational Environment." *Library Trends*, April 1971, pp. 447-466.

Warren Spring Laboratory. *A Specification for Microfiche Copies of Periodicals.* Stevenage, England, 1968.

Weber, Hans H. "The Librarian's View of Microforms," *IEEE Transactions on Professional Communication*, vol. PC-18, no. 3, September 1975, pp. 168-173.

Weber, Hans H. "Serials '73-Review and Trends." *Library Resources and Technical Services*, vol. 18, no. 2, Spring 1974, pp. 140-150.

Williams, Bernard J.S. *Miniaturised Communications: A Review of Microforms.* Hatfield, England: The National Reprographic Centre for documentation, 1970.

SERIALS MANAGEMENT AND MICROFORMS
A Reader

I ■ MICROFORMS AND SERIALS: THE USER'S POINT OF VIEW

INTRODUCTION

A library can only afford to engage in an on-going microform program for the maintenance and extension of its serials collection if it can also correspondingly insure that users will both accept microforms and utilize the collection. User acceptance of microforms is the first hurdle to be overcome. And, concomitant with this, it is of primary importance to ease user acceptance through a careful choice and maintenance of equipment which is well-designed to meet the users' needs, is not injurious to the microforms themselves, and is simple to use.

This chapter presents studies which detail the resistances, successes, and pitfalls experienced by various libraries in their attempts to encourage microform usage. Susan Nutter's "Microforms and the User" spans the overall problems of the environment of the microform reading area, maintenance and administration of the collection, and access to it. The setting up of a microforms reading area is crucial to the success of a microforms program; the best intentions can perish in the wrong surroundings. Some environments are conducive to microforms, some are detrimental, perhaps even lethal to them. This issue is of prime importance. The keynote to be remembered: the needs of *both* users and microforms.

Crucial problems for microforms in libraries are that of the interdependency between users' preconceptions of microforms and the frequency of their use and the twin problems of storage and distribution of microforms. Users' acceptance can only be brought about if microforms are in good condition, and this, in turn, depends on how they are stored, i.e. properly or improperly. If properly stored, their archival longevity varies, in relation to the type of film used, the process of production, storage conditions, etc.; if improperly housed, a deteriorated product is placed before the user for his acceptance. His only response can be negative; this form is not adequate for his needs. The librarian's task must be to insure that this does not happen. And this posits knowledge of the medium as a necessity. The study conducted by Ann DeVilliers and Barbara Schloman on microform acceptance and usage instances the growing trend of users to replace the lack of hard copy with microforms; startling as it may appear, they conclude that some users even *prefer* microforms. Claridge's article looks at the microformat of periodicals from the user's point of view, based on his needs and expectations. Starker's article makes the telling point that user acceptance of microforms has been enhanced by the improved technology of the necessary reading equipment; without this, the user literally cannot *see* the medium. The developments of cartridge-loaded film and motor-driven reader/printers are specifically cited as having aided acceptance. Rapid searching and convenient prints are indeed assets in the struggle for acceptance. Economic considerations are not to be overlooked here (or elsewhere!) either. Space savings as well are involved. Yet these are advantages to the library and the librarian, not necessarily for the user. His concern is for the acceptability for his needs of the materials set before him. He simply cannot use blurred fiche to be read through smudged lenses. Care for microforms and equipment are essential. Kaback cites the improved methods of searching brought about by microform technology. Ease of copying and preparing bibliographic reports are also added to the list of microform accomplishments. Indexes are another area to be considered here, since microforms offer manageable units capable of quick exchange (microfiche) in the reader. With new technology, microforms will be offering further refinements in utilization.

It is at this point that users be involved in the process. Carl Spaulding's article deals directly with the techniques needed for staff training in usage and maintenance of equipment; furthermore, it bridges the problem in the gap of communications with users. If microforms are alien to the staff, they must be (and will remain) even more so to the user. It is this lack of familiarity with the medium and its equipment that must be overcome for a successful microform program. Looked at from the side of the user's needs, machine manufacturers must take into account ease of usage for their equipment and not design machines in the abstract, relying only upon the specifications of the type of microform medium involved. Faulty machines greatly hinder the acceptance of microforms on the part of the user; an ill-designed reader may turn off a well-intentioned user, making him "once burnt, twice shy." It's as simple as this: a well-designed machine for user convenience is a necessity for microform acceptance. The Tannenbaum and Sidhom article provides an overall estimate of the environment requirements and the corresponding user - microform interaction in a large university microform center.

Additional Readings

"ARL-USOE Micro Study Pegs Library Use Problems." *Library Journal*, vol. 94, October 1, 1969, pp. 3394-5.

Asleson, R.F. "Microforms: Where Do They Fit?" *Library Resources and Technical Services*, vol. 15, Winter 1971, pp. 57-62.

Bock, D. Joleen. "Microform Usage in Two-Year Colleges." *The Journal of Micrographics*, vol. 7, no. 5, May 1974, pp. 231-233.

Conners, Richard. "Microfilm: Past, Present, and Future." *Infosystems*, March 1973, pp. 39-41.

Crawford, Franklin D. "The Significance of Micropublishing to Libraries." *Information and Records Management*, vol. 7, March 1973, pp. 62-64.

Gaddy, Dale. *A Research Project to Determine the Student Acceptability and Learning Effectiveness of Microform Collections in Community Junior Colleges*. Washington, DC: American Association of Junior Colleges, 1971. (ED 071 662).

Holmes, Donald C. *Determination of the Environmental Conditions Required in a Library for the Effective Utilization of Microforms*. Association of Research Libraries Interim Report, November 1970. (ED 046 403).

Kottenstette, James P. "Microform Utilization: The Academic Library Environment." *Library Resources and Technical Services*, vol. 16, Winter 1972, pp. 115-116.

Kottenstette, James P. "User Characteristics and Micropublications." National Microfilm Association, *Proceedings*, vol. 20, 1971, pp. 153-154.

LaHood, Charles G., Jr. "Use of Microforms in Libraries." National Microfilm Association, *Proceedings*, vol. 19, 1970, pp. 160-161.

Leisinger, Albert H., Jr. "User Evaluation of Microfilm Readers for Archival and Manuscript Materials/ Special Report." *Microform Review*, vol. 2, July 1973, pp. 177-209.

Lewis, Ralph W. "User's Reaction to Microfiche, A Preliminary Study." *College and Research Libraries*, vol. 31, July 1970, pp. 260-268.

Miller, Roger C. "Why Don't They Make Microform Machines for Libraries?" *Microform Review*, vol. 2, April 1973, pp. 91-92.

Morgan, Candace. "The User's Point of View." *Illinois Libraries*, vol. 58, 1976, pp. 216-219.

Salmon, Stephen R. "User Resistance to Microforms in the Research Library." *Microform Review*, vol. 3, July 1974, pp. 194-199.

Schwarz, Philip. "Instruction in the Use of Microform Equipment." *Wisconsin Library Bulletin*, vol. 67, Sept.-Oct. 1971, pp. 341-343.

Schwarz, Philip. "Learning to Use Microform Equipment: A Self-Instructional Approach." *Microform Review*, vol. 4, no. 4, October 1975, pp. 262-265.

Scott, Peter. "Scholars and Researchers and Their Use of Microforms." National Microfilm Association, *Journal*, vol. 2, Summer 1969.

Spreitzer, Francis F. "Library Microfilm Systems—Past, Present, and Future." National Microfilm Association, *Proceedings*, vol. 19, 1970, pp. 161-164.

Wallace, D. L. "A User Viewpoint on Microfilm with Particular Reference to an Updatable Microfiche System." Microfiche Foundation, *Newsletter*, no. 23, October 1971.

Whalen, Richard. "Microfilm in the Seconday School? Definitely!" *The Journal of Micrographics*, vol. 8, no. 3, January 1975, pp. 153-156.

Wooster, Harold. "Microfiche 1969—A User Survey." *Journal of Chemical Documentation*, vol. 10, no. 1, February 1970, pp. 13-17.

MICROFORMS AND THE USER: KEY VARIABLES OF USER ACCEPTANCE IN A LIBRARY ENVIRONMENT

by Susan K. Nutter

The success or failure of the utilization of microforms in libraries will be determined by the response of the user. Microforms will not reach their full and remarkable potential as a tool of education and research unless user needs are met. Therefore, any system design for conversion to increased and significant microform collections must have as its constant focus the needs and reactions of the user.

Traditionally, microforms in libraries have reflected an administrative solution to the problems inherent in the acquisition and storage of specialized materials. This has resulted in a limited number of applications and, therefore, a limited and exceptional use pattern and user group.[1] Application of the medium for its own merits, accompanied by a sensitivity to the needs of the user, could result in a utilization of microforms that would benefit both the library system and the user. Determination of user requirements can lead from the use of microforms as a storage medium to their utilization as a communications medium for information control and dissemination.

As long as user requirements are poorly defined, the use of microforms will be limited. A review of the literature for significant studies evaluating user acceptance of microforms shows that most studies relate to commercial or governmental applications that have little in common with library applications. Also, the studies run the range from carefully controlled, scientific investigations to whimsical evaluations of voluntary user comments. For the purposes of this article, an attempt has been made to identify the key variables

Reprinted from *Drexel Library Quarterly*, vol. 11, no. 4 (October 1975), pp. 17-31, by permission from the author.

of user acceptance in a library environment that emerge from those reliable user studies. The elements of user acceptance presented here as essential to a systems design for microform utilization in libraries will be limited to elements that libraries can affect and control. There will be no discussion of those elements of user acceptance, such as film resolution, whose control lies with the manufacturers, publishers, etc.

Key Variables of User Acceptance

User acceptance of microforms is absolutely dependent on a total system design that incorporates users' needs. Most microform applications in libraries have failed to grow due to a lack of system design, and the loose application of systems components in libraries has frequently resulted in prejudice against the entire concept.[2] The development and application of user-oriented systems require financial resources often outside the library budget, particularly since few libraries have adequate research and development funds. Unless there are adequate financial resources to provide for a system approach which will allow efficient use of the variety of microforms available today, libraries run a high risk of confusing, frustrating, and discouraging the user who will resist, and may ultimately reject, microforms.

A total approach to library microform handling and use must be developed around the three key variables of user acceptance in a library environment that have been identified in an examination of the literature of user reaction to microforms. These are:

1. The acceptance of microform presentations is controlled by the value of the information to the user. One study has shown that application of microforms in an academic setting has suffered from a lack of truly relevant and current materials and textbooks in microformat.[3] Serious, meaningful uses of the microform minimize the user's awareness of the details of presentation, while frustrating or trivial uses maximize the user's awareness of discrepancies in the presentation.[4] Microform collection development must focus on the new and relevant materials available through advances in micropublishing.
2. The user must have easy access to microform materials; an effective system of bibliographic control must provide identical access to both hard copy and microforms.
3. A microform area must be successfully designed and administered so as to provide a comfortable physical and psychological environment for microform use.

All three user requirements must be met for a successful system design. It must be emphasized that the following are guidelines, not specifications. Creative innovation is vital so that individual needs at a given location dictate the system.

Collection Development

The publishing industry is on the brink of a very rapid expansion in the use of the microformat to a point where it could become commonplace as a method of textual and graphical communication.[5] It has been predicted that microforms will become the major medium for "new information" in reference and research libraries,[6] and that, in the future, "90% of new material will, by necessity, be published and/or available in microform."[7] During the past decade micropublishing has undergone a radical change. Initially, microfilming was thought of as a technique for space reduction or in connection with the need for preservation of materials. However, there are now two types of micropublication—retrospective and original. The former deals with materials which originated prior to the widespread use of microphotography and were not originally intended or designed for micropublication. The latter deals with materials specifically designed and produced for micropublication.[8] Microform applications are pertinent to those areas where the form and content of the material itself offer benefits in microformat which are not necessarily available in hard copy. Therefore, if the choice of medium is that which is appropriate for a particular application, materials in both hard copy and microform should be equally acceptable to the user. The principle of selecting the communications medium offering the greatest benefits should guide collection development.[9]

Creative publishing concepts have led and will continue to lead to enhancement of the information value of materials in microforms. The U.S. government has led the way in simultaneous publication in microform and has become the largest producer of microforms in the world.[10] The government changed from roll microfilm to microfiche in 1963; this coincided with the beginning of a new library concept within the federal government—that of a distributing, rather than a circulating, library or information facility. Documents are not to be returned; they are kept or discarded (such a concept is quite practical with microfiche). NTIS, ERIC, DDC, NASA, and AEC reports are now available in microfiche. The Government Printing Office [has embarked] on a distribution program of depository government documents on microfiche. The DOD federal catalog system (MINI-CATS) is also a microfiche system. Patents, census data, congressional hearings, etc., are all available in microformat.

The government is not the only active micropublisher. Other examples of current materials available in microform include lists, indexes and manuals; directories; manufacturers catalogs; journals; monographs from selected publishers; society papers; theses; college catalogs; annual reports, etc. Since materials are now published in microform only, the information can be made more widely available more quickly and cheaply in microform,[11] bypassing the traditional publishing process. One reason for the growing popularity of microforms for presenting certain new material is the ease with which constantly evolving or changing data bases can be revised or added to. Standards, manufacturers' catalogs, and college catalogs are examples of frequently updated services. Since these are usually bulky, shelf-eating and time- consuming to update, the microforms also solve manpower and space crises in the library.[12]

More innovative library uses will be possible with the advent of SOM (Small Office Microfilming) Products. These are systems made up of inexpensive equipment for every phase of microfilming production, duplication, storage and retrieval. These developments in self-service camera processors will permit the library instantly to create microcopies of material selected by form or subject. The implications for reserve materials, special bibliographies, etc., are obvious.

The choice of a microformat is important. The selection of a type of microform for any acquisition should be based primarily on the nature of the information itself and on the constraints and limitations of the form. If reduction ratio is not a limiting factor, the selection of the microformat used should be based on the characteristics of the information to be reproduced.[13] If possible, an arbitrary confusion of forms within one discipline should be avoided.[14]

Certain types of material are not suited for micropublication. Reference books, for example, should rarely be issued in microform, nor should early printed books which are to be studied in their original state, books of art reproductions, or other books in which the quality of the illustrations is important,[15] although this situation should improve in the next few years. The humanities and the social sciences should remain primarily in book form, while that material which is predominately scientific facts or data should probably be preserved in different forms. There will be an increasing use of microforms for a wide range of purposes, and there should also be many books—it should not be an either/or situation.

Thus, the growing trend toward simultaneous publication in microform and print has expanded the opportunities for collection development. This, in turn, will bring about a change in use pattern. When microform materials are generally consistent with limited usage—out of print material, storage, archives, preservation, etc.—and with a limited user group, the use is *excep-*

tional, not routine. The difference between exceptional and routine use is an important one.Routine use means frequent and sustained use of the microform in satisfaction of numerous individual user requests. There is an intrinsic difference between a system used once by one hundred people and a system used one hundred times by one person. When microform materials are of a current and pertinent nature, the use is broad on a routine basis. Routine use and a broad base of users requires that the user needs be the primary focus for any microform system development.[16] Routine use also necessitates a detailed examination of the considerations of access and environment involved in the implementation of a microform system.

Bibliographic Control

A significant and unresolved problem in the utilization of microform collections is that of bibliographic control. If microforms are ever to realize extensive or routine use, bibliographic controls are an absolute necessity.

Physical and Psychological Environment for Microform Utilization

The design and operation of a microform area must provide a comfortable physical and psychological environment for the utilization of the microform collection. The design must follow a systems approach that places the user needs at the focus of all decisions. This section will set forth the environmental conditions required in a library for the effective utilization of microforms as determined from the user studies.

The use of microforms requires the same environmental conditions, with the exception of lighting, as are found in any well-designed library area. Microform areas must offer facilities designed both for the comfort and service of the user and the protection of the microforms. The proper utilization of a large microform collection precludes the ''stepchild'' approach to the servicing and storage of the microforms. No longer is it acceptable practice to locate an unattended reading machine in a remote stack area, more or less near the microform collection, and expect the user to ''help himself.''[17] A good indication of a library's attitude towards microforms is the ease with which it is possible to locate the microform area! A poor-quality facility indicates a library's disdain for microforms to patrons.[18] Too often microform areas are in the dreary basements of libraries—this relegation of users to work in semi-darkness and remote isolation has scarcely encouraged the exploitation of microforms by the user.

An important consideration in the location of the area is that of centralization vs. decentralization. The decision is a function of the size of the microform collection as well as the administrative organization of the library. If the size of the collection is very small, it may not be economically effective to decentralize. The microform facilities ideally should parallel the organization of the library system and its collections. It has been shown that when microforms are separated from their subject collection because of form, the user's and the librarian's resistance to microform increase.[19] Ideally, microforms in a particular discipline should be located in the same facility as the hard copy in that discipline. Although it is generally true that it is more efficient to centralize microforms in one location, such centralization may effectively discourage their use. The most heavily used microforms are likely to be those located near related hard copy materials. In a library system arranged according to broad disciplines, with departmental, branch or school libraries, it is to the user's advantage to have some decentralization of the microform areas.[20]

Administration of the Microform Area

The responsibility for the administration of the microform area should be with a staff member who is a specialist, one who has a strong interest and background in the format and the equipment.[21] At least one well-trained assistant (depending on the use and size of the area) should be in the facility during all of the hours it is open, to provide service for the material, instruction in the use of the equipment and maintenance of the expensive equipment.[22] Unless staff thoroughly understand microforms, their use and the operation of the equipment, they will not be able to persuade reluctant users as to their real utility and relative ease of use. The staff working in the microform area must have a positive attitude, based on experience and training, toward the medium. A negative attitude on the part of the staff will easily spread to the user, creating barriers to wide use of the materials.[23]

The importance of a staff member's presence in order to provide service for all the hours that the area is open cannot be emphasized strongly enough. User assistance is the most important responsibility of that staff member. Potential users need personal instruction initially—this generates positive attitudes. Most first-time users will experience some difficulty with microforms and unless they are helped through their initial difficulties, they may not try again. The importance of the user's attitude should not be underestimated. Users are confused and discouraged by the various forms of material and the different reading devices required. Careful explanation of the operation of the devices, coupled with printed instructions at the machines and signs indicating which formats the machines accommodate, will enable the user to do a satisfactory and satisfying job.

The actual condition of the microform itself and the equipment will have much to do with the user's attitude towards the medium. Proper inspection of microforms before they are added to the collection is a necessity. Technical inspection should ascertain that the microform is on a safety base carrier and that all images are properly aligned, fully legible, clear, sharp and evenly lighted. Scratches, abrasions, dust and dirt impair both the use and life of the microforms, as well as of the reading equipment.[24] The failure to maintain the reading equipment has an adverse effect on the user; consequently, any microform program must entail routine, careful maintenance of the reading equipment.

Readers and Reader-Printers

Present technology does not permit the design within reasonable economic limits of a reading machine that is both convenient and versatile enough to permit the input of any microimage form, reduction ratio, or image orientation.[25] The specific choice of format and reduction ratios requires both total system planning and experimentation as to avoid the frustration and resulting negative attitude due to the incompatibility between an available microform and the reading device at hand. There must be a match between the various formats in the microform collection and the reading machines in the area.

Just as the library attempts to provide enough reading and study seats for its users, it must provide enough reading equipment for its users. Queuing problems associated with a new service the library is trying to encourage could be disastrous. Deciding how many readers to provide must involve an analysis of the various formats included in the collection, the size of the collection within each format, and the size of the user community.

Among the readers purchased for the library must be a large percentage of reader-printers. The reader-printer is a necessity if microforms are to be widely used. The blow-back capability in microphotography is as crucial as the photocopying capability is in hard copy. Reader-printers meet the user's need to juxtapose several pages of information, to underline, to make marginal notations, etc. The majority of the studies of user acceptance stress the need to have reader-printers in the microform area and point out that the traditional resistance of information users to microforms was significantly overcome by reader-printers. With the more advanced and experienced users, there is an ever-growing requirement for faster, higher quality, cheaper, dry-process, hard copy print capability from microforms. These users foresee a legitimate continuing demand for hard copy from microforms.[26] Based on the evidence from the studies, it appears that, at a minimum, at least half of all the readers purchased for the microform area should be reader-printers.

Hopefully, the readers of the late 1970's will be small and well-designed, taking advantage of the human engineering experiments of the past years. There may never be a "universal reader," due to both the varieties of formats *and* users to be accommodated; hence allowances must be made, in the purchasing of reading equipment, for the whole range of user needs.

Storage and Handling

Microforms require proper storage and care in handling; and these requirements further support the argument that a staff member should be present in the microform area during all operating hours to provide for the proper handling of the microforms, since the user obviously will not be, and should not be expected to be, knowledgeable in this area.

The preservation of the microform collection through proper handling will have a large impact on the user. If the user finally reaches the point of reading the microform and finds that it is scratched, the image is blurred, or the reel broken, he will probably quickly develop a strong preference for hard copy. User acceptance of microforms is dependent on the quality of the microform, maintained through proper handling.

Microform use copies are presently stored (shelved) in a variety of ways, usually dependent on the number of microforms involved. Small collections of microfiche (500-1,000) are often stored in small cardboard and metal file containers, which are easily picked up and moved about. This "shoebox" approach is totally inadequate for large collections of fiche. A method frequently employed for shelving microfilm reels is open-stack shelving—placing reels in their labeled container boxes on regular stack shelves. The disadvantages are strong: space utilization is not efficient; dust protection is not offered; and losses easily occur. Specially constructed slide-drawer metal cabinets are designed to accommodate reels of microfilm or sheet microforms. There are advantages in their use: microforms are protected from dust and dirt; incidents of misfiling and loss are minimized; and floor space is efficiently utilized. These cabinets are designed primarily for medium-sized mixed collections of fiche and film. Large collections of microforms can be optimally stored through the recent development of the cartridge carousel filing system for both roll and sheet microforms. They range in size from single-tiered, desk-top units, housing 5,000 microfiches to seven-tiered, motor-driven units up to 9 feet in diameter, housing more than 125,000 microfiches. The cost of this equipment is justified by the need for compact storage of high use material requiring rapid access.[27]

There is a growing demand for the expansion and upgrading of manual storage files. As collections continue to expand with a subsequent demand for rapid retrieval rates, mechanized files are essential. There is a psychological value as well, both for the staff member retrieving and for the user, of having "push button" access to microform collections. A System Development Corporation study concluded that mechanized carousel storage systems would promote user acceptance of microforms.[28]

General Microform Area

The use of microforms requires the same physical environmental conditions, with the exception of lighting, as are found in any well-designed library area. General lighting should be of low intensity. The lighting should be adjustable, through a dimming device, and, if the area is large, it is desirable to control separate sections in accordance with the needs of the users working in particular areas of the room.[29] If the room has windows, curtains or shades should be provided to control entering light which can interfere with the reading machine screen image (reader screens should be turned away from the windows a full 180°).[30]

Acoustical treatment of the microform area should be provided to reduce noise created by reading machines, typewriters, and conversation. Carpeting will further reduce noise levels.[31]

The area must be air conditioned and have proper air filtration, humidity level, and temperature. Temperature control for greater than average reading room capacity will be required. The temperature must range above 65°F for the comfort of the user and below 80°F for the protection of the microforms. Ideally, the temperature should be as close to 70°F as possible. Recommended relative humidity levels are between 30 and 50 percent.[32]

Duplicating Library Concept

Almost every user study where the prevailing microform was microfiche found that the acceptance of microfiche and a growing preference for microfiche resulted from the operation of a "duplicating library." (The duplicating library concept is limited to microfiche, as only fiche-to-fiche duplications are economically feasible for microform consumers.) Microfiche, as a low capacity microform, is the most appropriate dissemination media (except for aperture cards) for supplying separate units of information to meet specific user requests.

In the duplicating library, the master microfiche is never circulated. Instead, it is duplicated on demand through diazo or vesicular fiche-to-fiche copies, and is then immediately available for the next request. The user receives his own permanent non-returnable copy of the material.[33]

There is a growing requirement, among libraries with large microfiche collections, for low volume fiche-to-fiche duplicating capability. The library can more economically meet multiuser demands for the same document by making and disseminating duplicate microfiche. The library may or may not make a charge for the copy transmitted to the user. It can be less costly to give away a microfiche copy than to circulate a book, since the expensive labor costs are reduced.[34] Doing so eliminates the time and expense of the book-keeping involved in charging the user for the microfiche.

Keeping a master microfiche file reduces loss through theft and wear—security is no longer a costly problem. "On demand" service can be provided without delays—the turn-around time for completing a microform copy transaction is about 30 seconds. (This service cannot be duplicated, nor even approached, by hard copy service.) The implications for interlibrary lending are exciting! For library networks it will be even more advantageous.

The availability of circulating portable readers is much to the user's advantage. The combination of a duplicating library of microfiche and port- able readers available for loan eliminate any disadvantages and emphasize the advantages of the microformat. The user will be happy with the fact that he can get materials more quickly, that the access is guaranteed, and that the materials can be used outside of the library. Once again, every user study that dealt with microfiche as the prevailing microform indicated that the deciding factor between acceptance and rejection was the ability to have fiche copies and borrow readers.

The users like portable readers that are light in weight (under 15 pounds), that can be easily carried, and that are human-engineered so that little instruc- tion is necessary for operation. They want readers that can be used under lighting conditions found in their offices. A minimum loan period of one week is desirable. It has been a successful practice in many academic libraries to make some portable readers available for semi-permanent loan for those groups, remote from libraries, who have a fairly constant need to view fiche.[35] (With the duplicating library concept, these users can telephone their fiche requests and have copies mailed to them.) An adequate suppy of portable readers must be available. Because of the loan period a higher number of portable readers than stationary readers would be required for the user community. A further advantage of portable readers results from the lessening of the demand for expensive stationary readers and carrel space in the library itself.

In adopting the duplicating library concept, the library can optimize its economc costs, facilitate interlibrary lending, keep the master microfiche file intact, provide immediate and guaranteed access, and incur the acceptance of microfiche on the part of their user community.

Guaranteed Access

A significant, and increasing, number of users in one study cited guaranteed, immediate access as the prime motivation in their preference for microform.[36] The variable of guaranteed access has not yet been carefully measured and evaluated in any of the user studies. It is quite possible that this concept may have tremendous impact on user acceptance of microforms.

The increasing number of users and the growing interdisciplinary emphasis of their research have brought about an intense and severe competition for access to library collections. Users going to the traditional library often do not find the items they seek. When outside requests and interlibrary lending requests are added to local demands, acute problems develop, often resulting in a lack of trust in, and support of, libraries on the part of the users. However, libraries can rebuild the user's confidence and support if they can guarantee immediate access to documents in the collection.

Guaranteed access can be provided through the use of microform copies. While it is impractical, very expensive, and probably ineffective, to buy an additional hard copy of every book in the collection in order to provide file integrity, it is possible to provide file integrity economically and efficiently through the use of microforms.

Microform technology has brought us to the brink of a new integrity for library collections. It just may be that the opportunity to have any document in the library's collection, and to have it immediately at the moment of request, will prove to be the most important variable in user acceptance of microforms.

Conclusion

Microform technology offers the potential for major improvements at the user-collections interface. The question is no longer one of *can* microforms be utilized in libraries, but one of *will* microforms be utilized in libraries. If a total microform system is designed with the needs of the user as its constant focus, the answer to that question may well be a resounding "yes."

References

1. Robert R. Grausnick and James P. Kottenstette, *A Performance Evaluation: Microfiche Versus Hard Copy. Final Report* (Lowry AFB, Colorado: Air Force Human Resources Laboratory, 1971), p.1.

2. Peter R. Scott, "Appendix K. Project Intrex and Microphotography," in *INTREX. Report of a Planning Conference on Information Transfer Experiments,* ed. Carl F. J. Overhage and R. Joyce Harman (Cambridge: M.I.T. Press, 1965), pp. 203-214.

3. Dale Gaddy, "Microforms in the Classroom," in *Microform Utilization: The Academic Library Environment.* Report of a Conference Held at Denver, Colorado, 7-9 December 1970, ed. Alta Bradley Morrison (Denver: University of Denver, 1971), p.131.

4. James P. Kottenstette, *An Investigation of the Characteristics of Ultrafiche and Its Application to Colleges and Universities* (Washington, D.C.: U.S. Dept. of Health, Education, and Welfare, 1969), p. F-14.

5. Bernard J.S. Williams, *Miniaturised Communications* (London: The Library Association, 1970), p.24.

6. Klaus W. Otten, "A Hypothesis, Microform Will Become the Major Medium for 'New Information' in Reference Libraries," *Journal of Micrographics* 4 (1971):266.

7. Ladd Z. Sajor, "Preservation Microfilming. Why, What, When, Who, How," *Special Libraries* 63 (April 1972):196.

8. Allen B. Veaner, *The Evaluation of Micropublications,* Library Technology Program LTP Publications, no. 17 (Chicago: American Library Association, 1971), p.3.

9. Kottenstette, *An Investigation of the Characteristics,* pp. G-18—G-19.

10. Felix Reichmann and Josephine M. Tharpe, *Bibliographic Control of Microforms* (Westport: Greenwood Press, Inc., 1972), p.4.

11. Williams, *Miniaturised Communications,* p.79.

12. C. Edward Carroll, "Some Problems of Microform Utilization in Large University Collections," *Microform Review* 1 (January 1972):22.

13. James P. Kottenstette and K. Anne Dailey, *An Investigation of the Environment for Educational Microform Utilization* (Washington, D.C.: Office of Education, 1971), p.8.

14. Peter R. Scott, "Scholars and Researchers and Their Use of Microforms," *National Microform Association Journal* 2 (Summer 1969):126.

15. Rolland E. Stevens, "Microform Revolution," *Library Trends* 19 (January 1971):388.

16. Kottenstette, *An Investigation of the Environment,* p. 2.

17. Hubbard W. Ballou, "Microfilm Technology," in *Annual Review of Information Science and Technology,* Volume 8, edited by Carlos G. Cuadra (Chicago: Encyclopedia Britannica, Inc., 1974), p. 132.

18. *Microform Utilization: The Academic Library Environment,* Report of a Conference Held at Denver, Colorado, 7-9 December 1970, edited by Alta Bradley Morrison (Denver, University of Denver, 1971), pp. 204-205.

20. Carroll, "Microform Utilization in Large University Collections," pp. 22-23.

21.   David C. Weber, "Design of a Microtext Reading Room," *UNESCO Bulletin for Libraries* 20 (November/December 1966):307.

22.   Weber, "Design of Microtext Reading Room," p. 303; Fair, "The Microtext Reading Room: Part V," *Microform Review* 3(January 1974):11.

23.   Carroll, "Microform Utilization in Large University Collections," p.23.

24.   Donald C. Holmes, *Determination of the Environmental Conditions Required in a Library for the Effective Utilization of Microforms, Interim Report* (Washington, D.C.: Association of Research Libraries, 1970), p. 19.

25.   Scott, "Scholars and Researchers and Their Use of Microforms," p.125.

26.   Arthur A. Teplitz, *Library Fiche: An Introduction and Explanation* (Santa Monica, Calif.: System Development Corporation, 1967), pp. 2-15.

27.   This discussion of storage equipment is primarily derived from: Holmes, *Determination of the Environmental Conditions;* Roger F. Wicker, Roy M. Neperud, and Arthur A. Teplitz, *Microfiche Storage and Retrieval System Study* (Falls Church, Virginia: System Development Corporation, 1970).

28.   Ibid.

29.   Holmes, *Determination of the Environmental Conditions,* p.7; Kottenstette, *An Investigation of the Environment,* p.35.

30.   Holmes, *Determination of the Environmental Conditions,* p.7.

31.   Ibid.

32.   Conversation with Peter R. Scott, Head, Microreproduction Laboratory, M.I.T. Libraries, on 10 January 1975.

33.   Lawrence B. Heilprin, "The Economics of 'On Demand' Library Copying," National Microfilm Association, *Proceedings* 11 (1962): 311-39.

34.   Teplitz, *Library Fiche,* p. 4.

35.   B.W. Campbell, "A Successful Microfiche Program," *Special Libraries* 62 (March 1971):136-142.

36.   Susan K. Nutter, "User Preference Studies of Microfiche: The M.I.T. Project INTREX and Barker Engineering Library Experiences," *Running Out of Space—What Are the Alternatives?* ALA Preconference, San Francisco, California, 26-28 June 1975 (forthcoming).

EXPERIENCES WITH SCIENTIFIC JOURNALS ON MICROFILM IN AN ACADEMIC READING ROOM

by Ann M. DeVilliers and Barbara Frick Schloman,
Massachusetts Institute of Technology, Cambridge, Mass.

The MIT Ford Reading Room has been in operation as an official part of the MIT library system since April 1970. The Reading Room provides convenient access to a basic core collection of research journals and monographs in chemistry and biology, duplicating material in the more comprehensive Science Library collection. The room is located in the Camille Edouard Dreyfus Chemistry Building and is open to the entire MIT community Monday through Friday, 9 AM-5 PM; faculty and graduate students in the Chemistry Department and researchers with related interests can obtain keys to the room for use after hours. It is presently staffed by one librarian and an assistant, who work a combined total of 40 hours per week in the facility.

In planning for the room, the decision was made that backfiles of the more highly used journals would be kept on 16 mm microfilm only. This decision was instigated by several faculty members who were aware of a succesful film operation in an industrial chemical library. For the library staff there were two immediate advantages to the use of microfilm: 1) the possibility of acquiring complete backfiles of journals that might not otherwise be available from book dealers; and 2) the ability to store lengthy sets *(1)*.

The complete reliance on microfilm for journal backruns has given the staff of the Ford Reading Room a unique opportunity to observe both user and staff reactions to the microfilm.

Contrary to an earlier impression that microforms would not find acceptance in academe *(2)*, the limited experience of this reading room indicates that a

Reprinted from *Special Libraries*, vol. 64, no. 11 (December 1973): 555-560, with permission of the publisher. © 1973 by Special Libraries Association.

microfilm facility can successfully be integrated into an academic library system.

A user survey has shown a general acceptance of microfilm, rather than the frequently mentioned reluctance of patrons to use microforms *(3,4)*. The survey results were comparable to the experiences of industrial chemistry libraries which have reported general satisfaction with using chemistry journals on microfilm and increased ease and efficiency in doing a literature search in *Chemical Abstracts (5, 6, 7, 8)*.

User and staff criticisms of this microfilm experiment have largely been directed at problems with the available microfilm readers and printing attachments and at shortcomings in film quality. The dry-process reader-printer was a significant improvement over the wet-process machine initially employed; but both staff and users look forward to a more flexible machine, such as the reader described by Stevens *(9)*.

Although the quality of the microfilm acquired has been improving, the staff strongly agrees with Veaner that micropublishing has to be recognized as a complex manufacturing process and that standards need to be established *(10)*. Patrons rightfully expect to find microfilm journal editions to contain what is present in hardcopy.

The Collection

The present book collection contains approximately 1,800 volumes. The chemistry faculty participated in the initial selection of monographs and serial titles. The 100 journal titles under regular hardcopy subscription were chosen entirely by the faculty and represent the basic journals in the field, as well as specialty journals for specific research.

The microfilm plan for the journals has been to acquire complete backfiles in 16 mm cartridges for 40 of the most frequently used titles (including *Chemical Abstracts)* and to update these film runs yearly. For another 30, the film backfiles date only to 1970 because of cost considerations, but are updated yearly. Also due to cost, there are no microfilm plans for the remaining 30 journals, and they are accumulating in hardcopy at this time. The Appendix lists the journals in these three groups.

The microfilm is all 16 mm negative and is loaded in cartridges. The hardcopy journal volumes are removed when the microfilm editions arrive. As of Feb. 30, 1973, there were over 1,700 cartridges in the collection, representing approximately 1,600 cumulative years of journal volumes.

Film Acquisition and Quality Control

As much film as available was ordered commercially. To insure long-term stability of the microfilm after its receipt, an MIT micro-reproduction facility has made spot checks for residual thiosulfate; there has been a minimum amount of rejection due to this.

When the cartridges are received in the reading room, the staff checks the film for image quality, proper film exposure and contrast, complete pagination, and proper labeling. The majority of the film cartridges have been found to be satisfactory, although enough have been returned to make an initial check worthwhile.

In addition, all reels are checked for an index, and the label is marked indicating the presence of an index and its location on the reel. To the dismay of staff and users, many indexes, as well as supplementary material, have been omitted from the microfilm journal editions although they exist in hardcopy. Also, publishers generally do not indicate the presence or position of special material on the reel.

Film Costs and Space Savings

As expected, purchasing journals on microfilm in addition to having hardcopy subscriptions is a strain on the budget. As part of the MIT library system, the reading room does not directly benefit from hardcopy sales to dealers since the money goes into a general fund.

Unfortunately, many titles are not yet commercially available on film; and custom filming is almost prohibitively expensive. For those journals that are available on microfilm, the film costs for the recent year can be as high as the hardcopy subscription although this is not usually the case. Several publishers have offered to trade the microfilm edition for the hardcopy volumes—either on an even exchange basis or at a sizeable discount. Hopefully, the market for microfilm will increase sufficiently to induce publishers to make the journals available on film to their hardcopy subscribers at a cost dramatically lower than the hardcopy subscription rate.

The reading room still has adequate room for a moderate growth in the collection. This freedom is entirely due to the reliance on microfilm for journal backfiles; comparable backfiles in hardcopy could never have been accommodated. For example, the hardcopy volumes for the *Journal of the American Chemical Society* from volume 1, 1879, to volume 94, 1972, occupy about 60 feet of shelf space; each volume measures 11½ inches tall. The comparable film run uses about 12 feet of shelf space, and the cartridges are only 4 inches tall.

Microfilm Machines

During the operation of the reading room, both Recordak Lodestars and Recordak Microstars have been used. The Lodestar, which has a wet-process printer, is being phased out by the manufacturer. It is being replaced by the Microstar which, among its several improvements, has an optional dry-process printer.

The room now has two Microstar readers and two Microstar reader-printers. Equipment costs remain high and have restricted the number of machines it is possible to have in the reading room. It should also be noted that, because cartridges of different manufacturers are presently not compatible in competitors' machines, the initial choice of equipment has to be recognized as a long-term commitment.

The staff performs basic machine maintenance, including changing the toner every 300 prints and replacing the paper and projection lamps when needed. The wet-process printer required periodical flushing of the system and changing of the fluid, a messy and unpleasant task.

Also, the staff has become adept at troubleshooting for machine problems and at correcting some difficulties which previously required a service call. Nonetheless, the staff feels strongly that service contracts are indispensable. Servicing is periodically needed to readjust the optical system, to check for mechanical wear, and to correct printer difficulties.

Copy charges are passed on to the patron. With the wet-process printer it was necessary to charge 10¢ a copy if cash was paid (and 15¢ if charged to an account to cover the copy plus bookkeeping). However, since the dry-process printing attachments were installed in September 1972, the print cost has been lowered to 5¢ for a cash copy.

User Response

The most pleasant surprise has been the ease with which our users have accepted microfilm despite machine problems and gaps in film holdings. Since the opening of the reading room, during the public hours, the staff has kept an hourly count of the total number of people in the room and of the specific number using the microfilm machines, with a breakdown by the type of machine used. These figures have consistently shown that both the room and the film receive active use. There is no reliable measure of the extent of use the room and/or machines receive in the evenings or on weekends. In addition, it was noted that when there was a choice between using a Lodestar or a Microstar reader, the Microstar was invariably selected.

Another measure of user reaction was made in September 1971, and again in September 1972. Machine users were asked to indicate their reactions ("prefer," "accept," or "dislike'") to using both journals and *Chemical Abstracts* on film. A copy of the questionnaire was placed by each machine for a period of a week; written comments were also solicited. The results of the two surveys are shown in Table 1.

Table 1. Users' Response to Journals and CA on Microfilm 1971 and 1972

	1971 Survey.*			
	Journals		CA	
Response	# Users	%	# Users	%
Prefer	54	59%	71	76%
Accept	17	19%	3	3%
Dislike	20	22%	20	21%
Total	91		94	

	1972 Survey**			
	Journals		CA	
Response	# Users	%	# Users	%
Prefer	59	62%	67	87%
Accept	15	16%	8	10%
Dislike	21	22%	2	3%
Total	95		77	

* Machines included 3 Microstar readers and 3 Lodestar reader–printers.
** Machines included 2 Microstar readers and 2 Microstar reader–printers.

The percentage of users who preferred using the microfilm editions of the journals and particularly of *Chemical Abstracts* increased in 1972. Many users said they prefer doing a literature search in *Chemical Abstracts* on film because they find it more efficient and less exhausting physically. Other comments indicated that the accessibility of all journal volumes of a given title make searching more convenient. Enthusiastic users are quite so, giving such comments as "great," 'excellent quality," and "hooray for microfilm."

In both the 1971 and the 1972 surveys, the written comments directed criticism toward machine inadequacies. The Lodestar had been a particular target for criticism. Patrons indicated the Microstars were preferred because of: 1) the zoom attachments (optional on the machine) which make reading easier and reduce eyestrain; 2) a more sensitive advance/rewind knob that improves scanning; and 3) the dry-process printer for its cleaner, faster, and more inexpensive copies. Several patrons wished the Microstar had a surface on which to place a notebook while taking notes from the screen. Also, there was an expressed interest in a more horizontal or an adjustable screen.

Conclusion

Based on operating experience in the MIT Ford Reading Room and on the results of two user surveys, it is apparent that a retrospective journal collection on microfilm can be a substitute for a comparable hardcopy collection. While the results of the 1971 and 1972 surveys discussed here indicated strong support for the use of microfilm, it must be recognized that there is no available measure of the attitudes of faculty and student nonusers who may have a basic resistance to using microfilm, or who may have tried it at one time and found it unsatisfactory.

While users have recognized and appreciated recent improvements in microfilm readers and printer attachments, there remain valid criticisms of the quality of commercially available microfilm. Editorial and technical criteria for the preparation of microfilm journal editions must be established to make them as acceptable as hardcopy editions. Despite present shortcomings, user and staff responses have been very positive. In the short time the reading room has been in existence, some machine and film improvements have been noted, and it remains our feeling that journal collections on microfilm do have a future.

Appendix

Journal holdings in the Ford Reading Room

    I.   Current subscriptions in hardcopy; complete backruns on microfilm:

Accounts of Chemical Research
Acta Chimica Scandinavica
American Chemical Society Journal
Analytical Chemistry
Angewandte Chemie
Archives of Biochemistry and Biophysics
Biochemical and Biophysical Research
    Communications
Biochemical Journal
Biochemistry
Canadian Journal of Chemistry
Chemical Abstracts
Chemical Reviews
Chemical Society, London. Journal

Chemische Berichte
Coordination Chemistry Reviews
Faraday Society. Transactions
Helvetica Chimica Acta
Immunochemistry
Inorganic Chemistry
Inorganic Nuclear Chemistry Letters
Inorganica Chimica Acta
Journal of Biological Chemistry
Journal of Chemical Education
Journal of Chemical Physics
Journal of Chromatographic Science
Journal of Molecular Biology
Journal of Organic Chemistry
Journal of Organometallic Chemistry
Journal of Physical Chemistry
Justus Liebigs Annalen der Chemie
Macromolecules
Nature (all sections)
Organometallic Chemistry Reviews (A and B)
Quarterly Reviews
Royal Society of London. Proceedings (A and B)
Société de Chimie. France. Bulletin
Tetrahedron
Tetrahedron Letters

II.   Current subscriptions in hardcopy; backruns from 1970 onward on
      microfilm:

Acta Crystallographica (A and B)
Biochimica et Biophysica Acta (all sections)
Biophysical Journal
Canadian Journal Research
Experimental Cell Research
European Journal of Biochemistry
FEBS Letters
Federation Proceedings
Genetics
Journal of Bacteriology
Journal of Biochemistry (Japan)
Journal of Cell Biology
Journal of Experimental Biology

Journal of Immunology
Molecular Pharmacology
National Academy of Science. Proceedings
Physiological Review
Quarterly Reviews of Biophysics
Science
Scientific American
U.S. National Cancer Institute. Journal
Virology

III.   Current subscriptions and backruns dating from 1970 in hardcopy:

Applied Physics Letters
Canadian Journal of Physics
Chemical Physics Letters
Current Contents: Physics & Chemistry
Developmental Biology
Journal of Applied Physics
Journal of Molecular Spectroscopy
Journal of Physics (A-F)
Journal of Statistical Physics
Molecular Physics
Physica
Physical Reviews (A-D)
Physical Society, Japan. Journal
Physics Abstracts
Physics Letters A, B, C,
Physics of Fluids
Progress in Theoretical Physics
Reviews in Modern Physics
Soviet Physics J.E.T.P.
Studies in Applied Mathematics
Zeitschrift fuer Physik

References

1. Stevens, Rolland E. / The Microform Revolution. *Library Trends* 19: 379-395 (Jan 1971).

2. Veaner, Allen B. / Reprography and Microform Technology. In *Annual Review of Information Science and Technology,* v.4. Chicago, Encyclopaedia Britannica, 1969. p.193.

3. Stevens, Rolland E. / The Microform Revolution. *Library Trends* 19: 379-395 (Jan 1971).

4. Lewis, Ralph W. / User's Reaction to Microfiche: A Preliminary Study. *College & Research Libraries* 31: 260-268 (Jul 1970).

5. Weil, B. H., et. al. / Esso Research Experiences with Chemical Abstracts on Microfilm. *Journal of Chemical Documentation* 5: 193-200 (Nov 1965).

6. Starker, Lee N. / User Experiences with Primary Journals on 16 mm Microfilm. *Journal of Chemical Documentation* 10: 5-6 (Feb 1970).

7. Kaback, Stuart M. / User Benefits from Secondary Journals on Microfilm. *Journal of Chemical Documentation* 10: 7-9 (Feb 1970).

8. Duncan, Virginia L., and Frances E. Parsons / Use of Microfilm in an Industrial Research Library. *Special Libraries* 61 (no.6): 288-290 (Jul/Aug 1970).

9. Stevens, Rolland E. / The Microform Revolution. *Library Trends* 19: 379-395 (Jan 1971).

10. Veaner, Allen B. / Whither Micropublishing? *Micrographics News & Views* 2: 2, 6-7 (May 15, 1971).

11. Starker, Lee N. / User Experiences with Primary Journals on 16 mm Microfilm. *Journal of Chemical Documentation* 10: 5-6 (Feb 1970).

MICROFICHING OF PERIODICALS FROM THE USERS' POINT OF VIEW

by **P. R. P. Claridge**, *Warren Spring Laboratory, Stevenage, Herts*

The microfiche has become widespread in its use in recent years largely through its standardization by the United States Government for reports. Based on a process invented by J. Goebel in 1939, it owed its rapid development in Europe to the efforts of Dr. L. J. van der Wolk, who created the Netherlands Microfiche Foundation. Now that there is some standardization of microfiche size and format, this microform has a much greater chance of success than it did when each manufacturer or publisher produced microfiche to his own sheet size and frame spacing and, in general, to an inadequate standard of quality. The 6 in. by 4 in. COSATI format[1] is a most suitable standard and this agrees with the preferred size in the British Standard[2].

In any microform system three, if not four or five, different organizations are going to be involved, all of whose interests must be safeguarded if the system is to be a success. These organizations are the copyright owner of the material, the original publisher in hard copy form, the microform publisher who produces the microfiche edition, the librarian or professional user who has to buy, store and index it and make it available for the fifth group, the individual users. It is the individual user's views on the suitability of the system, as he sees it, which will determine whether the system will be used or ignored, but, for both professional and individual users, the microfiche offers considerable advantages provided certain definite conditions are met.

Reprinted from *ASLIB Proceedings,* vol. 21 (1969), pp. 306-11, by permission of the publisher.

Basic Requirements

What is it that the user needs and what is it that he wants; these are not necessarily the same? Basically, all a user needs is a legible microcopy and the use of a viewer*. However, if he is to accept the microform as a practical alternative to hard copy, he will want a little more than that.

For consulting abstracts the user would be prepared to go to the library to consult the indexes. It is suggested that the currently provided 16-mm film in cassettes is the most convenient format for microfilming an abstract journal. In these circumstances to select a cassette, place it in a viewer and press the button for the correct page, or to follow indexing marks on a scale would not be more difficult than to find the place in the hard copy volume. However, for his reading of periodical articles, particularly those which he has set aside for future reference, the user wants to have the material in which he is interested available immediately wherever he may be and to be able to store it for future reference in a place where he can retrieve it easily. This the microfiche makes possible, provided he has either a personal viewer on loan to him or a viewer readily accessible in his immediate group of colleagues, so that he can consult the article without delay during working hours or can borrow the viewer whenever he has need of it outside those hours. To satisfy this need any viewer for personal use must be portable; that is, capable of being carried in one hand and put into the boot of a car.

Together with ready accessibility, an essential requirement is adequate quality; that is, the user must be able to read the projected microform as easily as he would be able to read the original. The question whether the image should be negative or positive is tied up with the type of viewer that is being used. A downward projection viewer will be viewed by reflected light and requires a positive image to give adequate illumination of the screen. This has the advantage that half-tones, which are sometimes very important in the interpretation of a paper, will be shown in an intelligible form. Back projection, in general, requires a negative image so that the background is dark and does not strain the eyes or show undue hot spots. In the last year or so, users have become more tolerant of back projection, which can perhaps be ascribed to the improvement of screen quality and decrease of glare, and perhaps in part to their becoming more used to the idea of reading on a machine. However, at Warren Spring Laboratory the users expressed a very strong preference for reading in their normal position, that is to say, at desk level with the image projected from above. Then they could make notes alongside while reading as they were accustomed to do. Also the image would be at the normal distance

---

*To avoid the ambiguous term ''reader,'' the term ''viewer'' is used for the equipment and the term ''user'' for the person using the equipment.

and direction for which their spectacles were adjusted, particularly necessary in the case of bifocal lenses.

Quality Requirements

The quality of the microfiche is the requirement which, at the moment, is giving the most trouble. For easy reading the standard of the final projected image must be at least 6 lines per millimetre and there is some evidence that an even higher definition than this still increases legibility. At twenty times reduction this means that the microfiche distribution copy must have a definition of at least 120 lines per millimetre. The British standard for microfiche does not emphasize this requirement and to date it has proved impossible to obtain any microfiche of Warren Spring Laboratory journal runs up to this required standard, although some US AEC reports seen have been of adequate quality.

To the suggestion that present quality is inadequate, the objection has been made that engineering drawings have been used with success for a number of years on aperture cards at the present standards. However, to gain adequate definition for an engineering drawing when enlarged from microfilm, firstly, it is only necessary to be able to see whether a line is there or not, and background is deliberately shown to ensure this, and, secondly, the drawings are specially made with print large enough to allow for the degree of reduction desired. The equivalent for a periodical would be to ask the publisher not to print anything in less than 12 point type, especially if it has subscripts. The equivalent of 6 point type with subscripts would be regarded as completely unacceptable in an engineering drawing. In fact, the standards of quality required by libraries are an order of magnitude higher than those required by the drawing office.

Copy Microfiches and Copyright

In the past, when the user received a recently published journal in which there was an article in which he was very interested and to which he would have liked to make future reference, he would have written to the author requesting a reprint and would have waited for this to arrive. Now, in the majority of cases, he sends the journal to the reproduction services and gets an electrostatic copy. In the case of an active microfiche system he will apply to the library and get a copy microfiche of the article. For this use the published microfiche has to be available as soon as the original hard copy. The cost of producing such a copy microfiche on demand will be considerably less, as is shown later, than that of making an electrostatic copy.

On the question of copyright, the making of a microfiche of a single article in a journal should not be considered any less fair dealing than the making of an electrostatic copy of the same article. Even if two articles happen to be on the same microfiche, the second paper will, from the point of view of the user, in most cases be irrelevant and the copy will thus not be of any detriment to the publisher.

All copy microfiches made in the Warren Spring Laboratory library will be issued in envelopes, printed with

This copy microfiche was made under the provisions of Section 6 of the Copyright Act, 1956, and is supplied for the use of the recipient only for purposes of research and private study.

Savings in Costs and Space

The cost of providing microfiches must be set against any savings. As the cost of making a master microfiche is likely to be of the order of £1 to £1 10s, and the cost of making each distribution microfiche of the order of 5s, the unit cost of producing a microfiche in an edition of, say, fifty will be about 5s 6d. The selling price of a journal on microfiches, including the copyright fee, may well be the same as, or even down to a half, that of the hard copy edition. Present cameras capable of attaining the requisite quality are slow and expensive, so that the amortization charge to be included in the price of the master is of the same order as that of making the microfiche. If a fast, automatic camera were available, this cost, and the cost of staff time, would be reduced and the cost of a microfiche master could fall as low as 10s, which would make even smaller editions than fifty economic.

For the library, there is a cost saving in buying cabinets to store microfiches instead of new bookshelves, and a further cost saving in that binding can be dispensed with. But the biggest cost saving is that of replacing full-sized prints, which at present are made by the thousand and which are not as cheap as the advertisements imply. The accepted view, taken from several authorities, seems to be that an electrostatic print costs between 1s and 1s 3d per page, so that the cost of a copy of an average eight-page paper will be between 8s and 10s. The cost of making a copy microfiche is of the order of 1s 7d (material 1s 2d, staff time 2d, overheads 3d): with the cost of purchasing a microfiche of the order of 5s, plus copyright fee, if only one copy is made in lieu of electrostatic copying, a clear saving is already shown and this could be extended considerably.

In terms of convenience, the individual user can keep all his notes and the copies of articles for reference filed together as a compact card index, while, for the library, journals of different formats are replaced by the uniform-sized microfiches, which simplifies the assessment of space left for future growth.

In most papers on the economics of microfilming the space-saving aspect has been emphasized almost to the exclusion of all others. This may be a very potent argument for a business firm where the actual space used is costly, and is costed to the last square foot, and where changes at short notice are possible. In the case of research establishments one has a space allocation; this may be generous, it may be cramped (it usually is) and it may become impossible. It is only in this last case that the space argument can really be costed because then the cost of an extension to the library can be compared with the cost of installing microforms. Nevertheless, the degree of space saving is considerable, although not as much for large collections as is made out in the advertisements for microfilming. In the Tables 1 and 2, 1 million pages of journal material has been taken as the unit. As shown in Table 1, a number of assumptions have to be made, but these are all within the limits of normal library practice and holdings. In each case the shelves and cabinets are assumed to be comfortably full, and the figures would all have to be increased to allow room for expansion. Several densities of microfilming are shown, and it is suggested that 33 frames full per microfiche on average is the figure to calculate on. Similarly with microfiche storage, two densities are given, four cabinets high (up to 5.5 ft) and three cabinets high (up to 4.375 ft). The first represents the closest practicable storage and the use of library steps to reach the top cabinets; the second would be the maximum useable with ease; if space allowed, it would be comfortable to have cabinets only two high, in which case the space taken would be twice the minimum floor area quoted. With the middle density, the gain by microfilming is approximately 90 per cent space saved.

Table 1. *Comparison of space occupied by hard copy and by microfiche*

	Hard copy	Microfiche 50 frames	Microfiche 33 frames	Microfiche 25 frames
Unit of quantity [a]	10^6pp.	20,000	30,000	40,000
Shelf space, [b] ft	200	20.8	31.25	41.7
Volume, [c] ft^3	120	3.5	5.2	7.0
Volume as stored, [d] ft^3	180	8.8	13.0	17.5
Minimum floor space, ft^2	71	3.8	5.5	7.4
Average floor space, ft^2	71	5.1	7.3	9.9

(a) The unit of hard copy is taken as 1 million pages, photographed at three different densities.
(b) Conversion factors are: hard copy, 400 pp. = 1 in.; microfiche in envelope, 80 = 1 in.
(c) Volume of hard copy is based on an average journal size of 8½ in. by 10 in.

(d) Hard copy on shelves; microfiche in cabinets. Shelves are stacked seven high with 3-ft gangways between double stacks. Cabinets (4-drawer, $20 \times 16 \times 13.5$ in.) are on stands 1 ft high, stacked up to 5.5 (four high) with 3-ft gangways between double stacks for maximum storage, but stacked only three high (4.375 ft) for average storage density.

Table 2. *Space requirements for microfiche expressed as percentage of requirement for equivalent hard copy*

	Microfiche		
	50 frames	*33 frames*	*25 frames*
Volume	2.9	4.3	5.8
Volume as stored	4.9	7.2	9.7
Minimum floor area	5.4	7.7	10.4
Average floor area	7.2	10.3	14.0

Experience at Warren Spring Laboratory

Every user has some form of prejudice. The student starts off with few and can easily be taught to use microforms as quickly and effectively as normal books. But the older user has become accustomed to, and has formed his reading habits around, the book or paper format. This prejudice must be recognized, met and overcome if microfiches are to be accepted. But if the users are consulted, are asked to express opinions and invited to discuss equipment which is shown to them, they respond with enthusiasm; and although the users will never admit that the microfiche might be a possible or acceptable alternative to the paper hard copy (except in those cases where the hard copy is unobtainable), in fact they will often quite happily accept reports on microfiche and will ask for some of their own records to be microfilmed for convenience in use. When that happens, it can fairly be claimed that the users have accepted microforms.

At Warren Spring Laboratory the first need to do something came up some four years ago when the library was running out of space and there was no chance of having any further building for at least five years. The obvious first solution tried was to discard unwanted material, and to rely on borrowing unstocked items from the National Lending Library on telex requests. Experience shows that 50 per cent of such requests arrive the following morning and this is as good a service as could be expected in retrieving material from an outside store. However, users complained that the material they needed for reference and browsing was no longer on the library shelves. The only alternative was to reduce the bulk of the material stored and, as a number of reports from NASA and other sources were already being recieved on microfiche, it was clear that whatever solution was chosen, microfiches would be received and would have to be dealt with, so that microfiche seemed to be the inevitable conclusion.

The users were consulted to hear their views on the proposals and a library committee was set up to meet the objections they had raised and to decide the backrun which should be kept for each periodical in the library, a ten-year period being taken as the normal maximum. It was agreed that microfiches for the backruns, after the first heavy usage, would be acceptable provided that caution was exercised. The users required, and were promised, that the hard copy would continue to be available for early consultation. Next, an exhibition was held of the portable microviewers which were available at the time. This was well attended by the staff and eighty-seven copies of a questionnaire were returned completed, in which a request was made for comments on each of the viewers, for a vote of the order of preference, and for a declaration of any prejudice the user might have. These forms were analysed to find which was the most popular viewer and ten viewers were purchased. For about 120 regular users (those who borrow regularly two or more items per month) it is intended eventually to have between fifty and sixty viewers. Only with such a level of equipment can the need be met for a viewer to be on permanent loan to any individual user or be readily accessible to him at all times. In addition, there is a high-quality viewer in the library to deal with very difficult material, together with means of duplicating microfiches and of making enlarged paper copies when necessary. The system has been in use now for about a year and a second batch of ten viewers has been ordered, once again after an exhibition to the users, and as the result of the voting preference shown by completed questionnaires.

It was decided that it would not be economic for Warren Spring Laboratory to set up its own microfiche camera. It would be preferable for the publisher of the hard copy to produce the microform, but various microform publishers already exist and are acceptable sources for microfiche at commercial prices, provided that the quality is adequate. A specification of quality, etc., has been drawn up for this purpose[3] but, as already mentioned, adequate quality has proved difficult to obtain, particularly for definition.

The difficulty is to break out of a vicious circle. Manufacturers cannot produce equipment down to a reasonable price because there is insufficient demand, and there will be no demand of any magnitude until the prices become reasonable. There are signs, however, that the circle, although not yet broken, is at least being enlarged. The number of makers of microfiche equiment is growing enormously, the price is coming down and the quality is rising, and, at the same time, there is considerable interest in the production of cameras and new equipment. If more libraries become interested and are prepared to buy, the trend should be accelerated.

References

1. USA FEDERAL COUNCIL FOR SCIENCE AND TECHNOLOGY. *Federal microfiche standards, adopted by Committee on Scientific and Technical Information (COSATI).* Washington, Office of Science and Technology, 1965, (PB 167630).
2. BRITISH STANDARDS INSTITUTION. *Specification for microfiches.* London, 1967, BS 4187: 1967.
3. WARREN SPRING LABORATORY. *A specification for microfiche copies of periodicals.* Stevenage, Herts., 1968.

USER EXPERIENCES WITH PRIMARY JOURNALS ON 16-MM MICROFILM

by Lee N. Starker, *Warner-Lambert Research Institute, Morris Plains, N.J.*

For several years now, many of us have been looking toward the day when we would be able to replace the bound journal holdings in our libraries with microfilm copies. We all knew that a tremendous educational job had to be done, but none of us really knew what was the likelihood for success.

Publication of *Chemical Abstracts* on 16-mm film in cartridges solved many of these problems. Users were enthusiastic, and began to urge acquisition of other microfilm materials. The problem, now, was that although many scientific journals were available on 35-mm film, and a smaller number in one or more of the other formats, virtually none was obtainable in the desired 16-mm size. Cartridges and motorized reader-printers for 16-mm film were an integral part of the *Chemical Abstracts* success, and it was very important that this format be maintained.

In the course of a casual discussion at the American Chemical Society's Spring Meeting in 1967, it was discovered that concurrent efforts were being made by Ben Weil of the Esso Research and Engineering Co. and myself to stir up interest in this area. Mr. Weil was working with the petroleum and chemical companies, and I had been proselytizing the pharmaceutical companies, both of us working to put pressure on the several microfilm-publishing companies to make more scientific journals available on 16-mm microfilm. Our ultimate success is attested to by the fact of this symposium.

As a result of our 1967 discussions, the now-famous "Grass-Roots" meeting was held in New York on May 29, 1967. This meeting brought

Reprinted from *Journal of Chemical Documentation*, vol. 10, no. 1, February 1970, pp. 5-6, by permission of the publisher.

together representatives of a number of information groups, all of whom were interested in developing a collection of scientific journals on 16-mm microfilm in cartridges, in order to take advantage of the breakthrough achieved by *Chemical Abstracts*. As a result of this discussion, several microfilm publishers announced their willingness to offer scientific journals on 16-mm film. Most interesting, also, was an announcement that the Council of the American Chemical Society had before it a proposal to make all American Chemical Society journals available in microfilm editions.

Time does not permit a full recounting of the history of all the events that led to making the journal literature available in this new format, but substantial progress is now being made. However, the total number of journals that can be made available has not yet been approached.

We at Warner-Lambert received our first journals on microfilm late last year. Having been forewarned by earlier recipients, we carefully checked our films for the presence of poor-quality reels. Although our experience in this respect was good, we did find it necessary to return several reels of film to the publishers for replacement. It should be noted, too, that delivery periods have varied widely from one publisher to another.

In addition to *Chemical Abstracts* on film, we now have *Biological Abstracts, Journal of the American Chemical Society, Journal of Organic Chemistry, Analytical Chemistry, Journal of the American Medical Association, Journal of the Chemical Society (London), Chemische Berichte, Annalen der Chemie, Chemical Engineering News,* and *Industrial and Engineering Chemistry.* Our experiences are still young, but in general we can say that this method of using the literature is gaining ready acceptance by the laboratory scientist, and is proving to be a worthwhile addition to the tools available to literature science.

Our initial expectations were that journals on microfilm were not likely immediately to replace the hard copy versions of these materials in all instances. At the same time, however, it was obvious that published materials were growing at a much faster rate than we were able to add the physical space necessary to contain them. We considered raising the height of our stacks, and reducing the distance between stacks, so that more journals could be fitted in the same area; but such gains were minimal. Other suggestions included cutting back on the number of titles to which we subscribe, and removing older volumes to nonlibrary storage areas. Both of these latter approaches were obviously not suitable, because the major function of the library is to shorten the period required for the achievement of company goals, and to be as useful as possible to the personnel engaged in this activity. These suggestions would obviously have slowed the information-transfer process.

How then, could we have our cake and eat it? How could we store more and more materials in an unchanging physical space and still keep everything readily accessible? The answer was microfilm.

We had, of course, to overcome the user's historical objections to microfilm—in most cases based on reasons that were no longer valid. The answer came with *Chemical Abstracts* in cartridges, and in readers with motor-driven film transports and rapid printout facilities. Once users became accustomed to the ease of handling cartridge-packed film, to the speed of searching *via* motorized transports, and to the convenience of rapid, on-the-spot copies, we found that our former recalcitrants were actually requesting that more journals on microfilm be obtained.

Table 1. Journal Requests by Date

Up to two years old	695	74%
Two to twelve years old	197	21%
Over twelve years old	50	5%

Because we still anticipated negative reactions from our nonchemically-oriented users, we made a brief study of our clients' use habits (Table 1) and found that 74% of the requests were for copies of journal articles less than two years old. Accordingly, we decided that as we were able to bring in microfilm editions of these journals, we would remove the hard-copy editions of all materials that were over three to five years old. This would permit the majority of users to choose which form of publication they preferred. For journals that were more than three to five years old, however, only microfilm would be made available, and this would force the most reluctant to become acquainted with this new medium. Economically, it also made sense to retain the latest three to five years in hard copy, since it is still less expensive to provide copies of papers *via* Xerox than *via* the usual microfilm reader printer.

Because we have both *Chemical Abstracts* and *Biological Abstracts*, it appeared logical to develop a users' center for abstract journals built around these collections and serviced by two 3M cartridge reader-printers. Then, as we added film of primary journals, we planned to develop a second users' area centered on these journal collections. We would thus have a collection of primary journals on film and a separate collection of secondary film publications. Presumably, a user would check the abstract journals for appropriate references, and then move to the primary journal center to view the complete papers that had been selected.

This approach did not develop, however. We acquired primary materials at a relatively slow rate, and we therefore initially added them to the abstracts area. Since these were chemical journals, the first comments that came to us were praise for the ability to search *Chemical Abstracts* and then to be able immediately to check the journal articles without moving from the microfilm reader.

These results have changed our thinking as to the best arrangement for these materials. We are now considering a station which will contain *Chemical Abstracts* and the appropriate chemical journals in one location, and *Biological Abstracts* and the biological and medical publications in a second center. We may eventually keep all film together, but current space allotments do not conveniently provide one area of sufficient dimensions for this use.

Economically, it would appear that reinvesting in microfilm editions of journals after having purchased one or more hard copy subscriptions would put a severe strain on any library's budget. In most instances, however, purchase of the film will be offset by the money that need no longer be spent on binding. The cost of the readers and other capital equipment can be offset by savings in the purchase of additional stacks, and one can expect, in addition, to recover some investment by selling the no longer needed printed editions.

These factors, while painting a very favorable economic situation for microfilm, do not even begin to take into account the huge reduction in cost achieved by limiting the physical space necessary to house bound volumes.

In our own instance, we had reached the position—after doubling our library's area only seven years ago—where we no longer had stack space for additional bound volumes. As a result, materials that would normally have remained in this area had to be removed to less-accessible places. Not only did this impose an inconvenience on the user, but it substantially increased the amount of time that library personnel had to devote to supplying these materials and then reshelving them. We were, in fact, beginning to approach a situation where we had a dual operation, using both open and closed stacks. Moreover, the size of our staff was such that we could not afford the personnel time needed to function in a closed-stack situation.

A hidden benefit in the acquisition of microfilm editions of primary journals is that in many instances this permits the replacement of an incomplete or broken run of a journal with a complete sequence of issues. Needless to say, such an occurrence permits some additional savings, since interlibrary loans, or outside copies of material from the nonavailable copies, are then no longer needed.

A final economic offset to the purchase of microfilm editions is the practice of at least one publisher in accepting hard-copy journal issues in exchange for the film. This, of course, provides a very simple method by which the budget-tight library can begin to assemble a microfilm collection without expenditure of large sums of money.

In conclusion, it might be well to indicate the primary suppliers of these 16-mm microfilm editions of the scientific literature.

The American Chemical Society now supplies all of its publications in this format. With several exceptions, these are available as complete runs. Princeton Microfilms, Inc., is providing a steadily expanding list of publications, while Atlantic Microfilm Corp. is beginning to supply materials primarily in the medical literature field. University Microfilms, which has a very extensive collection of materials available on 35-mm film, is preparing to republish much of its collection in the 16-mm format.

USER BENEFITS FROM SECONDARY JOURNALS ON MICROFILM

by **Stuart M. Kaback**, *Chemicals and Patent Information Group, Chemicals Corporate Services, Esso Research and Engineering Co., Linden, N.J.*

At the September, 1965, meeting of the American Chemical Society, B. H. Weil and a group of his colleagues at Esso Research and Engineering Co. presented a paper describing some joint experiments by Esso, the Chemical Abstracts Service, and the American Petroleum Institute, in which a microfilm version of part of *Chemical Abstracts* was used in the Esso Research library.[1] The resounding success of those experiments led directly to today's widespread use of *CA* microfilm.

The traditional resistance of information users to the use of microforms, rather than original hard copy, is a familiar phenomenon. The advent of the modern, cartridge-loaded reader-printer has gone a long way toward overcoming this resistance. It is no longer necessary for the user to thread the film through the machine. Further, he can make photocopies of as many pages as he wishes, right on the spot. Certainly there is still room for improvements in equipment, and several suggested improvements are presented below. Nevertheless, we have found that equipment representing the current state of the art is quite satisfactory and is readily accepted. It should be emphasized that the comments presented here are predicated on the use of a reader-*printer*, which produces copies in a matter of seconds. In the author's opinion, print capability is an essential feature for the effective use of microfilm versions of secondary journals, primary journals, patents, or any other documents.

At Esso Research we use reader-printers exclusively. Our collection of

Reprinted from *Journal of Chemical Documentation*, vol. 10, no. 1, February 1970, pp. 7-9, by permission of the publisher.

secondary journals on microfilm includes *Chemical Abstracts*, the American Petroleum Institute's abstract bulletins and their dual-dictionary indexes, a large collection of author- and subject-classified abstracts taken from internal abstract bulletins from 1920 through 1963, and several recent, specialized, internal abstract bulletins. We expect soon to add the microfilmed abstracts from *Plasdoc*, a documentation service for polymer patents produced by Derwent Publications, Ltd.

The first point at which user advantages from microfilm show up is in the ease of look-up of the abstracts. Microfilm cartridges are considerably less bulky and easier to handle than are bound volumes. Weil in 1965 presented data on time savings in look-up. These data are certainly in agreement with the experience of the present author, a frequent user of the microfilm. It is certainly easier and quicker to find what you're looking for on the microfilm than it is with something like bound *CA* volumes, especially when a large group of abstracts is involved. The process is made still easier by the various codes available on the microfilm for locating the desired abstracts. My own experience is confined to the Kodak Lodestar equipment that we use, and our chief reliance is on the Kodamatic counting lines. We also have one Lodestar equipped with an IC-3 automatic keyboard, and while this automated machine is relatively popular with users, we do not find that its use results in any appreciable time saving. The more-expensive IC-4 keyboard, or a Miracode apparatus, would probably speed look-up somewhat—but we have not been able to justify their acquisition on the basis of economics.

In fact, it is possible to get rapid look-up using just the Kodamatic lines. Weil's data indicated a look-up time of about 1 minute per abstract. Experience and a healthy propensity for man-*vs.*-machine competition enable this rate to be bettered by a substantial margin. For example, the author was once able to check through a group of 400 references, and print out more than half of them, in the space of four hours and ten minutes—an average of under 40 seconds per abstract for the entire operation, including printing, which takes about 15 seconds per print.

A secondary benefit of the simple microfilm look-up is that it is possible, when a large number of abstracts are desired, to have the copying done by a clerk. This saves quite a bit of professional time, and is frequently done in our organization.

The second big bonus to the user lies in the ease of taking information away from the library. No longer is it necessary to take voluminous notes, and perhaps miscopy some information. Nor is it necessary to make photocopies from bound volumes, which is often clumsy with large volumes, is hard on bindings, and might in some cases be a violation of copyright law. The *CA* microfilm lease, however, includes the right to make copies. Thus, the user may choose to photocopy any abstracts he wants, and can attach them for inclusion in his personal information file.

For the information specialist, these copies can be used to prepare bibliographies. It is convenient to cut up the copies, arrange the abstracts in any desired format, and make single or multiple xerox copies for distribution to laboratory or management personnel. This technique often allows the inclusion of peripheral information in an information report at minimal expense, where the time involved in transcribing and digesting the information would not be justified.

One of our constant hopes has been for the availability of *CA* subject indexes on microfilm. By marking up a copy of an index printout to indicate entries selected for look-up, one can provide a useful permanent record of a search and its strategy. The possibility of transposition errors is also diminished. Recently, the Chemical Abstracts Service provided an experimental set of microfilmed indexes for testing in several libraries, including ours. As expected, we found legibility problems with some of the very small print used in the indexes, and could not term the experiment an unqualified success. At present, the best alternative is to prepare xerox copies from bound indexes, although this gives some problems, especially with print near the binding.

Microfilms of API abstracts are handled in a manner similar to that used with *CA*. A special benefit accrues, however, for the indexes to the API abstracts. These are coordinate indexes, arranged in a dual-dictionary format. By preparing prints of the index entry pages, it is possible to carry out multiple-level coordinations in a single step. An example of a simple coordination is shown in Figure 1 (see next page).

The subject here is the thermal cracking of methane to give acetylene, ethylene, or both as products. The first step is to identify the relevant search terms—here, methane, thermal cracking, acetylene, and ethylene—and to make copies of the listings from the microfilmed index. The most important term is selected as the base, and here methane was chosen. Where terms are judged to be of equal importance, the most heavily posted term is usually selected. Each of the other terms is then coordinated against the base, using a different marking for each term, and using the base photocopy as a work sheet. In this way, one readily determines which documents were indexed by all of the terms and are thus most likely to be relevant, but one also identifies the documents indexed by two or more (but not all) terms, with a somewhat lower relevance probability. Depending on the yield of "most relevant" documents, one can decide whether or not to consult the "less likely" documents.

In the sample shown in Figure 1, 24 documents were indexed by methane and at least one other term. Five of these were immediately eliminated on the basis of the assigned role indicators. Of the remaining 19 documents, three were indexed by two other terms in addition to methane, and all three were relevant. The other 16 were indexed by methane and one additional term. Of

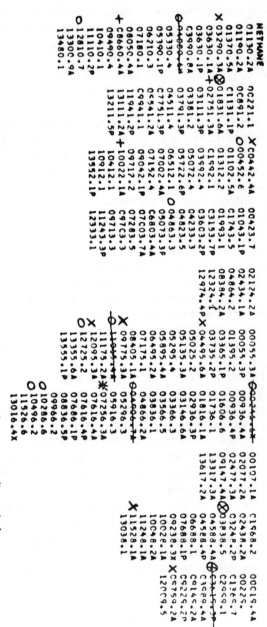

Figure 1. Multi-level coordination using a microfilm printout from a coordinate index

Subject: Thermal cracking of methane to ethylene and/or acetylene

Terms coordinated: Thermal cracking (+)
                       Acetylene (X)
                       Ethylene (o)

Relevant documents: 1831, 3838, 7256 (3 terms coordinated)
                       442, 3290, 4495, 9775, 11528, 12095 (2 terms coordinated)

Marginal documents: 2751, 8660, 9759, 10022 (2 terms coordinated)

Note: "Hits" eliminated by role indicators have been crossed out

these, six were relevant, four were marginal, and six were not relevant.

The conversion of our classified abstract files of about 2,000,000 cards to microfilm allowed the removal of many space-consuming cabinets from our library. However, microfilmed files such as this are not ideal for the user, since they are by nature browsing files. Microfilm is well-adapted to use for look-up of identifiable abstracts, much less so for browsing through abstracts as they move by sideways; this leads to considerable eyestrain.

It would be incorrect to assume that all of the problems relating to the use of microfilm for secondary journals have been solved. The image on the screen is quite good in the equipment that we use, but leaves room for better resolution and brilliance. More important, the focus is not always uniform over the whole screen. This problem became especially noticeable in our tests with the *CA* indexes, though it is not a major problem with *CA* abstracts themselves.

As noted above, the Kodamatic lines on the microfilm make possible relatively rapid look-up, although expensive equipment such as IC-4 keyboards or Miracode apparatus can probably speed this somewhat. It would obviously be desirable to have less-expensive equipment to do this, but again, the problem is certainly not acute.

We often find that microfilm quality is variable. In particular, there can be substantial variation from cartridge to cartridge in the film exposure and contrast, and this requires considerable adjustment of print controls. It is often difficult to obtain a set of prints with consistent quality, and this poses a problem when one wants to make second-generation xerox copies. Cartridges substantially off the norm are returned and replaced, but in practice one tends to live with moderate variation. Nevertheless, more-uniform film quality would certainly be desirable.

Occasionally, the page image on the film is so high that the top of a *CA* page is cut off in the print. This can cause the loss of column numbers and volume number, and a control which would allow the image to be raised or lowered on the screen would help here. Zoom lenses, not available on Kodak or 3M reader-printers, would probably help in handling very small print such as is found in *CA* indexes. Finally, the Kodak machines produce a damp copy that curls badly if it is not placed face down until it dries, and is hard to write on while damp. The 3M machines are less objectionable in this respect, but their prints have less contrast which makes them less adaptable to the preparation of xerox copies. There is certainly room for a cartridge machine which would produce a completely dry copy with good contrast, on uncoated paper which is easy to write on.

But while these problems do exist they are, as I have indicated, relatively minor ones. They are far outweighed by the various user benefits associated with microfilm, and the whole pot is sweetened by various economic advantages. It is certainly reasonable to expect considerable expansion in the use of microfilmed editions of secondary journals.

References

1.   Weil, B. H., W. G. Emerson, Shirley W. Bolles, and G. F. Lewenz, "Esso Research Experiences with *Chemical Abstracts* on Microfilm," J. Chem. Doc. 5, 193-200 (1965).

TEACHING THE USE OF MICROFILM READERS

By Carl Spaulding, *Program Officer of the Council on Library Resources*

Few persons not in the business of selling micropublications or reading machines would claim that roll film readers incorporate a high level of human engineering. In fact, most first-time microfilm users will, if left strictly on their own, have at least a little difficulty, and some will make a complete botch of things. But almost anyone, if given a brief tutorial session and a user's manual, can, with a modicum of practice, develop the proficiency needed to make the machine a useful tool rather than an additional hurdle when retrieving information. In this regard, the most important detail to keep in mind is that it is highly desirable to assist the new user initially so as to help preclude his developing a negative bias toward microfilm as a result of inept attempts to use a reading machine.

Training the Staff

Because of their crucial relationship to patrons of the microtext reading room, it is most important that personnel who work there be thoroughly trained in the operation of reading machines. In addition to the obvious reason for this requirement, there are justifications:

1. A person who has limited knowledge of, and competence with a machine is liable to feel self-consciousness when trying to instruct another in the

Reprinted from *Microform Review,* vol. 6, no. 2 (March 1977), pp. 80-81. © 1977 by Microform Review Inc.

use of that machine. In this circumstance, the instructor may well develop a hostility toward, or aversion to, the machine and the medium used with it. The user, perhaps having difficulties, may find it easy to adopt similar attitudes and thereafter be inclined to avoid using microfilm.

2.   Inadequately trained staff members and the users they teach are relatively likely to damage machines and film. Besides the cost of such damage, its occurrence, by embarrassing the individual who causes it, tends to prejudice her/him against microfilm.

Microtext reading room personnel should also be taught to perform those machine maintenance procedures which do not require a technician's skills. (Increasingly reading machine manufacturers are designing machines which the layman can easily learn to maintain in most regards.) It is especially important that reading room attendants know how to clean reading machines and how *not* to clean them, for it is quite easy to seriously and permanently damage the optical components by improper cleaning methods. (For this reason users should be discouraged from attempts to clean any part of a reader. It is best to dissuade them by obviating the need for cleaning, that is, by establishing a program for inspecting and cleaning of each unit according to a regular schedule.)

An individual being taught to operate a reading machine should be given a careful and patient demonstration. He should then be given hand-on experience to reinforce what he has learned and should be provided with a set of printed operating instructions for reference. Thereafter these instructions should always be available to him. It is worthwhile to prepare a specially designed strip of practice film which incorporates various special cases, such as positive and negative images, out of focus images, and images requiring 90° rotation. Instruction should include explanations of how to use reading equipment to the best advantage, as well as techniques for circumventing or lessening the effect of limitations of microfilm, e.g., using a lens of higher magnification than normally called for in order to read small print more easily.

Manuals

There should be a clear and concise manual of operating instructions for each type of reading machine in the library. Each manual should incorporate illustrations including, particularly, an easily understandable film threading diagram. A threading diagram should also appear on the front of each reader when its design permits. Alternatively, the diagram can easily be reproduced on a card kept near the machine. Controls should be clearly and unambiguously labeled and the locations of any that are out of sight for an operator should be indicated by labels he can see.

Manuals should include explanations of how to detect various conditions caused by human error or machine defect or malfunction, e.g., a misaligned mirror or film improperly wound on the supply reel. When such conditions can be easily and safely corrected, the manual should advise the user to seek assistance without attempting to operate or repair the reader. (A reader needing maintenance should not be left in the reading room for any appreciable period. It should be serviced immediately or removed to a nonpublic portion of the library until it can be serviced.) User manuals should not contain maintenance instructions because it is easily possible for an unqualified person to damage the reader or to suffer personal injury from electrical shock or hot interior surfaces if he tries to carry out maintenance procedures.

Teaching the User

The principal differences between teaching the user to operate microfilm readers and training the staff about them are: (1) the user does not need to be taught to clean and maintain the equipment, and (2) attitude plays a major role in dealing with the user.

With regard to the latter of these, it should be noted that while every assistance should be given the user of the microfilm collection, in some cases an attendant can easily be overly helpful even to the point of being intrusive, especially for a user who is self-conscious because of difficulty he is having with the machine. This matter of how much help is too much can became particularly important if the reading room staff includes individuals who have limited experience and skill in interpersonal relations.

Another aspect of attitude which is of importance in dealing with the microfilm user, is the tendency of some librarians to inhibit use of film by over-emphasizing the danger of damaging it or the reading machine. Although it is true that microfilm is in some regards more susceptible to injury than books and that readers can be easily damaged by certain types of misuse, this consideration is of secondary importance to that of encouraging free use of microfilm which, after all, has value not in its existence but in its utilization. Users should be encouraged to systematically report damaged film and reading machines without being concerned about paying for the damage. Such reporting can be implemented as a part of a general procedure wherein each user comments on any aspect of the total microform system which he finds deficient, whether it be defective microfilm, malfunctioning equipment, unsatisfactory environmental conditions in the reading room, inadequate bibliographic aids, incorrect shelving, or any other unsatisfactory condition. Where this approach can be made to work, it offers an excellent means of keeping tabs on a number of factors affecting the utility of the system. Toward this end it is worth considering the design of a simple reporting form, copies of which can be kept near each reading machine.

USER ENVIRONMENT AND ATTITUDES IN
AN ACADEMIC MICROFORM CENTER

by Arthur Tannenbaum and Eva Sidhom, *Microform Center,*
Bobst Library, New York University

User Environment was the subject of a paper[1] presented at the Fall 1975 ASIS meeting in Boston, where interest in the topic suggested that user convenience is a continuing problem when people face machines, whether these machines be coin-operated photocopying machines, microform readers, or computer terminals. Attention given to environmental factors and a staff service commitment at New York University's Bobst Library, specifically in the Microform Center, resulted in such increased activity and appreciation by the center's users that it may provide guidelines for microform center designers of the future.

The NYU planners were aware of the negative attitudes library users in general had towards the use of microforms. The Association of Research Libraries, also sensitive to this issue, asked Donald Holmes to make a study of the necessary requirements for proper environmental conditions to satisfy microform readers. Holmes made two reports, both available on microfiche in the ERIC Documents series. The first report[2] summarized the problems faced by users. These included: 1) light in area not controlled; 2) assistance not provided in placing films on reading machine; 3) reading machines often in a poor state of repair; 4) scratches and breaks in films; 5) microforms improperly filed; 6) some reading machines not projecting clear images; 7) machines incapable of being adjusted for height and reading angle.

The second study[3] suggested a design for a new custom-made reading carrel to provide the necessary mobility, as stated in problem No. 7 above. In fact, since Holmes reported that the single most fatigue-causing factor for readers of microforms is the rigid line of sight normally encountered between reader and machine, it became obvious that the more dynamic the space becomes between reader and machine, the more comfortable he becomes with the format.

Observation

The NYU planners, conversant with Holmes' observations, next made visits to microform sites. Typically, these installations (educational, commercial, government, etc.) were casual, not designed with solving, or coming to grips with the following fatigue-causing items: noise, lighting, machine height, seating, viewing perpendicular or parallel to the writing surface, scanning or reading activity, etc. These factors became vital for consideration when establishing the Microform Center at the Bobst Library. Although the point can be made that for the academic researcher content is more important than format, it is also true that physical discomfort retards the rate of comprehension and period of use with printed materials. Since hard copy is preferential to microform for prolonged reading in the opinion of most users, solutions for fatigue items are most welcome in encouraging microform use. It was decided to engage Dr. Holmes as a consultant to the project, to benefit from his personal experience. This decision was fostered by the increasing conviction of the importance of the environment after seeing the typical microform settings already described. Working with Dr. Holmes provided the following information; these remarks are derived from a combination of reports to the Dean of the Libraries.

Centralization

Many microform collections are dispersed in departmental libraries according to their subject content. From the standpoint of providing reference assistance to patrons, such dispersal offers much to recommend it; however, practical considerations of providing microforms as satisfactory substitutes for the full-size printed page required controlled conditions that would be almost impossible to achieve except in a reading room designed especially for using microforms. A microform reading room should have facilities designed for the storage, maintenance, and protection of the microforms as well as for the comfort of the users. The assembly of most microform reading equipment in a single location will make its use far more efficient than if it were dispersed.

Furthermore it will provide the opportunity of making and carrying out a much-needed machine care and maintenance program. Such a program will minimize machine damage to microforms and provide patrons with the full potential of the equipment used. Cabinets designed especially for microform or microfiche storage provide the best protection for software as well as the most efficient methods of putting them away. These cabinets can be arranged also as useful room dividers to block out undesirable lighting or noise conditions.

Room Conditions

Microform reading machine screen images are visible only when their brightness exceeds the ambient light in the area in which they are viewed. Ideally, the general lighting in the microform reading room should be of low intensity. It should be adequate for moving about, but should be of lower intensity than that required for reading or other desk work. If at all possible, indirect lighting with local switches and dimmer capability should be placed in the area where the microform readers are to be installed. Direct or daylight lighting may cause reflections on the microform reading screens and thus depreciate the screen image quality. The ability to adjust the angle of the reading screen is critical to overcoming lighting problems with the environment, although fresnel lenses, screen hoods and general machine portability are aids to the user in his individual adjustment.

The light measured by meter at the work surface in the microform reading area may be 15 to 20 foot candles as a rule, with capability for the reader to increase or diminish this lighting via local adjustment. The question of proper lighting, both for the illumination level on the screen and the work surface, has been subject to much scrutiny and opinion. A recent study involving microform reading generally supports Dr. Holmes' recommendation of 15-20 foot candles measurement on the writing surface, actually broadens these measures to 10-30 ftc., and further suggests 41 ft.-1 as the proper luminance on the reading screen. However, the same study admits that the best reading condition vis-à-vis performance was not entirely consistent with the study groups preferences and therefore the conclusion as to "ideals" remains subjective.[4]

Sound dampening is an important consideration in the microform center. The clustering of equipment that cranks and spins is bound to distract readers if the use is heavy. Placing readers in partitioned areas like carrels or divided tables will isolate the noise somewhat. Carpeting is the best way to achieve the sound muffling desirable in this area.

It should also be remembered that film tends to become brittle when subjected to low humidity. While it will at least partially return to its original condition when the relative humidity goes up to the desired 50 percent, this should not be counted on, and if film is not in an air-conditioned, humidified library, special humidification should be provided.[5] People also respond beneficially to a controlled climate. Proper humidification and temperature arrangements make studying a more agreeable and pleasant task.

The Microform Carrel

The ARL study of the microform carrel concerned itself in part with the line of sight established by reader and machine. It was felt that this line of sight should be as flexible as possible. Traditional microfilm viewing places a machine on a table and provides a stationary chair for the reader; this position can become unbearable for the person doing intensive study. The ARL prototype tried to prevent this situation by designing the machine platform to revolve sideways, in a lazy susan fashion, and tilt backward and forward. Room was provided for a typewriter. A library furniture company built a pilot model and demonstrated it at Penn State University in mid-1971. Librarians at the site reported that the model turned too stiffly, flopped instead of tilted, and that typewriter vibrations had adverse effects on the machine reader causing hazy focus and a shortened bulb life.

NYU decided to design its own microform reading carrel, which was demonstrated in Chicago at ALA Midwinter 1974 and delivered to NYU in early 1975. Student and faculty reaction has been quite positive. The outside dimensions of a single station were to be 4 × 4½'; however, for space economy, a double station unit was built, with dimensions approximately 5'5" × 4'6". This space includes a writing area, book shelf, and small lamp. The movable platform can be raised or lowered a maximum of 3", more than enough to adjust for glare or the height of the reader's neck. The reading machine can easily be turned laterally by hand. A secretary chair is surprisingly efficient for creating additional lateral and vertical movement for the reader. The carrel has been modified to fit the university's needs. A decision was made to house film readers only. They are larger and bulkier than fiche readers, where flexibility can be achieved in a variety of less expensive ways. The university already owned a considerable number of Kodak manual readers and had chosen the Kodak Motormatic as the upgrade model. Thus, the carrel was specified with the equipment in mind. Parenthetically, the machine used in the ARL report was the Kodak MPE manual reader, now regrettably off the market. In any case, instructions were placed right on the machine or in the carrel, indicating simple, step-by-step procedures for machine use.

Work Room

At the NYU Bobst Center a corner has been walled in for use as a work room. Ideally, there should be a work room in every library's microform center, but if this is not possible, a special work area should be provided to give the staff a quiet spot for inspecting, cleaning, and repairing microform. Repair of films is not a simple operation, and should not be treated as such. Allen Veaner was trying to emphasize this point when he said that "the use of pressure-sensitive tape for making splices is a violation of accepted practices and is generally considered a mark of poor quality work."[6] If microfilm cartridges are not employed, this cleaning and inspection function becomes doubly significant. Equipment in the work room should consist of a film inspection and splicing desk, fitted with a light box, rewinds, and a splicing machine; reading machines for roll film and microfiche inspection and identification, and shelving for temporary storage purposes. The work room should also house machine space parts (projection bulbs, optical flats, etc.) which can be replaced by staff.

Since the NYU Library has insituted a portable fiche reader loan-out program, and it is policy not to loan original fiche, a fiche duplicator has been acquired for noncopyright materials. The work room at NYU is a convenient area for the fiche-duplication operation.

Staff

Since users of microforms need varied kinds of assistance, no facility can be truly successful if library personnel work apart from the operation. The quality of staff assistance in any library's microform center is one of the major factors of its success. It should consist of persons who appreciate microforms as a 20th century form for the storage and retrieval of information and who are dedicated to the service of the center's users. Besides cleaning and maintenance activities, the staff provides assistance with mounting films on readers, making hard copies and fiche duplicates, guiding the user into the complex of materials that are the "catalog " of the collection, and being generally helpful.

Staff availability is important whenever a situation breeds confrontation between man and machine. Coin-operated photocopy machines predictably cause trouble with the public far beyond their reasonable expectation. As a result, staff-operated copy centers have emerged. We must admit that a certain apathy does exist between the microform hardware and the shotgun user (shotgun as in marriage). Philip Slater, in *The Pursuit of Loneliness*, describes this man/machine apathy: "Americans are always hung over from some blow dealt them by their technological environment and are always looking for a fix—for some pleasurable escape from what technology has itself created.'' In the library's case, the "fix" is the microform staff who provide the bridge to ease the user into the technology. The staff is the energizer between the passive if not downright reluctant user and the impassive, inert reader/printer.

A special head should be appointed for the microform center. Qualifications should include a degree in library science, some administrative ability and experience, and mechanical aptitude. Since it may be difficult to find a candidate who has had experience in microform technology, the alternative is to provide the appointee with scope for training in this area. This may be accomplished by reading selected literature, visits to institutions known for their successful use of microforms, visits to commercial microform production laboratories, and membership in the National Micrographics Association and perhaps in a local NMA chapter. Most important is that this person be a believer in the worth of the format.

Users

After the Bobst Microform Center was opened in the fall of 1973 and was used on a regular basis, it soon became apparent that the efforts, time, and planning in creating this Center were worthwhile. Statistics showed an increase in the use of materials and in the number of users. By early 1975 these figures had increased so dramatically that they appeared to substantiate the Holmes premise that user activity and acceptance of microforms rises when care and attention are directed towards the environment.

For example, room count figures from October 29, 1973 to January 20, 1974 showed 3,660 users. The count for the same 12-week period in 1974-75 revealed 6,739 users or an increase of 84.13 percent. At the same time, user statistics for the library at large demonstrated a less significant increase in activity. The 12-week period 1973-74 shows 147,579 books reshelved, and the same period 1974-75 is 193,029 books reshelved. This is a 31 percent increase from the previous year.

An idea of the traffic and current use of the Microform Center is revealed in the Fall 1975/76 statistics following.

Microform Center Statistics—Fall Semester 1975/76

Period	No. of users	Help with machines	No. of ref., access & other Q's	No. of printouts	No. of fiche dups	No. of portable readers lent
Oct. 1-31, '75	4169	850	967	3148	159	25
Nov. 1-30, "	3236	793	789	3841	258	28
Dec. 1-31, "	3554	832	725	3965	375	29
Jan. 1-31, '76	2937	778	532	4260	125	21
Total	13,896	3253	3013	15,214	917	103

I. Questionnaire

The expression of appreciation and delight by some users denoted that their attitudes towards microforms were becoming definitely positive. It prompted a decision to make a study of these attitudes through a questionnaire to be answered by users. It was believed that such a survey would be of interest to the library community. Users were selected at random, requested not to sign the questionnaire, and to answer it very freely, making any constructive criticism they thought would help the Center meet user needs and correct any condition complained of. As it turned out, complaints were minimal and user attitudes were definitely positive.

The questionnaire looked long, but because the user was requested to check only one answer out of a number of stated possibilities, the time needed to fill it out was not more than 10 or 15 minutes, and all those who answered did so willingly. Out of a total of 120 answered questionnaires, 77 contained comments and 43 had none. The highly favorable tone of the comments, and of the questionnaire answers altogether, was both impressive and rewarding. The questionnaire consisted of five major categories, each sub-divided into a number of sections.

The following is a report on the results of the questionnaire.

Type, reason for, and frequency of use: Of the users, 4 were faculty, 9 were visitors, 63 were graduates, and 44 were undergraduates. Thus faculty and visitors together constituted only 11 percent, while graduate and undergraduate students constituted 89 percent. The graduate users outnumbered the undergraduates, and their reasons for use were different. The latter came primarily for assignment preparation or study; the graduates came mostly for research, either intensive or occasional.

Frequency varied considerably: Of the 120 users, 55 or about 46 percent used the Center either seldom or occasionally; while 65 or about 54 percent used it often—i.e., once a month at least; or frequently—i.e., once a week or more often.

Average amount of time users spent in Center: 81, or just over two-thirds of the repondents, used the Center from a minimum of one hour to over four hours—a rather good testimonial for the user's abilities for sustained microfilm-reader use; only 39, or just under one-third, used it less than one hour. The exact breakdown of the time spent in reading is shown below.

TABLE I

No. of users	Approx. amount of time spent reading
3	15 minutes
12	15-30 minutes
24	30 min.-1 hour
Total: 39 users	Spent a maximum of one hour
39	1-2 hours
28	2-4 hours
14	more than 4 hours
Total: 81	Spent one to over 4 hours

TABLE II

	Strongly agree	Agree	No opinion	Disagree	Strongly disagree
A: I appreciate microforms because they provide me with otherwise unavailable or inaccessible material.	90	26	3	1	
B: When I find what I want, it makes no difference whether it is in regular form or microform.	31	33	19	31	6
C: Working with microforms usually bothers my eyes.	5	28	10	54	23
D: The advantages of microforms outweigh the disadvantages.	55	47	12	4	2
E: The environment and equipment at the Bobst Center nullify whatever I regarded as disadvantages.	36	44	25	11	4

II. User's Attitudes

The second category of the questionnaire concerned user's attitudes to microforms as media for research and information-gathering. Five clear-cut, specific statements were given, with five optional columns to be marked for each statement. The results revealed overwhelmingly favorable attitudes to the utilization of microforms in a research library and an appreciation of their value. The last statement (given under E in Table II) showed also that 80 of the 120 respondents thought the environment and equipment at the Center helped nullify any possible disadvantages microforms may have had in their views. The attitudes and the number of the positive or negative feelings are given above.

III. Reaction to Environment

The third major question requested an expression of opinion on five considerations that are liable to affect the user-attitudes to microforms: a) room comfort; b) equipment provided; c) the microforms themselves; d) staff assistance; and e) ease of access provided. Each of these was divided into several items. The preponderance of favorable replies is shown below.

TABLE III

	Excellent	Very Good	Good	Only Fair	Poor	Total
A. Room Comfort						
1. General Lighting	35	43	32	8	2	120
2. Lighting in Carrels	39	34	34	11	2	120
3. Chairs Provided	65	35	17	1	2	120
4. Arrangement of Room	44	40	30	4	2	120
5. Air Conditioning	47	35	30	8	1	120
6. Adjustable Carrels	35	30	31	5	3	104
B. Equipment Provided						
1. Evaluation of microfilm readers	45	42	26	3	-	116
2. Evaluation of microfiche readers	24	33	14	2	-	73
3. Evaluation of micro-opaque readers	17	31	13	3	-	64
4. Evaluation of reader-printers	26	30	19	4	-	80
5. Ease of use of machines	48	46	21	5	-	120
6. Quality of images as to their clarity	43	43	26	7	1	120

	Excellent	Very Good	Good	Only Fair	Poor	Total
7. Your sense of comfort while reading	45	40	30	5	-	120
C. The Microforms Themselves						
1. Their Quality	55	35	27	1	-	118
2. Their Condition	53	31	30	-	-	114
D. Staff Assistance Received						
1. Explaining Use of Machines	67	28	16	1	2	114
2. Helping to Find Needed Material	56	30	16	3	-	105
3. Explaining Indexes and Finding Aids	55	24	20	3	-	102
E. Ease of Access to Microforms Provided by:						
1. Room Arrangement	53	47	12	2	1	115
2. Degree of Assistance	56	36	17	4	-	113

IV. Comparing Facilities Used

Part IV of the questionnaire was aimed at finding out how users reacted to our new structured environment, and what they thought of it as compared to: 1) The microform facility in the old NYU library before the move to Bobst; and 2) Other microform facilities they might have used elsewhere. The questions and the number and types of response follow:

1. Did you use the old NYU microform facility before the move to Bobst Library in (month, year)? Responses: 22 yes; 95 no.

If the answer was yes, the user was asked to select the phrase that best described his own attitude toward the new NYU microform facility in the Bobst Library. The results follow:

The new Bobst facility is a more pleasant and attractive place to work than the old facility: Strongly agree, 18; Agree, 2; No opinion, 1; Disagree, 1; Strongly Disagree, 0.

It is less fatiguing to read from microforms in the new facility: Strongly agree, 15; Agree, 5; No opinion, 2; Disagree, 0; Strongly disagree, 0.

2. Have you used microform facilities at other institutes? Responses: 56 yes; 53 no. The 56 positive respondents gave names of public, university, and government libraries each had used in various localities around the country.

Answers to the question of how the Bobst Center compared to whatever other microform areas had been used were as follows:

The Bobst facility is a more pleasant and attractive place to work compared to other facilities: Strongly agree, 45; Agree, 10; No opinion, 0; Disagree, 1; Strongly disagree, 0.

It is less fatiguing to read from microforms in the Bobst facility as compared to other facilites: Strongly agree, 40; Agree, 10; No opinion, 2; Disagree, 4; Strongly disagree, 0.

V. Personal Evaluations

The fifth and last question, a simple request for each respondent's opinion on the Bobst Microform Center and any other personal comments, was worded: "All things considered, what is your opinion of the Bobst Microform Center. You may comment on any of the topics mentioned above or on any other topic you may feel is important. State any suggestions you may have to help us know your needs and serve you better." Of the 120 respondents, 77 or almost two-thirds took the time to answer this question and make comments, and 43 (or just over one-third) did not answer at all.

The answers were almost unanimously favorable and complimentary both to the Center and the type of service received in it. They varied in length from a short phrase or sentence to a more elaborate description of personal reaction to the Center. The following statements are given as samples:

1. "The facilities and staff at Bobst have made microform as pleasant to use as it can be."
2. "Overall the quality is excellent, the staff helpful and the atmosphere perfect."
3. "You are doing a great job..."
4. "The facilities are excellent. The staff is extremely helpful!"
5. "I have been thrilled by the new set-up..."
6. "If I must use microfilm, I'd rather do it here than anywhere else..."
7. "Wonderful place. Staff is always helpful. Materials easily accessible. Just great—no complaints at all!"

The seven quotes give an idea of the general tone of the comments. However, let us end by quoting the only two comments that were signed by the two visitor-users who made them. One of them was a visiting professor who had used our Center regularly, and the other was the Vice-President of the Economic Research Institute in New York City.

Prof. Philip S. Foner of Lincoln University, Pennsylvania, typed his questionnaire answers (which he returned by mail). In his comment, he said: "I have found the facilities excellent, and am deeply indebted for this assistance and the ability to use the facilities in connection with a number of books I am preparing for publication."

W. Homer Graham, a former NYU alumnus and the Vice-President of ERI wrote: "One of the finest installations of its type in the country, including Washington and NASA."

Conclusion

Biotechnology is one of those words you have to look up. It is, according to Webster's, "the aspect of technology concerned with the application of biological and engineering data .   )blems relating to man and the machine." This discipline appears to be a logical one to study certain fatigue factors caused by reading microforms for extended periods. For instance, English ergonomist (biotechnologist) Prof. E. N. Corlett states the following in a recent paper: "Many workers have to achieve their objectives in spite of the equipment they use: the lifting and handling done by transport and delivery workers, typists with inadequate desks and chairs, assemblers on product lines, or the posture of machinists."[7] It isn't difficult to apply that statement to the microform bugaboo, fatigue. Holmes recommended in his second report that "a comprehensive and in-depth study of the possible physical and psychological factors involved in the use of microforms"[8] be made.

The authors heartily endorse this view. In the meantime, it appears plain that sprucing up the microform reading area, with attention given to the human and environmental aspects discussed here, will contribute to changing users' attitudes from negative to positive regarding this format.

References

1. Tannenbaum, Arthur C. "Human Engineering Factors Help Determine Microform Use in the Research Library," American Society of Information Science *Proceedings*, 1975, 12, p. 97-98.

2. Holmes, Donald C. "Determination of User Needs and Future Requirements for a System Approach to Microform Technology." Washington, D.C., Association of Research Libraries, 1969, 35p. (Ed-029-168), p. 6-15.

3. Holmes, Donald C. "Determination of the Environmental Conditions Required in a Library for the Effective Utilization of Microforms," Washington, D.C.: Association of Research Libraries, 1970 (ED-046-403), p. 12.

4. Lee, David R. & James R. Buck. "The Effect of Screen Angle and Luminance on Microform Reading," *Human Factors*, October 1975, 17 (5), p. 461-69.

5. Metcalf, Keyes D. *Planning Academic and Research Library Buildings*. McGraw, 1965, p. 173.

6. Veaner, Allen B. *The Evaluation of Micropublications, a Handbook for Librarians* (LTP No. 17). American Library Association, 1971, p. 41.

7. Corlett, E.N. "Human Factors in the Design of Manufacturing Systems," *Human Factors*, April 1973, 15 (2), p. 106.

8. Holmes, *op. cit.* (ED-046-403), p. VI.

II ■ THE ECONOMICS OF MICROFORMS & SERIAL CONVERSION PRIORITIES

INTRODUCTION

What are the economics involved in the conversion to microforms? Will there be savings? If so, how much? Does a library buy a dual subscription of the same journal, one in hard copy (to be disposed of in time) and one in microform (to be kept as part of the permanent collection)? Should the library even buy the hard copy if the microform is also initially available? Should the library engage in its own microforming, or should it have microforming done out-of-house by professional companies? What should be done with the hard copies already microformed ? What journals should be microformed? All? If some, which ones? What are the conversion priorities? What are the criteria to be used to gauge this?

Such a bewildering paragraph-load of questions! The articles in this chapter are addressed to these questions. Some proceed in one direction, some in another. The problems are aired and thrashed out. Each library must understand its own priorities and needs first, before it embarks upon any total microform program based on another library's example.

A University Microfilms International flyer lists the benefits that can be obtained by a utilization of microforms with regard to periodicals: 1) Backfile periodicals on microform can save over 90 percent of the space normally needed to store bound or loose issues.[1] 2) The purchase price of microforms is often less than the cost of binding paper copies. 3) Periodicals in microform are rarely lost, stolen or mutilated as are hard copies. This is particularly important in consideration of the cost of replacement of periodicals. 4) Complete runs of rare backfiles can be obtained at perhaps a lower cost in microform. [However, this certainly is not always the case.] 5) By means of a reader/printer, paper copies can be made easily and almost immediately. The University Microfilms brochure ("The Economics of Serials in Microform") goes on to delineate the three major areas of savings with regard to microforms and periodicals: acquisition, binding, and storage. Acquisition decisions about whether to purchase microform editions in place of multiple hard copy subscriptions, or the replacement of missing serial issues must be considered. It is of course this latter that is our focus: the contrast between the difficulty and expense of acquiring a back-issue of a journal and the ease and savings involved in purchasing this in microform. Binding costs are avoided by microforms. And storage space is saved in the process. Both the latter must figure strongly in any economic considerations regarding microforms and serials. The following articles in the chapter delve into the specifics of the above issues raised.

REFERENCES

1. Keyes D. Metcalf, *Planning Academic and Research Library Buildings,* 1965, p. 393

Additional Readings

Abell, D.F. "Guidelines in Recommending Back Numbers of Scientific Journals for Purchase." *Illinois Libraries,* vol. 54, March 1972, pp. 231-233.

Brookes, B.C. "Photocopies vs. Periodicals: Cost-Effectiveness in the Special Library." *Journal of Documentation,* vol. 26, no. 1, 1970, pp. 22-29.

Erbes, Ray, "Microfilm Solves Our Magazine Storage Problem." *Library Journal,* vol. 84, 1959, pp. 3601-3602.

Langlois, Dianne C. and Jeanne V. Von Schulz. "Journal Usage Survey: Method and Application." *Special Libraries,* May/June 1973, pp. 239-244.

Martin, Murray S. "Matters Arising from the Minutes: A Further Consideration of Microform-Serials Exchange." *Microform Review,* vol. 2, no. 2, April 1973, pp. 86-90.

Martin, Ron. "Microforms and Periodical Mutilation." (Letter). *Microform Review,* vol. 2, no. 1, January 1973, pp. 6-8.

Martin, Ron. "Mutilation - A College and University Survey Concerning Microform Replacement for Mutilated Periodicals and Circulation of Microforms." *Nebraska Library Association Quarterly,* vol. 3, 1972, pp. 18-20.

Maxin, Jacqueline A. "The Open Shelving of Journals on Microfilm." *Special Libraries,* December 1975, pp. 592-594.

"More Libraries Converting to Microfilm for Periodicals." *Advanced Technology Libraries,* vol. 2, no. 3, March 1973, pp. 1-3.

Patterson, Stephen L. "Patterns of Use of Periodical Literature." *College and Research Libraries,* vol. 30, no. 5, September 1969, pp. 422-430.

Peele, David. "Bind or Film: Factors in the Decision." *Library Resources and Technical Services,* vol. 8, Spring 1964, pp. 168-171.

Rush, Barbara, Sam Steinberg and Donald H. Kraft. "Journal Disposition Decision Policies." *Journal of the American Society for Information Science*, vol. 25, no. 4, 1974, pp. 213-217.

Shaw, Debora. "Classification and Arrangement of Microforms in Academic Libraries." 1976. (ED 125 537)

Snowball, George J. and Joseph Sampedro. "Selection of Periodicals for Return to Prime Space from a Storage Facility." *Canadian Library Journal*, November-December 1973, pp. 490-492.

Stevens, Rolland E. "The Microform Revolution." *Library Trends*, January, 1971, pp. 379-395.

Stewart, Blair. "Periodicals and the Liberal Arts College Library." *College Research Libraries*, vol. 36, 1975, pp. 371-378.

Stoness, B. Jeanne. "Integration of Print and Non-Print Resources." The New York Library Association, *Bulletin*, vol. 24, no. 8, October 1976, pp. 1 and 10.

Strain, Paula M. "A Study of the Usage and Retention of Technical Periodicals." *Library Resources and Technical Services*, vol. 3, Summer 1960, pp. 295-304.

Stuliglowa, Anna K. "Soviet Newspapers and Periodicals on Microfilm." *Microform Review*, vol. 1, no. 4, October 1972, pp. 289-291.

Wetzler, John. "Microfilm: An Answer to Your Periodical Space Problem." *Junior College Journal*, vol. 37, 1966, pp. 42-44.

Wootton, C.B. "The Economics of Microfilming Serials at the BLLD." *Microform Review*, vol. 7, no. 3, May/June 1978, pp. 137-138.

THE CONVERSION CONFUSION: SOME COMMENTS

By **Mary Jane Edwards,** *Head of Periodicals Section, Pennsylvania State Library*

The evergrowing demand for, and increasing use of, material from periodicals and newspapers in research by patrons of all ages presents a dilemma to the librarian in charge. Previously, this library medium was only another resource angle for the patron to explore—today it is the main one. In fact, I would venture to say that most modern authors have had to delve into magazines and newspapers for elusive facts or for additional color.

With this demand in mind, librarians suddenly find themselves overwhelmed with stacks filled with bound periodicals of all shapes, sizes, conditions, and runs. The answers—build, wear blinders, change jobs, retire, or convert to microfilm—all present frightening pictures to the librarian. A little common sense and preparation, however, will not only assist in building a more compact and useful collection, but will reduce the conversion confusion.

The advantages of converting to microfilm are many, of course, and have been listed many times before. But to reiterate briefly:

Savings in Space. The old argument about equipment needed for storage and usage equaling the space already used in the present system just does not hold true. Modern equipment is sleek, streamlined, smaller, and getting more so every day. Even used equipment that can be purchased at great savings from dealers does not present great difficulty, and you can usually find a nearly ideal place for a table and chair, reader and cabinet—it is shelf space that most libraries lack. After all, books need a place to sit, too!

Longevity. Let's face it. They don't make paper like they used to. It has been a mighty long time since we have had paper of archival quality. Also, an added

Reprinted from the *Journal of Micrographics*, vol. 9, no. 6 (July 1976), pp. 5167-8, by permission of the National Micrographics Association. ©1976 by the NMA.

point—why should librarians expect microforms to be of archival quality as long as the master is? Microforms with high usage will get scratched and sometimes torn but so do books,and microforms can be replaced more cheaply than can a bound periodical. Microforms with little usage will last indefinitely and will not disintegrate just sitting on the shelf.

Complete Holdings. One of the strongest selling points of microfilm is that the periodical will be complete. It seems that the missing or mutilated issue is the one that is requested most, but with microforms there are no gaps, no torn pages, and nothing cut out.

Okay, you're sold or, at least, half sold. Where do you begin? First, if possible, do it alone, especially the final decision as to what goes or stays. You know your collection best. If you have staff, of course, they may help collect pertinent information. But, remember, you have to live with wrong decisions and it is much easier living with your own. In a large system, subject specialists or interested co-workers may be called on for help; however, the more opinions that are involved, the more time it will take, and *you* have to work with the collection daily.

Next, resign yourself to the fact that conversion cannot be completed overnight.

Consult a reputable microform dealer. The National Micrographics Association would be glad to provide a free *Buyer's Guide*, which lists many dealers.

Then investigate the possibility of doing the microfilming in-house. The cost of purchasing the equipment may be fairly high, but if you have the funds it may be a good investment since there are many other library materials that may be microfilmed in the future. Also, you may contract a local service bureau to produce microforms of complete runs of periodicals.

Try to find book dealers who will purchase or extend credit for bound volumes; some book dealers will even exchange microforms for the volumes. If you cannot sell or exchange your old periodicals, offer them to other libraries. The blow of losing these old friends may be lessened if you receive something in return, even if it is only the satisfaction of knowing another library has given them shelf room.

Research conversion methods. Not too much information on conversion is in print, and it will probably take more time to find articles than to read them but a worthwhile alternative is to contact another library that has had experience with this problem.

Decide which microform suits your library best. Sixteen-mm or 35-mm film is immaterial for high usage purposes. Storage space is about the same in the drawers for either 16-mm or 35-mm film, and most readers or reader/printers will adapt to either 16- or 35-mm film. Microfiche, on the other hand, is difficult to file if used for high usage titles. The fewer types of microforms the better for a small library, and sometimes only one or two reader/printers are needed.

Next make a list of all the serials and include all pertinent information. Staff may help with this chore. (I prefer to list all the information on cards that can be shuffled and sorted.) The following facts should be included:

- Holdings in the library
- Where the periodical is indexed
- Usage
- Gaps
- Condition (paper quality, outline format, illustrations, etc.)
- Availability in other library organizations to which they belong—some titles need not be retained if they are readily accessible at a nearby library
- Necessity of item in collection—for example, one volume of some obscure foreign language title or unused podiatry titles may not be necessary items and may be discarded.

Using the above information about each item, divide your collection into the following categories.

Category 1. Items that must be converted (include in this most titles in the Wilson indexes, newspapers, serials with high usage, large gaps, poor condition, etc.)

Category 2. Items that probably should be kept

Category 3. Items that you are uncertain whether to keep or convert

Category 4. Items that you prefer to keep

Category 5. Items that must be kept.

Category 5 can now be immediately put aside. In this category would be items of definite value. Magazines or art should also be kept until colored microfilm becomes a more practical reality, as well as gifts from a patron who may check up now and then to see if they are still there.

Beginning with the items in category 1, contact dealers, buyers, and library friends to properly dispose of the serials. While working through this category, you will probably find that some items or portions of items in category 2 will automatically fall into place to be either kept or converted. Finish converting category 1 before proceeding to the other groups. If you are unfamiliar with microfilm, take a while to become used to dealing with it so that you can decide more easily whether to keep or convert the remaining periodicals.

Promote microform usage with your patrons. You may even have to do some diplomatic pushing with staff members who have negative attitudes, but, once the initial unfamiliarity is overcome, most people will be so glad to have the information available when they want it that they will readily accept using the readers.

By already eliminating the major share of obvious titles, you are now ready to consider the last four groups. Categories 2 and 3 can be tackled together. Evaluating each title individually, you can debate the merits of converting to microfilm or keeping in its present form. Delegate any item that will involve hours of indecision or controversy to category 4. Both categories 4 and 5 can be reviewed from time to time as your situation changes or as time warrants.

I think you will be pleased with your results. Microforms are no longer the material of the future. They are NOW! There is no getting around it, they will be used more and more often. They are economical, compact, and durable. Patrons are being exposed to this media at a progressively younger age and therefore accept it readily.

Libraries cannot possibly house all material requested, of course, but with serials, the more complete runs you have, the less frustration for you and for your patrons. Anyone working in a library that has anything to do with young people or in a specialized library knows the usage of periodicals today. Anyone working in research areas realizes the value of complete holdings of back material. In fact, any library should have some microforms so that its librarians and its patrons will be familiar enough with their usage that going into another library for research will not be a difficult transition or traumatic experience.

There is no easy or quick way to convert your bound serials to microfilm. There is no way to achieve 100-percent satisfaction, but the primary point is: If you are considering conversion at all, you undoubtedly need to do it.

MICROFILM AS A SUBSTITUTE FOR BINDING

by **Eugene B. Power**, *President, University Microfilms*

Of increasing urgency for libraries in the United States, and other countries as well, is a satisfactory solution for the storage problem. The number of books, periodicals and newspapers which must be saved for future use is rapidly exceeding the physical capacity of the buildings now available or likely to be constructed. Even if one discounts the estimates of reputable authorities that a research library such as Yale University will tend to double its size every sixteen years,[1] the growth of collections and rise of building costs present formidable difficulties.

Two classes of materials especially, periodicals and newspapers, crowd library shelves. Both have many issues each year, and both are bulky. Journals and newspapers have another characteristic in common—a high reader interest immediately following publication which diminishes more or less rapidly, depending on the subject. Recent studies by Fussler[2] and others reveal that in the fields of chemistry and physics interest rapidly declines after three years. This same pattern of use in a more intensive form surely holds for newspapers as well. Yet any good research library must have available back files of periodicals and newspapers, often covering 100 years and more, if it is to be worthy of the name. This situation presents an odd dilemma. The material is used but rarely and is filling space to overflowing, but still is essential when needed.

A possible expedient for the reduction of storage costs is the use of microfilm.[3] Under this plan the library circulates periodicals either unbound, or in inexpensive pressboard covers, for the 2-5 year period after publication, during which the use is the heaviest, and at the same time, a microfilm copy of

Reprinted from *American Documentation*, vol. 2 (1951), pp. 33-9, by permission of the publisher.

the same material is purchased. The cost of the microfilm is no greater and is usually less than the cost of binding, and there is consequently no increase in over-all expense. When the demand for the original paper copies tapers off, they are discarded and the microfilm substituted for general use.

Nearly 800 leading periodicals are already available to subscribers to this service. Through the use of high-reduction microfilm[4] it is possible to produce microfilm copies of journals to sell at the rate of ¼ cent per page, which is just about the cost of binding the equivalent material. The film varies in reduction ratio from 14-1 to 20-1 as a maximum, reproducing forty pages to each foot. On a reading machine with an enlargement ratio of 17 to 25 times, the resulting image is clear, sharp and satisfactory. Low enlargement readers are not satisfactory, since the type is too small for comfortable reading.

The virtue of the program just described is that the library is able to acquire the microfilm at no additional expense since the cost is no more than the charges for binding. When the paper copies are discarded, most of the shelf space that would be required by the bound volumes represents a net saving and all without restriction of library service, though with a change in the nature of the material offered [to] the reader.

A few detailed examples will make clear how great the saving really is. In terms of storage costs, a periodical fifty years old, used once in five years, is just as expensive as a periodical used fifty times in one year. When an estimate of what cumulative storage charges for a periodical purchased on subscription, bound and stored for a period of fifty years or more is made, the result is astonishing. A realistic method for making such an estimate is outlined below.

Assume t=time in years during which a periodical file is stored, and that

v = the number of volumes per year
a = cost of storing one volume for one year
k = cost of binding one volume
n = number of volumes stored
b = cost of storing one volume in microfilm for one year
m = cost of microfilming one volume of newspaper
e = cost per page of microfilm copy of periodical
p = cost of making one positive microfilm from negative
y = number of pages in one volume
c = cost

The cost of storing a completed file of a journal which is no longer published can be expressed by the formula

$c = a\,n\,t$, if bound, and $b\,v\,t$, if on microfilm

Further:

$$c = \tfrac{1}{2}\, a\, v\, t^2$$

represents the cost of storing a continuing bound publication, and k v t the binding costs.

$$c = m\, v\, t$$

represents the cost of microfilming a continuing publication, and

$$c = \tfrac{1}{2}\, b\, v\, t^2$$

the cost of storing a continuing periodical on microfilm.

(m + p)vt the cost of one positive microfilm, while (m + 2p) vt ÷ 2 the cost of one copy when two copies are made from the same negative.

y e v t would represent the cost of a positive microfilm of a continuing periodical where ''e'' is the cost per page.

When actual cost figures are substituted in these formulae, the results are revealing. While it is true that some of the necessary figures are not readily available, the estimates and formulae here provided are ample to enable any librarian to draw useful conclusions.

In a typical American library stack one square foot of floor space will accommodate on the average fifteen books, eight periodical volumes, or one volume of newpapers. Space of this type is worth from $1.50 to $2.50 per square foot on an annual rental basis, including heat , but not light or upkeep. This means then that ''a'' is at least $1.50 for each newspaper volume, 20 cents for a periodical, and 10 cents for each book. Binding a newspaper volume of approximately 700 pages costs $7, while for periodicals the average is $3.50 for a volume of 800 pages. The usual microfilm storage cabinet requires nine square feet of space for 612 volumes of books, newspapers, or periodicals, including the aisle space in front for use. Thus the figure for ''b'' is 2.2 cents.

If the cost figures for various methods of storage discussed above are computed and plotted on a curve, some interesting comparisons and relationships are revealed. Let us assume a newspaper of approximately thirty pages daily is stored over a period of fifty years.

Newspapers bound:

$$c = \tfrac{1}{2}\, a\, v\, t^2 + k\, v\, t$$

$$c = \tfrac{1}{2}(\$1.50 \times 12 \times 50^2) + (\$7.00 \times 12 \times 50)$$
$$\$22,500 + \$4,200$$

c = $26,700

Newspapers—microfilm:[5]

$c = \frac{1}{2} b v t^2 + (m + p) vt$

$c = \frac{1}{2}(\$.022 \times 12 \times 50^2) + (15 + 6) \times 12 \times 50$

$c = \$330 + \$12,600$

$c = \$12,930$

It will be seen that even when only one copy of the microfilm is made, film cost is substantially less than the storage of the original. If, however, two copies of the film are made, and the cost of photography divided between two libraries, it will be found, using the formula $c = \frac{1}{2} b v t^2 + (m + 2p \div 2) (v t)$, that the cost of bound volume storage equals film cost in ten years. After ten years the spread between cost lines which represents the saving becomes increasingly great. (Fig. 1) The same reasoning applies to periodicals using the formula $c = \frac{1}{2} a v t^2 + k v t$ for bound files, and $c = \frac{1}{2} b v t^2 + y e v t$ for microfilm, yields more impressive results, since a large number are already being offered on microfilm at a cost approximating that of binding the original paper edition. (Fig. 2)[6]

Frequently a library keeps a file of a journal no longer published. A comparison of the cost of storing a single volume in its original form or of purchasing a microfilm and storing the film is shown in Figure 3[7] using the formula $c = a n t$ and $c = b v t + y e$. From the graph it will be seen that the storage cost for ten years of a defunct periodical is just about equal to the cost of purchasing and storing a microfilm copy, thereafter a saving results. Where space is at a premium it may be more than merely a matter of dollars and cents. It may be a question of giving adequate library service or none at all.

Just as books require shelving, microfilm requires storage cabinets. A cabinet in popular use, costing $180, accommodates 612 100-foot rolls of 35mm film, or the equivalent of 612 volumes of newspapers, or the same number of volumes of periodicals. Double faced shelving will accommodate fifty volumes of periodicals and less than seven volumes of newspapers per running foot at a cost of $18. Thus, for periodicals, shelving costs 36 cents per volume. For newspapers the shelving cost is much greater than the cabinet cost for microfilm, or $2.57 per volume.

It should be noted here that this comparison of costs does not take into consideration other factors which have a bearing on the extensive use of

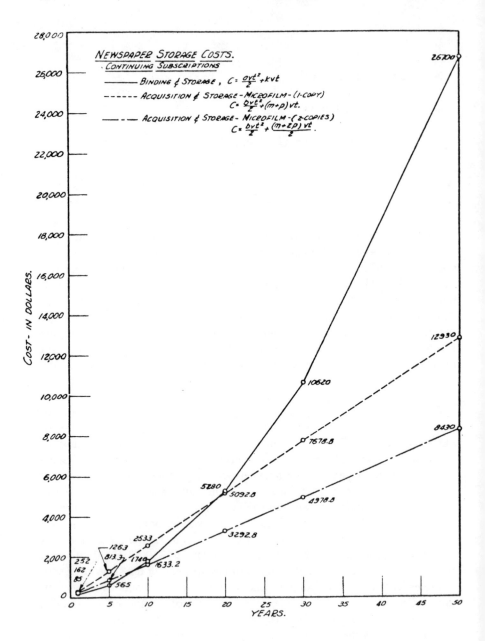

Fig. 1

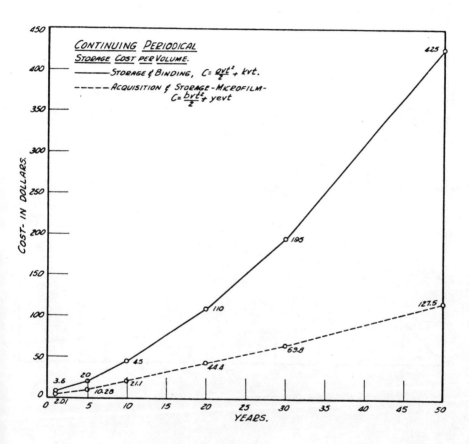

Fig. 2

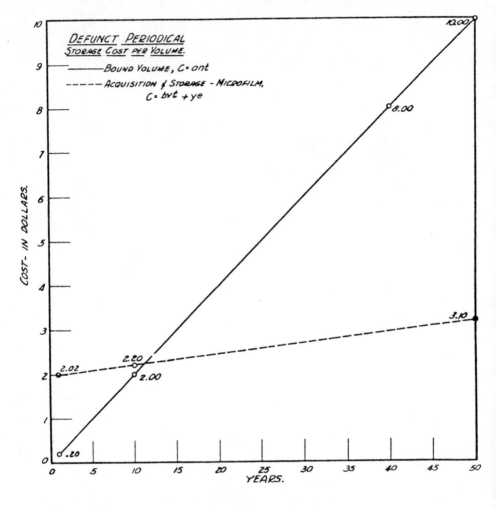

Fig. 3

microfilm. Among these certainly would be the cost of the reading machines necessary to service a large film collection, or additional space or facilities which the use of reading machines might require. Whether the cost of servicing the collection is more or less for film than for books is dependent upon a number of factors. For example, heavy newspaper volumes in a distant part of the stack are difficult to service, whereas the microfilm can be conveniently located and quickly serviced. Because of the small amount of space required, a substantial collection on microfilm can be kept readily accessible near the reading machines.

If the materials kept on film are only those items which there is a sub-stantially lessened demand, a few reading machines will serve for a sizable collection of periodicals or newspapers. Dr. Warner G. Rice, Director of Libraries at the University of Michigan, has estimated that a research library of the sort he heads would need one reading machine for each 100 graduate and faculty readers, even if a substantial part of the collection were on microfilm. Present day reading machines are well engineered and built and will, with reasonable care, last twenty years. Thus the annual replacement charges would not be more than 5 percent.

A table model reading machine together with its user requires not more than 50 percent more space for comfort than a reader sitting at a conventional study table. Since at any given time not more than a small fraction of places will be devoted to microfilm reading, space requirements should not be excessive. The recent appearance of satisfactory portable reading machines on the market means that like books, film and machine can be loaned for use in office or home.

There is no doubt in view of the comparative inexperience in the use of microfilm by scholars that some additional servicing is required. Inexperi-enced hands can thread film incorrectly and tear it, and many users require some assistance or instruction. It is equally true that a little practice greatly increases proficiency.

From the foregoing it can be seen that we now have techniques at our disposal to forestall to a considerable degree the mushrooming growth of library buildings costs, at the same time preserve material in a medium considerably more permanent than many paper copies current today.

If the possibilities outlined above are to be fully realized, certain decisions must be made. The initial success of high-reduction film may point the way to a solution for some of the perplexing problems surrounding standardization. If the two basic types of microfilm currently supplied in the United States, notably low-reduction 1-10 to 1-15 microfilm for copies of books, manuscripts and other originals made for individual users, and high-reduction microfilm 1-16½ to 1-25 for newspaper reproductions and for periodicals of the type mentioned above can be widely accepted and standarized, much existing confusion would be eliminated. Future models of reading equipment could be designed to provide dual magnification in low and high ranges and more attention could be devoted to considerations of legibility and use. Incidentally, on the basis of experience with high-reduction microfilm, the opaque screen seems to yield a sharper and more adequate image than the conventional translucent screen, though either may be used with good results.

Librarians, therefore, can meet the requirements and needs of users with two types of equipment. One type is the large permanent reading machine of finest quality and greatest flexibility. These may now be obtained on the market at a cost of from $300 to $725. The second type of reading machine is the smaller, less universal portable unit which should ultimately be available for from $75 to $150. The larger universal machines could be used within the library, and the smaller could be loaned to the user with the film for use outside the library. Instrument manufacturers have repeatedly pointed out that the problem of the small low-cost instrument is insoluble until definite use specifications are evolved. Once the requirements are known, the production of a suitable model is not a matter of great difficulty.

From the foregoing it would appear that a number of conclusions can be drawn from the data presented having a direct bearing on future library policy. Among these are the following:

1. The purchase of older back files of periodicals, often at premium prices, is not a wise investment. Age almost automatically means infrequent use. The same needs can be adequately served by a microfilm copy. In bound form space costs continue at a high rate year after year, whether the materials are used or not; in microfilm the fixed charges are greatly diminished.

2. Storage of newspapers in bound form is not warranted. The space required is excessive, the binding expensive, and the use after a short period of time is infrequent. Moreover the cheap wood pulp paper will disintegrate after 25-40 years and the total investment is lost. A microfilm copy is small, compact, satisfactory to use and permanent.

3. Through the proper use of microfilm pressing problems of space can be substantially eliminated. Files necessary for adequate library service can be kept and maintained without frequent expansion of stack capacity and new construction at the present high building costs.

4. Present library service can be maintained or expanded through the use of microfilm, as publications can be kept on microfilm that otherwise would have to be discarded because of space considerations.

5. As the number of desirable publications is itself increasing in a parabolic curve, storage of many titles on microfilm may become inevitable if costs are to be kept within manageable limits. With many libraries it may become a question of using microfilm to give adequate service, or severely curtailing the resources made available to their users.

References

1. Rider, Fremont. "The Scholar and the Future of the Research Library," New York, Hadham Press, 1944.

2. Fussler, Herman. "Characteristics of the Research Literature Used by Chemists and Physicists in the United States," *Library Quarterly*, XIX, 19-35, 1949.

3. For a full description and list of titles included in this service see "The Problem of Periodical Storage in Libraries," University Microfilms, Ann Arbor, Michigan, 1950.

4. Power, Eugene B. "The Use of High-Reduction Microfilm in Libraries." *American Documentation*, 1, No. 3, 139-143, 1950.

5. Microfilm negative of 100 feet per volume at $15, and positive at $6.

6. Based on an average of 800 pages per title per year, a binding cost of $3.50 per volume and a microfilm cost of ¼ cent per page.

7. A cost of ¼ cent per page can be realized only if ten or more copies are made over which the cost of the negative can be spread, combined with the use of high-reduction ratio.

SERIALS ON MICROFILM—THE QUICK SALES APPROACH

Bookdealer-Library Relations Committee, Acquisitions Section, RTSD

Sad as it may seem, many librarians have been persuaded by persistent salesmen to turn over bound volumes of periodicals in return for a promise to deliver microfilm and have, in effect, simply given away the bound volumes. It is possible for such an exchange to be advantageous to a library and some have benefited thereby, which makes it all the more depressing to report that librarians must be very suspicious of quick-trade offers.

Some time ago the Bookdealer-Library Relations Committee of the Acquisitions Section, Resources and Technical Services Division, reported on this practice in *American Libraries*[1] but reports continue to come in of exchanges which turned into give-away programs. The committee therefore feels bound to draw the attention of all librarians and dealers once more to this unfortunate situation. Without wishing to harm the activities of reliable firms, the committee recommends most strongly that any librarian asked to entertain a proposal for the exchange of serials for microfilms consult with the chairman, Bookdealer-Library Relations Committee, before closing any deal.

It is not the intention in this article to go over the relative merits of microfilm against hard copy. The data on the comparison are by no means all in. Rather the article will attempt to provide a framework within which to respond to an offer.

All libraries reach a time when they question whether long runs of serials are really earning their shelf space. Microfilm substitution seems a ready answer to the problems caused by those hundreds and thousands of little-used volumes. Cost of purchase, however, is high and libraries have also to consider the cost of special storage and reading facilities. In such circumstances an offer to trade bound volumes for microfiles at no cost to the library must seem attractive.

What is being offered, what given in return? What is the manner of presentation? Do not allow yourself to be browbeaten or dazzled by financial legerdemain, nor to be hurried into a limited-time offer.

Any approach which suggests secrecy should be rejected out of hand. Any dealer should be willing to have his proposal referred to the Bookdealer-Library Relations Committee or the library's own counsel.

What of the proposed exchange? The library will give up a collection of material that has taken years to assemble. Each title involved may have its own implications. Complete runs of a serial are much more valuable than broken holdings. Materials rich in illustrations cannot yet be adequately replaced by film. For that reason some serials, even in this age of the reprint, are relatively rare and valuable. The value of others such as little magazines, shortlived political or polemical publications, lies as much in their format as in their contents. Relationship to collecting policies may also be important. Local history, for example, is a field in which a discard proposal should be weighed carefully.

In return the library is offered microfilm of the material taken away. Sometimes only the volumes taken will be so replaced but frequently the offer will be extended to cover a complete run, or it may be other material such as an antecedent title. In the first instance the librarian would need to consider deeply the utility to the library of receiving certain volumes only on film. If, for example, use has been minimal, perhaps not even the bound volumes are needed, let alone microfilm. In the second instance, while it is obviously attractive to receive more than you give, there is the less obvious rider of how the extra material is to be made available. Perhaps the sponsor will say he is melding several libraries' sets. If so, ask to see a certified list of what he has available. The process of borrowing or building a set for filming is long and expensive, as can easily be learned from the experience of University Microfilms, Inc. If the dealer merely hopes to complete a set, the process may never be concluded. Perhaps microfilm is to bought from, or exchanged with, another company. Cost in such a case will be high and dependent on others not party to the transaction.

The balance of cost must be examined carefully. Check in your own library, or with libraries nearby, the retail price of the bound volumes, remembering the seller would be lucky to receive 50 percent of the retail price from a dealer. Check also the retail prices of the microfilms, if commercially available. Remember these prices are based on multiple sales, and may not be a very good guide. Nevertheless a comparison of the two totals will give some clue as to the financial viability of the proposal.

Technical capability. The quality of the image produced is important, but equally important is the physical quality of the film and its processing. Unfortunately some types of film are subject to deterioration if improperly processed. It has been reported that one brand of vesicular film emits small amounts of hydrogen chloride gas which can cause deterioration of cardboard containers and rusting of metal cabinets. All librarians should therefore determine the type of film proposed for use and the processing used, and compare these with the guidelines in Veaner's book.[2] At present the committee feels compelled to recommend against vesicular film, as not yet proven to be of archival quality.

Contract details. Some entrepreneurs offer for signature contracts which may be binding, but which offer no legal protection to the library.

Any exchange which involves the relinquishing of library property must be carried out under explicit authority only. In the absence of a clear statement on such authority, no transaction should be undertaken.

All contracts should state in detail all items covered by the agreement. No contract should allow anyone other than authorized library staff to remove library material from the shelves. Each title should be treated separately and a signed receipt be given for the volumes received. The next title should not be released until microfilm for the preceding title has been received and checked for quality and completeness, while unsatisfactory film should be replaced before any further transaction takes place.

All statements on time should be specific. Vague delivery periods such as "as soon as possible" are unacceptable. Wording such as "between ten and thirty days after receipt" is necessary, together with a statement that failure to meet such conditions will void the contract. All contracts should also allow for a "cooling-off" period before coming into effect.

All contracts should be submitted to the library's legal counsel to determine whether they are enforceable, but perhaps the primary rule really is when in doubt don't. The committee is willing to offer advice and assistance, but stresses the need for this to be done before and not after any loss is sustained.

References

1.   New microfilm for old books, *American Libraries* 1 (2): 137 (February 1970).
2.   Allen B. Veaner, *The Evaluation of Micropublications: A Handbook for Librarians* (Chicago: American Library Association, 1971). L.T.P. publication, No. 17.

SURGING SERIAL COSTS: THE MICROFICHE SOLUTION

by **Michael Gabriel,** *Government Documents and Serials Librarian, Memorial Library, Mankato State College in Minnesota*

The economics of serials acquisition and maintenance is becoming for libraries what a perpetually growing proboscis was for Pinocchio: an unendurable, unsightly monstrosity which threatens to topple the body that supports it. The problem is as critical for small and medium sized libraries as it is for the larger research institutions that are reeling from rapidly accelerating subscription, binding, replacement, and labor costs.

Increased costs of subscriptions are chiefly responsible for the current crisis in the continued development of viable serial collections. Rising prices of paper and escalating postal rates are the principal villains, and—combined with other general inflationary factors—they have pushed the average price of an American periodical from \$11.66 in 1971 to \$13.23 in 1972 (a 13 percent increase), and to \$16.20 in 1973 (a 22 percent increase). [1]

Research libraries are forced to continue to pour an ever larger slice of the materials budget into serials, or the quality of their collections will deteriorate and markedly impair graduate programs and general research. In the University of California system, for example, some of the smaller libraries have reduced serial holdings to cut costs, while other larger libraries in the same system have clear policies that affirm the relative importance of serials and have reduced the funds allocated for retrospective purchases, current monographs, and nonprint materials.

Often overlooked are the staff costs of coping with fluctuating acquisition

Reprinted from *Library Journal* (October 1, 1974), pp. 2450-3, with permission from the publisher.

and payment records. For the libraries which depend heavily on subscription agencies (and virtually all large libraries do), individual invoices announcing price increases are the pin-prick that can burst a growing boil of resentment. Verifying and recording an agency's annual invoice containing entries and prices for anywhere from 20 to 20,000 titles is a monumental drudgery requiring hundreds of hours of knowledgeable staff time. Unfortunately the job is not finished when the invoice is sent off to the business office for payment. Price changes (affecting about 10 percent of all journals in 1973) from publishers are routinely passed along by the agencies all year long, and each change must be verified and processed by serials staff. The agencies are reluctant to ameliorate this problem, but a little forceful arm twisting by librarians can induce revised billing procedures. Some firms will hold all added charges and submit a separate invoice for price increases at renewal time when both lists can be conveniently verified and recorded.

To be fair, subscription agencies also are squeezed by the inflationary spiral. Many publishers lowered or completely eliminated discounts ordinarily granted to agents. These added costs are being passed along to libraries. Agency service rates probably will climb in the near future as more publishers eliminate discounts to subscription agencies. Service rates charged to libraries by agents would have to multiply if direct subscriptions ever were able to compete with the economies possible with subscription agencies, when ordering, problem correspondence, claiming, and (especially) checkwriting are tabulated. [2] The frustration of dealing directly with publishers to resolve billing and continuation problems is further compounded by the recent reduction of fulfillment staffs by many periodical publishers.

The second most costly item in the serials budget is binding. Commercial binderies charge between $4 and $5 per volume for class A binding. Libraries at the mercy of state contracts often pay much more. The California state colleges are bound to the State Printing Office for the ludicrous sum of $8 per volume, class A binding. Special treatment (handsewn, recasing, folio, etc.) costs much, much more, and spiraling costs of materials such as buckram will push general binding costs even higher. If the average periodical volume translates into two physical volumes each year (and in some libraries the average is higher), binding costs alone can approach ten dollars per title. Add that figure to the average subscription cost and you have the princely sum of $26 required to obtain and bind one title for one year. Add another dollar to pay for storage and maintenance and multiply the total by the number of titles in your collection, and weep. For that is not all.

Open-stack periodical collections suffer annual rates of theft and mutilation that may start at a barely acceptable one percent and range upward to what only can be called grand larceny. Research libraries can spend tens of thousands of dollars each year on replacement issues alone. Back in 1963 the University of

Michigan completed one of the few studies of replacement costs and discovered that the average processing cost for a replacement issue was $2.10.[3] One shudders to think what that cost must be 11 years later, especially when added to the price of the issue itself.

Another interesting fact divulged by the Michigan study concerned the feasibility of reducing theft and damage by closing off free access to periodicals. At the University of Michigan, the cost of implementing and staffing a closed stack system would have cost more than twice as much as the total cost of obtaining replacements. So much for closed access.

In any case, there is a perverse logic at play when librarians spend so much to replace missing issues. Numerous studies have shown that 50 percent or more of the titles in any large periodical collection are used less often than once a year, and as much as 80 to 90 percent of all use is concentrated in a very small portion (less than 25 percent) of the total periodical list.[4] What point is there in expending scarce resources to obtain an item which, because of its relevancy, controversial nature, etc., is most susceptible to repeated theft? Rather depend on established inter-library loan networks similar to MINITEX in Minnesota or WILS in Wisconsin, to supply photocopies of the requested materials as demand arises, rather than buy a volume or an issue to tip in, only to find it missing again a short time later. The success of cooperative ventures like MINITEX surely has resulted not only from the increased access available to small and medium sized libraries, but also because a growing number of libraries no longer can justify a ballooning periodicals budget and have lavishly cancelled subscriptions and foregone new offerings, depending instead on networks to supply timely and inexpensive photocopies of virtually anything.

Others have argued that libraries need to retain only the most heavily used titles and rely on networks or research facilities such as the Center for Research Libraries for photocopies of requested articles. Sizable savings are possible with this approach, but there are difficulties here as well. Without a closed access system, or some other form of circulation procedure for periodical use, it is very difficult to identify low-usage items, or, if once achieved, to persuade the chairman of the English department that a number of his highly specialized, seldom used journals should be cancelled in exchange for access through inter-library loan.

There is a solution to virtually all of the problems afflicting serials, a panacea that has been available to libraries for several years, but for a variety of reasons its promise has remained unfulfilled. That solution is microforms, and in particular—microfiche.

Why do libraries continue to buy and bind vast stores of paper issues when so many periodicals are available in microform? Why, when the cost of a microform volume is routinely half that of annual binding costs for the paper volume, do libraries continue to spend vast sums to procure and maintain complete paper volumes and to allocate huge amounts of staff time to re-shelving and shelf-reading to maintain some sort of order, no matter how difficult or disorganized? The explanation most often tendered is user reluc-tance to accept microforms, which must be the most self-serving excuse on record, considering the treatment typically afforded microformats.

How many libraries position their microform collections in a well lighted, central location instead of some dark dungeon in a far off corner of the general collections? How many provide access to microforms through easily inter-preted catalogs or computer generated serial lists, and provide high quality, convenient-to-use readers with trained personnel to lend assistance?[5] Is it surprising to encounter user reluctance in the absence of such conditions?

Many special libraries (especially those oriented to science and technology) easily have achieved user acceptance with serials on microfilm cartridges and high speed motorized readers.[6] But reliance on cartridge-loaded film is pro-hibitively expensive for many general libraries. A cartridge volume costs between two and three dollars more than the same title on roll film,[7] and the cost of a motorized microfilm reader can be double that of a manual machine. A new library could achieve savings by subscribing to periodicals on cartridges and buying back runs in the same format instead of purchasing back files in paper. But for the thousands of libraries that already own sizable holdings on roll film, the price of converting back files from rolls to cartridges is a project fit to put wobble in the knees of the most courageous budget analyst.

Hence the appeal of microfiche. In the past year a number of micropub-lishers and distributors, including Johnson Associates, Bell and Howell, Updata Publications, University Microfilms, etc., have begun offering a wide variety of periodicals on microfiche, a medium that offers significant ad-vantages over film in terms of cost and use. First consider costs.

The price of fiche volumes is generally less than film, and the cost of buying general periodicals (or titles in almost any subject other than science and technology) in either medium is roughly half the cost of binding the same volume in paper. If all the related costs of binding (particularly including the budget required to staff a binding operation) are itemized, the cost of micro-forms is a fraction of the total binding outlay. Royalty agreements presently require libraries to continue paper subscriptions while buying microform volumes. But the paper can remain on the shelves unbound, and when the microform volume arrives, the paper issues can serve for a time as a second access point for users, or they can be discarded altogether to create badly needed storage space.

The storage advantages inherent in microforms have long been one of the most compelling arguments in favor of this medium. A periodical volume on microform occupies less than one-fifteenth of the space required to house a bound volume; and for all those libraries bulging at the seams with cluttered shelves and unmanageable maintenance problems, microforms are difficult to resist. And fiche occupies less space than film.

Third, obtaining replacement issues on fiche is vastly more convenient and less costly than replacing either paper issues or microfilm. A single replacement issue on fiche costs about seventy five cents, while microfilm volumes are priced at original costs. And paper volumes? Well, that subject has been covered already.

That brings us to the most important consideration: Convenience of use. If resistance to microfilm has been partly failure by libraries to offer adequate assistance and suitable conditions for use, and partly the formidable obstacles to convenient use posed by many microfilm readers because of elaborate controls, threading difficulties, and tiresome winding chores—consider the microfiche.

A single periodical issue most often appears on a single fiche. The user is not confronted by an unfathomable mechanical proficiency test whose successful completion requires the location of a spindle to which a roll must be attached before a film can be threaded (no matter how imperfectly) and finally driven to the desired page by a manual or power operated device that is susceptible to an amazing frequency of frustrating failures. Conversely, observe a ten-year-old child or a senior faculty member approach one of the newer fiche readers on the market (and good fiche readers can be purchased for much less than comparable film readers).[8] The user slips an easily managed 4'' x 6'' card between two glass plates, flicks the light switch, and focuses. If he chooses to relax on a reading room sofa with a lap reader—or checks out the fiche and reader for home use—all the better. The library can retain a permanent fiche copy on file and make duplicate copies to sell or give away, or produce inexpensive copies on a reader printer. Given suitable surroundings and easily operated readers, the user need never moan at the loss of that most cherished of all library shibboleths—the printed page. The purchase of the magazine being used may not have been possible without the savings achieved through microforms. Despite the initial costs of viewing and storage equipment, microforms afford the opportunity to build larger and more diverse serial collections in an era of dwindling resources and rampant inflation. For librarians, that should be the most compelling reason of all to accept the dark medium.

The development most urgently needed to optimize the potential of microfiche is publication of journals solely in fiche, or in paper and fiche simultaneously, and the removal of requirements imposed by publishers who insist that libraries subscribe to both paper and microform volumes. The American Chemical Society is considering offering its journals on current microfiche starting in 1975; and the American Institute of Physics already offers all of its journals on microfilm or paper, and the microfilm is available at approximately the same time the paper issues are distributed, but sells for about 25 percent less than the cost of the paper issues.

As other publishers watch paper prices and postal rates escalate, they too may see the wisdom of micropublishing. For libraries need the opportunity to buy, if they choose, current periodicals on microform only, and thus continue to build viable serial collections without the necessity of organizing ubiquitous cooperative acquisition and loan networks that are bound to drive prices even higher.

Ultimately, however, the successful conversion from paper to microform will depend on user acceptance. If we continue to treat the microform as if it were the untouchable in a library materials' caste hierarchy, publishers will go on as before issuing increasingly expensive paper journals that fewer and fewer libraries will be able to afford, and we all will suffer the consequences.

References

1. Brown, Norman B. "Price Indexes for 1973: U.S. Periodicals and Serial Services." *Library Journal*, July 1973, p. 2052-54.

2. For two discussions of the agents' role in serials work see: Smith, Katherine. "Serials Agents/Serials Librarians," *LRTS*, Winter 1970, p. 5-18, and Sineath, Timothy. "Libraries and Library Subscription Agencies," *The Library Scene*, Summer 1972, p. 28-30.

3. Wood, D.A. et al. "Investigation of the Cost of Periodical Replacement in the Periodical Reading Room of the University Library," in *Case Studies in Systems Analyses in a University Library* (ed. by Barton R. Biorkhalter), Scarecrow, 1968, p. 120-27.

4. Williams, Gordon. "Background and Proposal for a National Lending Library for Journals." Proposed by Cntr. for Research Libraries, 1972.

5. Fair, Judy. "The Microtext Reading Room," *Microform Review*, July 1972, p. 199-202; October 1972, p. 269-73; January 1973, p. 9-13.

6. Starker, Lee N. "User Experiences with Primary Journals on 16-mm Microfilm," *Journal of Chemical Documentation*, February 1970, p. 5-6.

7. Spigai, Frances G. *The Invisible Medium: The State of the Art of Microform and a Guide to the Literature*, ERIC Clearinghouse in Library and Information Sciences, March 1973, p. 20.

8. For information and standards concerning microform readers, see issues of *Library Technology Reports* and *Standards and Guidelines for Procurement of Microfilm and Microfilm Equipment* by the Libraries of the California State Universities and Colleges, adapted by the Council of Library Directors, June 22, 1973.

CONVERSION OF PERIODICAL HOLDINGS TO MICRO-FORM: A RATING FORM

by **Philip John Schwarz,** *Serials Librarian, University of Wisconsin - Stout*

The number of libraries utilizing microforms as a means of preserving their periodical collections has increased over the past decade. The rationales for the transformation from paper to microform as a storage medium are many and will not be recounted here. Let it suffice to say that once a library has decided to convert its holdings, it is faced with the very practical problem of determining which titles should be converted first. The purpose of this paper is to describe how the problem was dealt with by the University of Wisconsin - Stout.

A search of the literature did not reveal how other libraries approached this problem. Consequently we decided to develop a means of systematizing the process of evaluating our periodical collection for possible conversion to microform. We were looking for something that would be simple and yet would remove the decision making process from the "off the cuff" level. To this end we decided to develop a forced choice rating form similar to those commonly used in attitudinal surveys and preference testing.

Once we had determined the approach we would use in establishing a priority listing of titles, our next step was to identify the factors that would be considered in our evaluation. With this in mind, we attempted to identify the problems we were experiencing with our existing periodical collection. The outgrowth of this process was a list (example 1) of 8 factors, presented as positive statements, which we felt warranted conversion to microform. We do not consider this list to be definitive, nor do we consider these factors to be static. They were developed to fit our philosophy, needs and the state of

Reprint of ERIC Document ED 080 125, 1973.

microfilm technology at a given time. At another time or place, other factors should no doubt be considered.

EXAMPLE 1

MICROFORM EVALUATION FACTORS

1. There is a considerable number of missing issues in each publisher's volume.
2. There is a considerable number of worn or mutilated issues in each publisher's volume.
3. The title is heavily used.
4. The format presents storage problems.
5. The paper is of poor quality.
6. Articles are popularly written and of current interest.
7. Articles are short.
8. The title is indexed.

Once we had identified the factors that would be evaluated, our next step was to arbitrarily establish a rating scale of 0-8 for each factor. In this scale, if a factor was given a 0, it was considered to be false; if given an 8 rating, it was considered to be true. Each factor would receive a rating of anywhere from 0 to 8. The higher the number of evaluation points, the higher the holdings would be on the priority scale. In an effort to standardize our ratings, we refined the scale for each factor. In the case of factor number 1, a percentage of the number of missing issues was equated with a number on the rating scale. The same approach was used for factor number 2 relating to the number of mutilated issues. In the case of periodical usage, factor number 3, we equated each number on the rating scale with a range of numbers relating to the number of times a title was checked out. This approach was also used for factor number 7 where a range of page numbers was equated with the numbers on the rating scale. A similar approach was used for factor number 8 where a number on the rating scale was equated with the number of sources the title was indexed in. In the case of factor number 4, storage problems, a three point scale was used; 0 equaled no storage problem, 4 was equated with a magazine in a tabloid format, and 8 was equated with a bulky item such as a newspaper. In the case of the paper quality, factor number 5, two points on the scale were used, 0 for paper in good condition and 8 for paper likely to, or showing signs of, deterioration. The last factor, number 6, related to the type of writing and was the most difficult to judge. Three points on the scale were finally used as follows: 0 equaled popular, 4 equaled semi-popular, 8 equaled scholarly. If, for some reason data was not available for a given rating factor, it was recorded as zero on the scale. This had the effect of providing high ratings for only those titles where adequate information was available for decision making.

With the scale developed and refined, we then evaluated each title using the factors noted in example 1 and the guidelines noted above. The data for each title was placed on 3 x 5 cards for ease of interfiling with our other records. As mentioned earlier, the higher the evaluation score, the higher the priority assigned to the title. The completed cards were arranged in order, highest to lowest, and the money spent accordingly.

After using the scale for some time, it became evident that the entire holdings of a particular title should not be evaluated on a single form. By breaking down holdings into 10 year time segments, we found that the rating for each segment could vary considerably. Using this approach we found that we were better able to make a decision regarding holdings that could be converted, held in the paper form or discarded.

The use of the refined scale also removed much of the burden for gathering data from the shoulders of the serials librarian. Most of the data can be gathered and tabulated by students leaving the final decision up to the professional librarian.

This scale, or a version of it, has been used at the University of Wisconsin - Stout for several years. It has proved an effective tool in our efforts to spend money more efficiently and wisely.

MICROFORM SERIALS COLLECTIONS:
A SYSTEMS ANALYSIS

by **R. J. Coffman** *Director of the Library, Northeastern University*

TECHNICAL CONSTRAINTS AFFECTING SERIALS MICROFORM

Primary Issue: Linear versus Unitized Microformat

The purpose of microform serials is intimately related to the density of use of a title. In research done by Dr. Blair Stewart and Ms. Irma Lucht at the Associated Colleges of the Midwest in Chicago, it was determined that for a large group of academic and public libraries the density of use of serials was highest for the more popular titles. This phenomenon was attributed to the fact that the accessibility of a given title in a given system was inversely proportional to the level of its use by clients. The less a title was used the more accessible it was to the user, while the more a title was used the less accessible it was. This has important implications for the development of microform serials collections. [1]

If a group of 750 serial titles is known to have a high density of use, it may be advisable to purchase a microform edition to insure accessibility, but serious consideration should be given to replacing a hard copy edition if it has high density of use.

Reprinted from *The Serials Librarian*, vol. 1, no. 1 (Fall 1976), pp. 46-50, by permission of the publisher.

A solution developed at Northeastern University's Library in Burlington, Massachusetts was to retain hard copy for most periodicals for three years, while having concurrent microform subscriptions. The decline in use of those periodicals measured was substantial enough to warrant only a microform edition after that period of time. This threshold will probably vary from library to library.

Density of use intimately affects the selection of a particular microformat. Microforms are either linear (microfilm) or unitized (microfiche or microcard) in format. In applications where material is of low density use and archival, linear storage can be preferable because storage of roll film is more secure than storage of fiche or cards. Where density of use is expected to be high, the feasibility of automatic accessing of microforms must be weighed. Commercially available systems make use of both film and fiche for this purpose. Automated accessing can be accomplished by searching for specific frames or by searching binary coded chips or other magnetic or optical targets. In searching for specific frames, fiche are referenced by horizontal and vertical coordinates, while film is referenced by linear units into a given reel. In searching by binary coded chips or other devices, the search is accomplished by a Boolean combination of preselected criteria. Such systems are used extensively by police and criminal justice researchers. However, at present, none of these search systems is applicable to commercially available microform serials, but it should be a goal which the library community sets for the micrographics industry.

Unitized format is appealing for cases where high density of use is expected, since fiche to fiche duplication enables the reproduction of 98 frames (or pages) for approximately the same cost for one page in paper production, about five cents.

Thus, primary to deciding whether or not a title should be in microform and what format should be selected, a determination of density of use should be made. Only then can the question of unitized or linear storage be answered.

Secondary Issue: Quality of Image

This issue is all too often blandly disregarded by microform producers, even the largest, but it is of crucial importance to librarians and users of microforms in general. On this issues hinges, to a large extent, the capabilities of a microform system.

Basically, there are two aspects of image quality: resolution and stability.

Resolution can be measured in the first frame of the film or fiche, which should contain a National Bureau of Standards Resolution Test Chart - 1963A.

Acceptable resolution is 1.8 and 1.4 along the vertical and horizontal axes of the image,[2] that is, the targets at 1.8 and 1.4 lines/mm. are discrete and not blurred together. If lines blur in these resolution targets, the problem could be in either the film or the reader's lens, but in any case, the system is not functioning adequately.*

If it is anticipated that copies of fiche will be made, the acceptable resolution should be increased so that resolution fiche copies is 1.8 and 1.4. On the production side, this better than acceptable standard for commercially vended fiche is usually within the scope of fiche produced from master fiche filmed with a step and repeat camera. If, however, the vended fiche is produced from a second generation master which was in turn produced from a first generation strip up of 16mm film, quality of the vended fiche is questionable. It is therefore important for the serials librarian to be cognizant of the method employed by micropublishers in the filming process. Since 5-10 percent of the image is lost from one generation of an image on film to its copy, a third generation image has lost anywhere from 15 to 30 percent of the original information.

Stability of image is the second aspect of quality. When it is expected that microforms are to be stored for the indefinite future, archival quality as defined by the National Bureau of Standards and the National Micrographics Association is the standard. Generally, silver halide film is considered to be preferable to either diazo or vesicular for the permanence of its image. Microcards are also stable, but the restrictions of their use due to the susceptibility of their surfaces to scratching and alteration are factors which have to be carefully weighed in their selection.

Quality of Reproduction of Microforms

Obviously the quality of reproduction either in hard copy or in film or fiche is dependent on the generation and the quality of the image being reproduced. It is also dependent on the polarity of the image being reproduced.

---

*[It is incorrect to quantify resolution without at the same time specifying the exact reduction ratio at which the National Bureau of Standards Resolution Chart has been photographed. The correct number for resolution under such conditions is derived by multiplying the number next to the smallest resolvable pattern by the reduction ratio. That product is the resolution of that particular photographic system in lines per millimeter. (Orig. publ. abridged). Note by Allen B. Veaner.]

Some electrostatic processes have nonreversable polarity. This means that image reproduction is always from one polarity to its opposite, negative to positive or positive to negative. Since electrostatic processes print negative images (white print on black background) very poorly, the selection of negative polarity film should be made, since the printout will be positive.

If it is anticipated that a microform collection will necessarily contain both positive and negative polarities, then a reader-printer should be selected which can reverse the polarity of its printouts. This capability is called ambi-polarity.

Adjunct to this concern is the size of the blow-back of image. In some processes, the size of the print clearly reproduced is critical. When the size of blown-back characters is below a certain threshold, acceptable resolution of the printout is not achieved. Thus, parallel to the consideration of resolution of image in a microform reader is the resolution of image in a reader-printer. There is no substitute for factoring both of these components into a microform system, before any selection decisions are made.

The Bibliographic Accessing of Microform Serials

Accessing may be accomplished in two ways: by a unique, consecutive numeric or alpha-numeric sequence, or by a system of organization that reflects an integrated ordering of knowledge. In the first alternative a library may choose to number its serials by accession numbers, such as the Associated Colleges of the Mid-West Periodicals Bank in Chicago. This has proven to be an efficient device at ACM. Unique numbering arrangements of microforms are also used for major microform serial sets such as the Educational Information Resource Center (ERIC), National Aeronautics and Space Administration (NASA), National Technical Information Series (NTIS), and the Securities Exchange Commission 10K Reports. With these unique, consecutive numbering systems, additional microforms are added at the end of collections and there is no (or very little) expansion within consecutive arrangement.

On the other hand, there are arrangement schemes dependent on systems of organizing knowledge. The MARC Serials Format developed by the Serials Division of the Library of Congress is such a system. As more serials records are stored with the Ohio College Library Center this system will take precedence over all others, but not without some inherent difficulties.

The problems the MARC Serials Format creates for the microform serials librarian are two-fold. Each separate microformat is treated as a separate edition of the title, and separate records are entered as well as separate sets of catalog cards generated. For the same serial title one could have 16mm and 35mm positive microfilm coverage, followed by a microfiche edition. All three would have separate sets of cards and separate computer records to be searched by computer console. Whether cards or records, it means that search time for the particular desired holdings is either doubled or tripled, and thus, in an economic sense, it costs more to search this format than if the records were consolidated. Libraries will have to make this consolidation locally if it is deemed desirable from a client standpoint. Users of the terminal or the catalog will have to be trained to make these multiple searches for the same title, if records are not consolidated.

Physical Storage

The method of bibliographic accessing directly affects the means of physical arrangement and storage. Self-contained, unique consecutive numbering systems have greater packing density because no internal expansion is anticipated. Those systems based on a classification and arrangement of knowledge requiring materials to be constantly integrated demand that space be allocated internally for expansion.

Furthermore, the integration or separation of the various microformats creates special difficulties. Usually, the smaller the microform serials collection, the easier it is to service it by keeping an integrated collection where all microformats are shelved together. This is true of special libraries where the difficulties of large research collections are not anticipated. In other transitional cases, the change from integrated to separate collections may be required. In large research libraries, due to pressures of space, it is usually important to separate collections according to microformat since packing density, the number of microforms stored per unit area, is critical. In smaller collections, self-service outweighs this benefit, since the client only has to look in one location for a desired title. In transitional cases, a compromise can be achieved by separately storing all microform serials prior to a cutoff year (say, five years back) while more current serials are integrated. This is a solution the Northeastern University Library in Burlington has developed.

Goals

Improving service to clients should be the end goal of any microform serials system. This is predicated on staff awareness of the inherent complexities of microform serials and the ability to service and develop collections for their institutions, whether they be high school libraries, public libraries in a small town, or large academic and public libraries concerned with providing in-depth research collections.

To this end staff development programs must be directed to developing positive attitudes and technical skills required in the servicing of microforms. For instance, profiles of software and hardware can be developed to assist staff in understanding the dimensions and variety of collections.

Complexity in microform collections is with us to stay. The industry will always, and should, experiment with new techniques. As both consumers and developers, serials librarians, and indeed management personnel, must take initiative and leadership in directing the micrographics industry to ways which will better serve the ultimate user.

References

1. Stewart, Blair. "Periodicals and the Liberal Arts College Library." *College and Research Libraries* 36 (1975): 371—378.

2. National Micrographics Association. *Industrial Standard Facsimile Transmission of Microfilmed Documents*. Silver Spring, MD: NMA, 1972.

REPLACEMENT OF HARD COPY BY MICROFORMS

by **Frederick C. Lynden,** *Assistant Chief, Acquisitions Department, Stanford University Libraries*

As the library budget shrinks and as the issue of space becomes more significant, it is necessary to establish criteria for evaluating the purchase of microforms to replace hard copy materials. There is a number of factors to be
considered: the kind of material being replaced; the type of microform used as
replacement; the amount of space saved; the costs of hard copy versus film
copy, including the binding and equipment costs; the quality and durability of
commercial microform products; convenience to users; reliability of equipment and costs of maintenance; the bibliographic finding aids, internal and
external; availability of hard copy photocopies; microform/hard copy "trade"
plans; preservation of unique or deteriorating material; and cooperative microform plans.

Replacing bound volumes of newspapers, periodicals, or books with microforms is not yet a panacea for the library seeking extra space. With the present
state of technology in the microform industry, the problem of weighing the
pros and cons of such a course remains.

Selection of Materials for Replacement

1. *Space (linear feet) occupied by the original materials.* The late Roma
   Gregory pointed out that newspapers, periodicals, and government
   documents are the most likely candidates for acquisition in microform

Reprinted from *Microform Review*, vol. 4, no. 1 (January 1974), pp. 15-24. Copyright © 1974 by
Microform Review Inc.

since "some [are] very bulky publications, printed orginally on poor paper, consulted seldom but of vital importance to research collections..."[1]

2. *Questionable suitability of certain materials.* Certain types of material, such as reference books, are not suitable for reproduction in microform: Reference books are rarely, and never should be, issued in microform. Even the reference features of non-reference books, such as the index, are more and more frequently issued in original size, when the text is reduced to microform...Other kinds of library materials which are least suitable in microform, if the original form is available, are texts which must be compared with other similar texts for the purpose of collating or editing, early printed books which are to be studied in their original state for the placement of watermark or the positioning of separate pages, books of art reproductions or other books in which the quality of illustrations are important, reserve books, and other books which are used frequently.[2]

3. *Amount of use.* Material on film may not be as readily available to large numbers of users as the hard copy. In contrast to hard copies, microform copies are machine dependent, and an insufficient number of readers or inoperable readers make access more difficult. User access problems are compounded by the fact that materials covering a long span of time are often included in one reel or on one fiche, and cannot be divided among machines or users.

4. *Availability of commercial products.* It is often the case that no copy is available commercially and microfilming a local copy is frequently undesirable for two reasons: (1) the cost of high quality custom filming is usually too great (see section on In-House Filming of Hard Copies); (2) variable physical conditions of the original hard copies affect the reproducibility of the materials. William R. Hawken's *Copying Methods Manual* describes in detail the technical and physical problems associated with photocopying originals.[3]

5. *Bibliographic integrity of the material.* Often the microform files, assembled from many sources, may be *more* complete than the hard copy files which they replace.

6. *Preservation factors.* The condition of the paper original and the degree to which the original copy may have been mutilated are considerations when selecting hard copies to be replaced by microform. Two other factors which will be treated later in this paper are the binding costs and the uniqueness of the material.

Type of Microform for Replacement

When choosing the type of microform which should be used to replace the original materials, there are several important considerations. The A.L.A. handbook, *The Evaluation of Micropublications*, recommends that microfilm be used for serials such as newspapers or periodicals, and that microfiche or micro-opaques be used for complete bibliographic units such as "technical reports, individual journal articles, reprints of chapters, and relatively short monographs."[4] According to this handbook, it is wise to consider both file integrity and the frequency of use when deciding on the format of the microform. The less frequently used material can be put into serial or roll format, whereas the heavily used materials would be more accessible in a microfiche or micro-opaque format. Although the cartridge form allows motorized access to roll film, two developments which may weigh in favor of fiche for heavy use are the portable lap reader and inexpensive reproduction of fiche from fiche. However, Norman Shaffer asserts that "the service costs on fiche are probably higher. It requires different cabinets and the maintenance of file integrity can be a nightmare while the envelopes add significantly to the storage space required."[5]

a. File Maintenance Factors. The maintenance of file integrity can be a troublesome problem when microfiches are used to replace serials. When the entire run of a periodical is on microfiche, there may be hundreds of separate fiche to reference, handle, insert in envelopes, and re-file. For example, the *Colored American Magazine* (Boston, New York), volumes 1-17, no. 5, May 1900 to November 1909 is on 89 fiches. As the bulk of fiches becomes larger, the chances for misfiling them increase. Some libraries require an attendant to re-file all fiches in order to avoid mis-files.

The management problems of fiches are sometimes overlooked when considering the purchase of fiche. In a recent article on the rising costs of serials, the conveniences of microfiche are extolled, and it is suggested that journals be published "solely in fiche" in order to reduce costs.[6] Unfortunately the article does not discuss the inconvenient aspects of microfiche noted above, and problems associated with the use of fiche as replacements for serials are not conveyed to the reader. For example, without documentation, it is stated that a "single periodical issue most often appears on a single fiche."[7] With 98 pages on a standard fiche, how many single issues, from what population of journals, will fit on one fiche? As to publishing journals solely on fiche, it is certain that, although manufacturing costs would be reduced, the same front-end costs, i.e. the editorial, marketing, and initial production costs, would still have to be absorbed by the consumer. If journals were only available in fiche, the cost of fiche for these journals would probably increase significantly.

b. Durability Factors. The standards for archival permanence published by ANSI, the American National Standards Institute, are another consideration when purchasing microforms to replace hard copies. Unless the film or fiche meets ANSI standards PH1.28-1973 and PH5.3-1967 (R1973), its archival quality is dubious. The whole controversy over the permanence of silver halide versus the diazo or vesicular films has not yet seen a final outcome. Nevertheless the tendency for micropublishers has been to publish materials which require frequent updating or which become obsolete rapidly in diazo and vesicular film because these types of film are less expensive. However, diazo's "use for the preservation and dissemination of archival research materials is not yet recommended."[8]

c. Film Reduction Ratios. The film reduction ratio is also an important consideration, since the kind of microform reader and equipment is affected by the size of the image. The film used in replacement may be either 16 or 35 mm. 16 mm film can be stored more compactly than 35 mm, but it is not suitable for reproducing newspapers since the legibility suffers from the greatly reduced image size.

Space Savings

A major factor involved in microform replacement is the space saving aspects of film compared with hard copy. In a recent conversion of chemistry and biology journals to 16 mm cartridge film at the Ford Reading Room, MIT, Ann De Villiers and Barbara Schloman report the following:

> For example, the hard copy volumes for the *Journal of the American Chemical Society* from volume 1, 1879 to volume 94, 1972, occupy about 60 feet of shelf space; each volume measures 11½ inches tall. The comparable film run uses about 12 feet of shelf space, and the cartridges are only 4 inches tall.[9]

The space savings can be dramatic. With the present high cost of storage per square foot, typically ranging from $60.00 to $75.00 on today's market, a shelf space savings, such as that at the MIT Ford Reading Room, can mean considerable cost savings. Although it is necessary to consider the space to be occupied by microfilm or fiche readers, reader/printers, and microform storage cabinets when one is looking at space savings, in many cases there is already a microform room which may have area for expansion. In calculating the space to be saved, on must look at the following factors:

1) Space occupied by the bound volumes to be replaced; 2) Number of reels or fiche to replace bound volumes; 3) Space occupied by the storage units which will contain the microforms; 4) Space occupied by reader/printers and the space occupied by people; 5) Space taken by the supervisor/attendant.

By checking the number of reels or fiches required to replace the bound volumes one can then estimate the amount of space which will be occupied by the microforms, since the dimensions and capacities of microfilm and fiche cabinets are provided by the manufacturer.

In-House Filming of Hard Copies

The evidence indicates that the price of in-house filming of hard copy materials is prohibitive because of the cost of the master negative. This is the conclusion of Alan B. Pritsker and J. William Sadler in ''An Evaluation of Microfilm as a Method of Book Storage,'' *College and Research Libraries,* July 1957.[10] In a follow-up article in the January 1963 issue of *College and Research Libraries,* Verner Clapp and Robert Jordan concluded that the cost savings could be achieved for in-house filming if there was cooperation and the cost of the master negative was shared among several libraries.[11] The technique and technology of microfilming academic materials has not changed significantly since these articles were prepared. Microfilming is still an extraordinarily labor intensive process. With increasing film and labor costs, it is thus extremely dubious that a library can achieve cost savings by doing its own filming.

Although the Clapp and Jordan article noted that the use of high reduction microfilm might change the price situation radically, the response of the library community to published microform libraries employing high reduction film seems to signal slow progress towards the use of ultrafiche. The use of ultrafiche requires special equipment, and there has been controversy about the equipment and services which go with at least one microform library.[12] Another serious qualification to the conclusion of Clapp and Jordan is how copyright would affect the production of multiple copies for co-operating users. Certainly, copyright restrictions have been a handicap to the ultrafiche library projects which have offered almost exclusively titles out of copyright. With the uncertain acceptance of high reduction film and the high costs of in-house filming, it seems that the most likely alternative to filming one's own replacement microforms is commercial purchase of conventional microforms.

Commercial and Library Guides to Microforms

With the advent in 1961 of *Guide to Microforms in Print** (Washington, Microcard Editions, 1961-   ) and the beginning in 1966 of the *National Register of Microform Masters* (Washington, Library of Congress, 1966-   ), the problems of locating film copies have been reduced. Using the former tool it is possible to look up prices for microforms and make the comparisons necessary for the replacement of hard copies. Using the latter, it is possible to find microforms in other libraries and realize the economies of not having to re-make the master negative. Another library guide to available microfilm of newspapers is the successor to the 6th edition of *Newspapers on Microfilm*, now in two volumes, *Newspapers in Microform: United States, 1948-1972* (Washington, Library of Congress, 1973) and *Newspapers in Microform: Foreign Countries, 1948-1972* (Washington, Library of Congress, 1973), reporting positive and negative microfilm of domestic and foreign newspapers in the United States and Canada. A new guide called *International Microforms in Print*** (Weston, Conn., Microform Review, 1974-   ) covering solely microforms offered for sale by publishers outside the United States is now available. This purchasing guide includes monographs, journals, newspapers, government publications, and archival material.

It is not possible to purchase many current journals *only* in microform. According to Xerox University Microfilms, *Serials in Microform, 1973/74*, "libraries entering orders for current periodicals must certify that the library subscribes to the paper edition..."[13] Thus, the cost of microform replacement becomes an *incremental* cost and must be offset by significant reductions in other expenditures, such as binding, if any money is to be saved.

Binding Costs

Although the cost of filming has been raised by the increased costs of materials, the cost of binding is also rising due to shortages of binding board and cloth, and higher labor costs. According to a recent survey of binding, the average costs for binding 12" Class A periodicals ranged from a low of $3.85 to

*[Since the 1976 edition, published by Microform Review Inc.]

**[This publication has been merged into the *Guide to Microforms in Print*.]

a high of $7.88.[14] In calculating binding costs one must consider also the preparation costs and not just the binding costs per volume. Xerox University Microfilms in discussions with librarians at Columbia University estimated that it cost $2.75 per volume for preparation and $6.00 per volume for binding for a total cost of $8.75.[15] The Xerox University Microfilms' figure for binding alone is in the middle of the survey quoted above, but the processing costs raise it above the highest figure in the study. It is clear one must consider processing costs when figuring the binding costs.

According to Xerox University Microfilms the average microfilm price for a current periodical subscription is $7.11 per year.[16] Where the binding costs are high, there may be justification for the purchase of microfilm. At Stanford University Libraries, since 1966, the Engineering Library has purchased 100 titles in microfilm rather than binding them and holds overlapping subscriptions to microform and hard copy versions of these titles. Engineering Librarian Elizabeth Bates, who studied the question of microform replacement of library materials, concluded that "the users will accept microfilm in lieu of hard copy, and the use will increase rapidly if we have a reader/printer..."[17] However, user satisfaction with such a policy will depend upon how soon after the end of the subscription year the microform copy arrives. Until the microform copy arrives, the user must contend with unbound issues.

One problem when using microforms in lieu of binding is the relatively small number of titles available from commercial microform publishers. Although many titles are not available in microform commercially, the number of titles available from commercial firms is increasing. In an informal telephone poll of several major microform publishers, all had increased the number of titles substantially over the past four years.

There appear to be offsetting costs when replacing hard copies with microform in lieu of binding. On the one hand, substantial binding preparation savings can be achieved. It is not necessary to bind the current hard copy subscription because microform replacement is available. One of the advantages of overlapping subscriptions of hard copy and film that "the title is never absent at the binder or never on a processing shelf awaiting receipt of a missing issue so it can go to the binder."[18] On the other hand, to make the film readily available, additional purchases of equipment for the use and preservation of the microform may be required. In some cases products from one manufacturer may not be compatible with another manufacturer's equipment, e.g., there is incompatability among competing cartridge and cassette systems. The microtext room may need expansion or additional air-conditioning equipment or readers, or as noted earlier reader/printers. If a number of motorized readers are used in one facility, then some soundproofing may be necessary.

The calculation of the costs of replacement by microform will vary according to the local conditions in a library, but certainly some important considerations are: 1) The availability and cost of the film and its compatability with existing equipment; 2) The offsetting cost reductions in personnel and materials achieved through elimination of binding; 3) The additional costs for microform equipment and personnel; and 4) The cost of microform storage versus the savings in hard copy storage.

A look at the costs of hard copy versus film copy will look like a balance sheet with some offsetting savings and costs. A study comparing the costs for serials binding with microfilm replacement at Indiana University Libraries showed a total binding cost for 1449 serial publications ($6.89 per year average) which was slightly less than the total microfilm cost for the same publications ($7.20 per year average).[10] However, when the binding labor costs ($2.75 per unit) were added to the binding costs, the resulting savings by purchasing microfilm was approximately 34½ percent. When microform labor costs ($.55 per reel) were added to the total microfilm costs, the resulting savings by purchasing microfilm was slightly less - approximately 29½ percent. Despite these savings, the balance sheet will likely be different for each institution according to its size, academic programs, degree of centralization, and other characteristics. No "universal truth" can be stated about the question.

Maintenance of Microforms

Durability is affected by the care and maintenance of the microforms and microform equipment. One of the strongest arguments made in favor of microform products is their lasting quality in comparison with paper products. This argument is subject to some qualifications. Storage equipment can be damaged by chemical deterioration...Even tested and established products, such as silver halide, are subject to blemishes, fungal attack, or other deterioration when kept under improper conditions. Other factors can impair the quality of microforms. Frequent use causes wear, and improperly maintained equipment can result in damage to the microforms.

Another aspect to the maintenance of microforms is the treatment accorded the product by the user. Improper handling by the inexperienced user can scratch roll film and unlaminated fiche, reducing their legibility. Certainly it is necessary to staff microtext rooms with managers who are aware of, and implement, measures which will insure effective use of materials. Security for film is as necessary as for the bound copies of periodicals. What is the difference if someone damages some film by exposing it to too much heat or mutilates a journal by cutting out an article? Or what about the user who steals a fiche? Preservation problems are not eliminated by adopting microform instead of hard copy.

Quality of Microforms

If the library replaces an important set of a journal or newspaper with an inferior microform product, then any economic savings have been virtually nullified. Some kind of quality control is necessary to see if the entire run of a journal, including indices, has been filmed; whether it has been filmed in proper sequence; whether the film is always in focus; whether the pages of the journal are always filmed with the same page orientation; whether the original filmed by the commercial company or by a library was in as good condition as your copy; whether the boxes are labelled accurately and clearly and contain the film described on the label. *The Evaluation of Micropublications* (Chicago, A.L.A., 1971) contains an excellent check-list for quality control of microforms received in the library[20] The library community can also insure more quality control on the part of commercial microform publishers by returning materials which are unsatisfactory. This, of course, means checking microforms prior to use or before discarding the originals. For receipt inspection purposes libraries should have some kind of light set-up. (Various types of equipment for illuminated inspection, including a professional light box set-up are described in *The Evaluation of Micropublications.)*[21] Another aspect of quality control involves the careful evaluation of the catalogs and advertisements of micropublishers to determine whether their product will be compatible with local library equipment.

User Reactions

When considering microform replacement it is also necessary to think of the user. The user's reaction to microforms and the convenience to the user are two cardinal elements in the decision to replace with microforms. Two studies, Holmes (1969) and Lewis (1970), showed that given a choice, readers chose hard copy over microform. The study by Holmes of 1969 noted reader complaints about: problems of browsing for microforms; damaged microforms; and difficulties in finding misfiled microforms.[22] The study by Lewis of 1970 pointed out problems with the quality and number of readers available; restriction of material to one location where the machinery could be used; lack of standardization in films and equipment; and eye strain. The general user preference was for hard copy.[23] E.M. Grieder, former Associate Director for Collection Development at Stanford University Libraries, in analyzing two ultrafiche libraries consisting of general literature in the humanities and social sciences, described the microform user's problems:

...for treatises in the social sciences, *belles lettres* generally, biographies, and in fact for any lengthy reading task, or one which requires extensive reflection and rereading, use of microfiche at an immobile station is likely to be regarded more as a punishment than as a stimulating and satisfying intellectual experience.[24]

Other user problems which have been mentioned are slower speed of reference, more difficult shelf-classification, and infrequent availability of color film.

Although the user studies cited above indicated negative user reactions to microforms, each pointed out compensatory, positive factors which can contribute to a successful microform installation. According to Lewis, it is possible to overcome some inconveniences of microfiche by providing liberal copying privileges and making equipment readily available for reading fiche and printing hard copies. A user study by Harold Wooster, then Director of Information Sciences of the Air Force Office of Scientific Research, found that the major drawback for users of fiche was difficulty of access to readers or lack of readers for their own use. He noted that libraries which had used microfiche successfully had "adequate numbers of microfiche readers, reader/printers, and copiers (and filing boxes for individuals to use!)."[25] Wooster discovered that libraries which had favorable user reactions to microforms usually had enthusiastic librarians who made an effort to persuade users to give microforms a fair trial. In the MIT conversion noted earlier, a majority of users indicated a positive reaction to the use of scientific journals and *Chemical Abstracts* on film. Ann De Villiers who successfully replaced periodicals with microforms in the Ford Reading Room at the Massachusetts Institute of Technology concludes that acceptance by users can be encouraged by providing pleasant reading areas and "treating microforms like the rest of the collection as much as is feasible."[26] Taking this approach, complete cataloging, making microforms available for circulation, and providing reference services in the microform reading room might encourage greater user acceptance.

Selecting Equipment

In estimating the reliability of equipment and the costs of maintenance, it is helpful to consult some of the equipment guides and surveys. *Library Tech-*

nology Reports has a series of evaluations of microform readers which describe
the readers and give performance and price information. The descriptions
include information on the quality of the image; operator-machine relationships; hazards; the warranty; and maintenance. In November 1973 and January
1974, portable and lap readers were evaluated.[27] The *Guide to Microreproduction Equipment* and its supplements, published by the National Microfilm
Association (NMA), include technical information as well as special features
of readers and reader/printers.[28] There is a picture of each machine and the
price of the machine and the cost of extra lenses is indicated. NMA has also
published a handy booklet: *How to Select a Microform Reader or Reader-
Printer.*[29] In September 1973, the Defense Documentation Center published a
guide to equipment for microfiche viewing. Entitled *Microfiche Viewing
Equipment Guide*, this guide includes only technical information without
evaluation. There is a picture of each reader and the price and warranty period
for each device are also indicated. Available reader/printers are also listed in
this guide.[30] For information about the storage capacity of microform cabinets
and their prices, one should consult the *Library Technology Reports* of March
1972 published by the American Library Association.[31]

Finding Aids

Bibliographic finding aids, internal and external in the microform replacement, form another important consideration when purchasing film for
replacement. When a library replaces its hard copy which is bound in clearly
marked bibliographic segments, the microforms should be checked for
accurate headings on the boxes; properly placed target sheets; and target sheets
which designate any gaps in microform runs. Again, a thorough check of the
film when it is received is necessary to protect the library from sloppy work. It
is also very helpful - sometimes essential - to have a hard copy index of the
microform product.

Hard Copy Availability

When a library purchases microform replacements of materials, it is both
desirable and convenient to have a reader/printer which will allow hard copies
to be made from the microforms. If the microform replacements are housed in a
branch library, then it is politic to make available a reader/printer which has
the same access hours as the microform replacement. It is also important to

purchase a reader/printer which has few maintenance problems and dependable service agencies. Hard copy availability is a significant part of a comprehensive conversion program, for it allows the librarian to emphasize public service aspects of microform replacement.

Microform Trade-In Plans

There are several microform/hard copy replacement plans being advertised, and libraries must be cautious when requesting microforms in this manner. One of the most common replacement plans is the exchange of film for hard copies. To protect libraries from unscrupulous dealers, the Bookdealer Library Relations Committee of ALA prepared a list of questions to consult if asked by a dealer to exchange serials for microform. Libraries were advised to prepare a contract which would insure delivery before payment; to check the dealer's ability to provide quality film; to check the material included in the microform package and its price in comparison to the sale value of the hard copies; and finally, to notice the dealer's manner of approach.[32] Recently some legitimate publishers and dealers have offered lower prices or gratis microforms for the exchange of hard copies. In these cases the hard copies have been sold abroad. Some publishers have offered a discount rate on the price of the microform if the libraries trade in their back issue hard copy holdings. Others have offered complete files of film plus a reader in exchange for the hard copy back issues. Still other publishers have offered microfiche at no additional cost as part of their subscription to a hard copy original. One of the problems of accepting these fiche and discarding the hard copy originals is that there is no guarantee the supplier will continue making fiche copies available.

Preservation Filming

Some libraries replace their unique or deteriorating materials with a microform copy and report the existence of a negative to the *National Register of Microform Masters*. The Library of Congress and the New York Public Library have very extensive programs of microform replacement for their deteriorating materials. Writing in 1973, Charles G. LaHood, Jr., Chief of the Library of Congress Photoduplication Service, reports: "In 1962, current and past newspaper files were transferred to microfilm. Of the 165,000 bound volumes of newspapers on file, approximately 25,000 were printed after 1870 on pulp paper ... Since 1962, 25,000 bound volumes have been replaced by microfilm positives."[33] By 1973, the Library of Congress had at least 50,000 volumes on film, part of them from negatives already in existence and part of them for LC's own Photoduplication Service which uses 24 high resolution planetary cameras for filming. At the New York Public Library, the Library Photographic Service has a capacity of 2.5 to 3 million frames of master negative microfilm per year, although only about half of this capacity is being used presently due to budget restrictions.[34] According to Paul Fasana, Chief of Preparations Services, the New York Public Library is currently spending in excess of $150,000 a year to film materials from the collections that are on brittle paper and deteriorated, or serial publications which are printed on inferior paper.[35] The New York Public Library also uses negatives from other libraries when they are listed in the *National Register of Microform Masters*.

Experiences of Other Libraries

There are a few libraries where there has been extensive microform replacement of hard copy. Two of the libraries where this has been done, the Library of Congress and the New York Public Library, have converted primarily for the purpose of preservation. The Ford Reading Room at MIT is a relatively new library unit and is using microforms in place of back-sets due to space problems and the difficulties of obtaining back runs of older periodical titles. Indiana University Libraries replaced all of its newspapers lost in two fires with microfilm, and has made a detailed study, which was cited earlier, of the actual dollar savings of microfilm replacement over binding.

Cooperative Filming Projects

Replacement of microforms is an important area for potential cooperation. Libraries contemplating the replacement of hard copies may be able to share the costs of microform replacement with other libraries. Outstanding examples are the ARL sponsored Foreign Newspaper Microfilm Project and the Foreign Official Gazette Project which permit libraries to share the filming costs for the original negatives and purchase positive prints. If delivery schedules among the participating libraries are frequent and prompt, then one library might maintain the microform files and the other libraries might discard their hard copy originals. Such a system would require rapid communication, but this is now feasible due to the increasingly widespread installation of TWX terminals throughout libraries in North America.

Conclusion

Any conversion to microforms from hard copies should include a careful examination of the advantages and disadvantages of using microforms. Local decisions will be based upon local conditions, but certain factors remain constant. When microforms are used to replace hard copies, one must assess user requirements, equipment needs, film quality, staff requirements, and comparative costs.

Since user resistance to microforms is still prevalent, it seems logical to convert to microform only materials which do not receive heavy use. It is also generally accepted that certain materials are neither easy nor convenient to use in microform such as reference books, books of illustrations, reserve materials, and materials used for text comparisons. The relatively long time lag between the completion of hard copy volumes and the receipt of microform copies is also troublesome to users. If microform copies do not arrive quickly, missing issues can become a problem. Since it is not possible to browse in microform collections and locate the sought-after copy, users may also demand more service from the staff. Thus, additional support staff for maintenance, filing, shelving, and classifying of microforms may be considered an *incremental* cost, only partially offset by savings in binding and space. Patrons also seem to prefer portability when using materials, so it is important to provide hard copy service as well as high quality, portable readers. The library can encourage patron acceptance of microforms if an easily accessible, pleasant reading facility is provided. By purchasing the most current equipment and providing assistance to readers, libraries can make it easier for readers to use microforms.

There can be considerable shelf space savings and some binding cost reductions, although additional equipment costs may sometimes by required when purchasing microforms. Libraries should also be aware of the comparative costs and space requirements for microform storage cabinets, readers, and reader/printers. The microtext products should be shelved in an area which has humidity and temperature controls as well as an environment as free from dust as possible. If these conditions are not met, the durability of microform products may prove shorter than the purchaser expects.

The library should exercise careful quality control when receiving microforms. This means having a knowledge of the technical specifications required to promote archival permanence, and the evaluative procedures necessary to assure that the highest production quality is in the finished product. Some of the disadvantages of hard copies may also show up in microform. A poor image can be as serious as a mutilated page. Although paper copies may deteriorate, heavily used microforms will also wear out in time and need to be replaced. If precautions are not observed, a library may receive poor quality film or find its film deteriorating.

There can be staff savings in serial bindery preparation since it is not necessary to claim missing issues, order replacement copies, and recall issues for the purpose of binding when microform copies are available. On the other hand, some of these savings may be offset by the need for additional service staff to manage the microtext room, check-in microform products, assist users with machines, and perform the quality control tests needed. Filing and refiling microforms and maintaining security of the collections will be time consuming.

When considering conversion, it is also necessary to look at the direct costs of microforms. It is clear that commercial or cooperative products offer the best savings to libraries since the cost of making the master negative is borne by the publisher or filming library. One needs also take account of the type of film being used, and the related equipment requirements. Another direct cost of microform replacement is the incremental cost of the hard copy subscriptions which must be purchased in order to obtain the microforms.

In conclusion, a microform conversion project should not be regarded as a panacea; in order to insure user acceptance, cost savings, and quality control, a good program requires a careful, analytical study of all the benefits and problems associated with using microforms in place of hard copy.

References

1. Gregory, Roma S., "Acquisition of Microforms," *Library Trends* 18: 374 (January 1970).

2. Stevens, Rolland, "The Microform Revolution," *Library Trends,* 19:388 (January 1971).

3. Hawken, William R., *Copying Methods Manual,* Chicago, Library Technology Program. American Library Association, 1966.

4. Veaner, Allen B., *The Evaluation of Micropublications: A Handbook for Librarians,* LTP Publication no. 17. Chicago, Library Technology Program, American Library Association, 1971, p.6.

5. Webb, John, "ALA Las Vegas," from Norman Shaffer's address: Microforms in Serials Acquisition and Management, *Microform Review* 2:250 (October 1973).

6. Gabriel, Michael, "Surging Serial Costs: The Microfiche Solution," *Library Journal* 99:2453 (October 1, 1974).

7. *Ibid.*

8. Veaner, *Op. Cit.*, p. 15.

9. De Villiers, Ann M. and Schloman, Barbara Frick, "Experiences with Scientific Journals on Microfilm in an Academic Reading Room," *Special Libraries* 64:557 (December 1973).

10. Pritsker, Alan B. and Sadler, J. William, "An Evaluation of Microfilm as a Method of Book Storage," *College and Research Libraries* 18:290-296 (July 1957).

11. Clapp, Verner W. and Jordan, Robert T., "Re-Evaluation of Microfilm as a Method of Book Storage," *College and Research Libraries* 24: 5-15 (January 1963).

12. Spreitzer, Francis F., "Developments in Copying, Micrographics, and Graphic Communication, 1973," *Library Resources & Technical Services* 18:157-58 (Spring 1974).

13. Xerox University Microfilms, *Serials in Microform, 1973/74,* Ann Arbor, Xerox University Microfilms, 1973, p. ix.

14. Bright, Franklin, Memo to Technical Services Directors of Large Research Libraries on a Comparative Study of Binding Costs, December 27, 1973.

15. Xerox University Microfilms, *Customer Profile Analysis Report for Stanford University: Documentation,* Ann Arbor, Michigan, 1973, p. 31.

16. *Ibid.*, p. 34.

17. Bates, Elizabeth, Memo to Jack Pooler, Chief, Science Division, Stanford University Libraries, August 14, 1968.

18. Peele, David, "Bind or Film: Factors in the Decision," *Library Resources and Technical Services* 8: 169 (Spring 1964).

19. Indiana University Libraries. Serials Department. *Serials Binding and Microfilm Costs Comparison (July 1974 - revised)*, Bloomington, Indiana, 1974, p. 1-2.

20. Veaner, *Op. Cit.*, p. 25-28.

21. *Ibid.*

22. Holmes, Donald C., "The Needs of Library Microform Users," National Microfilm Association, *Proceedings of the 18th Annual Meeting and Convention* (Annapolis, Maryland, The Association, 1969), p. 256-260.

23. Lewis, Ralph W., "User's Reaction to Microfiche: A Preliminary Study," *College and Research Libraries* 31: 260-268 (July 1970).

24. Grieder, E.M., "Ultrafiche Libraries: A Librarians's View," *Microform Review* 1: 87 (April 1972).

25. Wooster, Harold, *Microfiche 1969 - User Survey,* Arlington, Va., Air Force Office of Scientific Research, July 1969, p. 4 (AD 695 049).

26. DeVilliers, Ann M., Letter to Fred C. Lynden, July 11, 1974.

27. American Library Association, Library Technology Program, *Library Technology Reports: Section P1: Microforms and Equipment - Readers,* January 1965-January 1974. Chicago.

28. *Guide to Microreproduction Equipment,* 5th edition, edited by Hubbard W. Ballou, Silver Spring, Maryland, National Microfilm Association, 1971, 793 p. and *1973 Supplement to the Guide to Microreproduction Equipment,* Silver Spring, Maryland, National Microfilm Association, 1973.

29. National Microfilm Association, *How to Select A Microform Reader or Reader-Printer,* Silver Spring, Maryland, National Microfilm Association, 1974, p. 19.

30.   Gordon, Ronald F., *Microfiche Viewing Equipment Guide*, Alexandria, Virginia, Defense Documentation Center, September 1973, 3rd edition, 161 p.

31.   American Library Association, *Op. Cit.*, March 1972, *Microform Storage Cabinets*, p. 26.

32.   "New Microfilms for Old Books," *American Libraries* 1: 137 (February 1970).

33.   LaHood, Charles G., Jr., "Microfilm for the Library of Congress," *College and Research Libraries* 34: 292 (July 1973).

34.   Sajor, Ladd Z., "Preservation Microfilming: Why, What, When, Who, How," *Special Libraries* 63: 200 (April 1972).

35.   Fasana, Paul, Letter to Maurice Lapierre, Sept. 11, 1973. Reprinted in Memo to A.L.A. Discussion Group, Technical Service Directors of Large Research Libraries, From Karen Horny, January 31, 1974.

COST COMPARISON OF PERIODICALS IN HARD COPY AND ON MICROFORM[1]

by Jutta R. Reed, *Collections Development Librarian, The Libraries, Massachusetts Institute of Technology*

What are the added costs or the potential savings when a library replaces paper periodicals with micropublications? Although much has been written on the general advantages and disadvantages of microforms in libraries, most studies lack the economic data to answer this question. Obviously, the precise costs and savings will differ from library to library. However, in each library the process of analyzing areas where periodicals on microform increase or decrease costs results in a set of cost factors which are similar in all libraries; and each library's particular cost analysis repeats a general pattern.

This article has a twofold purpose. The first is descriptive—the identification of the cost categories which apply to all libraries; the second is analytical—the simultaneous development of a generalized cost analysis. Although potentially a library has a number of alternatives when selecting periodicals on microform, this article will be limited to analyzing the economics of replacing current paper periodicals with commercially available micropublications. Specifically, the article evaluates the two alternative ways of retaining periodicals in terms of a series of cost factors; overall, it aims to answer the question: What are the added costs and potential savings when a library purchases micropublications instead of binding and retaining its hard copy periodicals?

Reprinted from *Microform Review*, vol. 5, no. 3 (July 1976), pp. 185-92. Copyright© 1976 by Microform Review Inc.

Acquisition Cost of Microforms

Foremost among the numerous cost factors which a library must consider when it replaces hard copy periodicals with microforms is the acquisition cost of the microform replacements. Since the microform subscriptions duplicate regular periodical subscriptions, they increase total acquisition costs. This increase is a function of the number of titles selected on microform: for example, if a library purchases 100 duplicate subscriptions for the microform editions of journals, the annual increase would be the sum of these subscriptions. Estimating the average cost of these subscriptions is difficult. There are no published price indexes for commercially available microforms, and the present pricing structure of microform subscriptions is complex. Some publishers offer discounts for dual subscriptions; some publishers allow discounts upon return of the paper copies; others charge the same price for the microform edition as for the hard copy subscription; and a few publishers charge more for the microform edition. Finally, subscription costs for periodicals in microform can vary from publisher to publisher depending on the medium selected; that is, the same title on microfiche may be less expensive than if purchased on roll film. The great disparity in the pricing structure of microform subscriptions makes most statements on the price ratio of microform to hard copy subscriptions hazardous. While the differential may range from fifty to zero percent, the price advantage of the microform over the hard copy subscriptions is generally only ten to fifteen percent. Increases in paper costs and further technological advances in micropublishing may enlarge this price differential; but the change in the publication medium will realize only limited savings since actual production costs are only a fraction of the overall costs of publishing a periodical.

In addition to actual acquisition costs a library incurs incremental cost increases to select, order, receive and catalog the microforms. These costs further decrease the differential between the hard copy and microform subscription.

While the existing price indexes for paper periodicals are not fully comparable, they can suggest general cost parameters for the microform subscriptions. For 1975 these indexes range from a high of $76.84 for chemistry and physics periodicals to a low of $4.69 for children's periodicals. The average price for a periodical subscription was $19.94.[2] Even if we assume a small price advantage for the microform periodicals, these figures indicate that duplicate microform subscriptions will significantly increase a library's acquisition budget.

However, this increase is counterbalanced by the concomitant reduction in the maintenance costs of the hard copy periodicals. Maintenance costs can be broken down into four categories: binding; replacement of missing issues;

rebinding and repair; and replacement of mutilated volumes.

Maintenance Costs

Binding each year's issues of a paper periodical is a major expense for libraries. A 1973 survey of binding charges in large research libraries found that "the average costs for binding 12" Class A periodicals ranged from a low of $3.85 to a high $7.88"[3] The midpoint of that range suggests an estimated general cost of $5.85 to bind one volume. In addition there is the labor cost to collect, collate and process each volume. A general estimate is that it costs about $3.00[4] to prepare one volume for binding. Finally, the total binding cost for a subscription also depends on the size of the periodical and the number of volumes to be bound each year. On the average a year's subscription in the humanities and social sciences consists of one volume, while there are probably at least two volumes for scientific and technical periodicals.

Binding costs for hard copy periodicals can be calculated as follows:

$$c = (l + b)v$$

where c = total binding cost
  l = labor cost
  b = binding charge per volume
  v = number of volumes bound per year

Using the estimated figures of:
  l = $3.00
  b = $5.85
  v = 1 for the social sciences and humanities
    2 for scientific and technical periodicals

suggests the following costs: $8.85 for binding a year's subscription in the social sciences and $17.70 for binding the two volumes of a science journal. Although the specific binding costs will vary in each library, these estimated costs highlight the substantial expense of binding hard copy periodicals generally.

Not only must hard copy periodicals be bound, they are also susceptible to loss, wear and tear, and mutilation. In most libraries some current paper periodicals require replacement of missing issues before they can be bound; later, some bound volumes must be repaired, rebound or even replaced.

These maintenance costs will be dependent on usage, library security arrangements, etc. Although they will normally be low on a per-title basis, loss and repair costs can mount over the life span of a periodical.

When hard copy periodicals are replaced with microforms, binding costs are eliminated and replacement costs are minimal. The resulting savings often equal or surpass the initial acquisition cost of the microform replacement. For example, a year's subscription to *Daedalus* on microfilm costs $7.50,[5] while it would probably cost $8.85 to bind the paper issues. Similarly, the microfiche subscription to *Scientific American* costs $12.00,[6] and it would cost more than $17.00 to bind the two hard copy volumes.

So far the cost analysis of periodicals on microform shows on one side added acquisition costs weighted against savings through the elimination of binding, repair and replacement costs. Periodicals on microform, however, incur two additional costs: these are the costs of the microform equipment and the costs to maintain that equipment.

Equipment Costs

The equipment needed to support a microform periodical collection presents a complex cost variable. In some libraries existing microform equipment can be used. In other libraries new equipment will be purchased to support the periodicals on microform. For all libraries it is almost impossible to quantify equipment costs on a per-volume basis. Equipment costs are highly sensitive to the amount and type of equipment, as well as the size of the collection. Even the minimum number of readers required to service a microform area is dependent on four variables: the number of potential users, the number of microforms, the number of hours the area is open, the level of use. While it may be possible to quantify the first three factors, and the level of use is difficult to measure. It is determined by the type of material on microform and user awareness and exposure to microforms. The experience in most library microform areas shows that the level of use determines the number of microform readers required.

Four other factors affect reader costs. First, the prevalence of roll film over microfiche or vice versa determines total reader costs. Since microfiche readers are far less expensive than film readers, reading equipment costs will be lower in a library with a predominantly fiche collection, than in a library with a large roll film collection. Secondly, the availability of portable circulating and/or personal microfiche readers reduces the number of readers required in a library. Thirdly, the type of reader selected is a major cost factor. Depending on the special features the cost of a microform reader can vary from a low of $200 for a manually operated fiche reader to a high of $3000 for a fully automatic microfilm reader. Finally, total annual reader costs are a function of the replacement schedule in a library. This schedule is determined by the quality of each reader, the frequency and type of use, and library budgetary demands. Depending on these variables, the probable life span of a reader falls between five and ten years; and the purchase price would be distributed over the particular amortization period.

Similar factors determine the costs for reader-printers. University Microfilms suggests a ratio of one reader-printer to ten readers. Active use of a microform area would alter this ratio. Ideally, at least half of all readers purchased should be reader-printers. The number of reader-printers will vary from library to library; and the purchase price will differ depending on whether the reader-printer accommodates film and/or fiche, handles different reduction ratios, or uses a wet or dry printing process. The same general considerations apply to the costs of microfiche duplicators and other supplementary equipment.

Although establishing ratios between equipment costs and periodical titles on microform is impossible, two positive generalizations can be made. The larger the microform collection, the lower per-volume equipment costs will be. While in most library systems per-unit costs rise as the size of the library increases due to the built-in complexities of large library systems, the equipment cost curve for microforms follows the opposite path. As the microform collection expands, the ratio of microforms to reading machines and other equipment increases, and unit costs decline. For example, in most libraries one microfiche duplicator will serve user needs and its purchase price would be distributed over a greater number of titles in a larger microform collection. Secondly, equipment prices will probably rise slower than costs of other library operations. Most library services are labor-intensive and have experienced a "relatively slow rate of labor-saving innovation."[7] Consequently the "costs per unit of library services have tended to rise far more rapidly than the general price level."[8] Microform equipment on the other hand has benefitted from technological advances in the manufacturing process, and increased productivity has resulted in a slow rate of price increases. Doubtlessly labor and material costs of microform equipment will continue to rise, but these price increases will be, in part, counterbalanced by technological improvements in the versatility and quality of the microform equipment.

Although the outlook for future microform equipment prices appears positive, this should not obscure the fact that a microform collection requires a substantial capital outlay to purchase the necessary readers and reader-printers. In many libraries periodicals in microform could be accommodated on already existing microform equipment. But, in those libraries where new equipment must be purchased, the costs will be high initially.

Equipment Maintenance Costs

In addition, the use of the microform equipment will cause periodic maintenance costs for replacement of worn-out parts or repairs of machine malfunctions. A major recurring replacement is the lamp in the microform readers. New lamps can cost from $1.50 to more than $5.00; they can last from a few hours to more than 500 hours. Potential machine repairs are even more unpredictable. They can involve a minor adjustment or require a major overhaul. The two components of repair costs, labor and parts, will vary substantially depending on the particular machine problems. Overall, annual maintenance costs will again be a function of the quality and quantity of the equipment, the amount of use, and the availability of staff to do preventive maintenance.

Environmental Costs

Finally, periodicals in microform may require potential expenditures to secure a controlled storage environment. To insure durability, microforms should be stored in an area with air conditioning and humidity control. Projections of potential expenditures are too complex to allow any estimates. Furthermore, hard copy periodicals would equally benefit from optimum storage conditions.

Storage Costs

A cost comparison of periodicals in hard copy and microform must not only consider the direct expenses, for example, subscription and binding costs, but it must also assess the indirect costs of storing the respective volumes. Storing the collection is a substantial part of the true cost of operating a library. Storage costs result from a combination of land, construction, shelving, and building maintenance costs.

A brace of caveats must precede this discussion of storage costs of periodicals in hard copy and microform. First, storage costs depend on local conditions, such as, real estate prices and the labor market. These costs will also fluctuate over time. Actually, only a few libraries have calculated storage costs.[9] Among these are the University of Chicago, Yale and the Massachusetts Institute of Technology. The available figures range from a cost of $0.135 to store an average book per year at the University of Chicago[10] in 1961 to $0.347 to store the same book in the M.I.T. Libraries in 1968.[11] There is no accurate method to estimate a general annual storage cost per library volume; in choosing the specific storage cost from one library, namely M.I.T., we should remember that this is merely an illustrative figure, and local conditions will either raise or lower the actual storage cost in each library.

Second, the use of uniform annual storage costs entails a number of assumptions and oversimplifications. Typically libraries increase storage space in increments, that is, through the addition of an extra room, floor, or a new building. Once the new space has been added, its costs remain fixed regardless of the actual number of volumes stored there. Thus the storage costs for a library actually grow in steps and will take a steep increase when the storage capacity is exceeded and new space must be added. The distribution of total storage costs per volume per year results at best only in an approximation of real costs.

Finally, storage costs are a function of storage density and are highly sensitive to the number of volumes stored. No measurement standards exist for comparing storage density of bound periodicals with micropublications. Storage density is based on the physical size of each volume and the consequent space requirements and depends on different criteria in each format. For bound periodicals the number of pages, thickness of the paper and, to a lesser degree, library binding policies determine the size of the bound volume. For microforms the type, that is, microfiche or roll film, and the reduction ratio determine the size. Although Keyes Metcalf and others have established guidelines for estimating the number of bound periodicals per shelf section, no one has outlined similar guidelines for microforms. Space requirements for microforms also vary greatly depending on the type of storage. For example, specially manufactured film cabinets will hold far more reels of film in the same square feet of space than open shelves.

With this last caveat in mind, the following parameters are used to arrive at comparative storage density figures for bound periodicals and microforms. The 3-foot shelf will serve as the storage unit, and only storage costs for film will be discussed. We will also assume that the reels of film are stored in film boxes with 6 reels per box and 16 boxes per 3-foot shelf, where 1 reel equals 2 volumes. Therefore 96 reels of film or 192 volumes can be stored on each shelf section.[12] The same 3-foot shelf on the average holds only 15 bound journal volumes.[13]

Since the cost to store a periodical volume is a function of the amount of space the volume uses, the increase in storage density when the periodical is stored on microfilm is matched by an equal decrease in storage costs. Assuming an annual storage cost of $0.38 for a bound journal volume[14] suggests an annual cost of $0.034 to store the same volume on microfilm; that is, the storage cost for a microfilmed volume is 9 percent that of a hard copy volume.

Cumulative storage figures for periodicals in hard copy and on microfilm can then be calculated as follows:

Assume: t = time in years volumes are to be stored
            v = number of volumes per year
            a = cost of storing one bound volume per year
            b = cost of storing one volume on microfilm
            c = storage costs

For a five-year period, storage costs for a periodical in hard copy would be:

	Year's Storage Cost
1st year	av
2nd year	$2av$
3rd year	$3av$
4th year	$4av$
5th year	$5av$

	Cumulative Storage Cost
1st year	av
2nd year	$3av$
3rd year	$6av$
4th year	$10av$
5th year	$15av$

This can be expressed mathematically by the formula:[15]

$$c = \tfrac{1}{2}av(t\,(t+1))\;.$$

The formula would be identical for storing the same file on microfilm, except b is substituted for a:

$$c = \tfrac{1}{2}bv(t\,(t+1))\;.$$

For example, the storage cost for the volumes of *Scientific American* for five years would be:

$$c = \frac{1}{2} \times \$0.38 \times 2\,(5(5+1)\,)$$
$$c = \$11.40 \text{ in hard copy and}$$
$$c = \frac{1}{2} \times \$0.034 \times 2\,(5(5+1)\,)$$
$$c = \$1.02 \text{ on microfilm.}$$

Although these specific results should be regarded with caution since v, a, and b will differ from library to library and will change over time, they demonstrate the dramatic reduction of storage costs of micropublications over hard copy periodicals. The time paths of storage costs of the two formats accentuate the advantage of micropublications: respective costs after 20 years would be $159.60 for the hard copy and $14.28 for the microform version of *Scientific American*.

Whatever the actual storage costs and space requirements of periodicals on microform in a particular library, micropublications will drastically reduce storage costs by requiring less shelving in all libraries. Generalized estimates of space savings when micropublications are substituted for paper volumes range from 85 to 98 percent, with a cluster in the 90-93 percentiles. Two further examples will highlight the comparative space requirements. The bound volumes of the *Journal of the American Chemical Society* from 1879 through 1972 require about 20 shelves. The microfilm cartridges for the same years would use 1.5 shelves when the cartridges are stored in film boxes. Similarly, four years of *Time* magazine occupy more than 3 feet of shelving; the microfiche edition for these years fits into a box using less than six inches of space.

However, both the microfilm and microfiche editions of these journals require reading equipment which takes up space. While a library with a small microform collection can utilize tables set aside for reading and does not need to preempt stack space to accommodate the reading equipment, a library with a large microform collection requires separate space for the equipment, or approximately 40 square feet of space for each microform reader according to planning guidelines.[17] Even in that case the necessary microform equipment uses only a small portion of shelving space saved by the correspondingly large number of periodicals on microform.

Although the microform equipment will slightly reduce savings in shelving space, the overall space savings of periodicals on microform are clearly substantial. In the long run microforms will increase the storage capacity of present library buildings and can postpone the construction of additional storage space. Because microforms allow a library to store information in far less space and consequently at far less cost than hard copy volumes, the reduction in storage costs for microforms gives periodicals on microforms a decisive economic advantage. The fact that storage costs primarily constitute capital funds does not alter this conclusion.

Service Costs

The use of periodicals in paper or on microform will entail service costs. The circulation cost is a major component of these costs. For those libraries where both paper and microfiche copies of periodicals circulate, the cost per transaction will be identical. However, for periodicals on microfiche an alternative exists to the high cost of circulation. A strong case can be made that it is more economical for a library to give out a duplicate microfiche at a nominal fee than to circulate it at a considerable cost.

A second service cost is the cost of reshelving the paper periodicals and of refiling the microforms. These costs will depend on a number of factors: size of each collection, space configurations, volume of material to be reshelved or refiled, and the hourly labor cost. No accurate data are available on shelving versus filing costs. But in a large library the labor cost for refiling the microforms in a compact area should be substantially lower than shelving the paper periodicals in widely dispersed stacks. Shelving in conventional stacks also requires frequent shifting of parts of the collection. Many libraries do not have sufficient expansion space on the shelves to absorb new periodical titles and the annual bound volumes without periodic shifting. One study suggests that at 90 percent capacity ''one fourth of the collection must be shifted each year to meet new accessions.''[18] The labor costs for shifting bound periodicals can be substantial. In comparison, the cost to shift microform files will be minimal.

The pattern is reversed for the third service cost category: the amount of library staff assistance users need to locate an article. While most hard copy periodicals can be used on a self-service basis, effective utilization of microforms depends on the availability of library staff to aid users with the microforms and the equipment (and to perform, coincidentally, basic preventive machine maintenance). In libraries where the microform area is part of a larger service department the staff already present can perform these services. But in libraries with a separate microform area a special microform assistant will be necessary.[19] Regardless of the particular circumstances in a library, user orientation or education costs at present will be high for periodicals on microform.

Overall, total service costs for periodicals on microform should be lower than for hard copy; this will be especially true as users become more familiar with microforms and will need less instruction in the use of the microform equipment.

Conclusion

An accurate assessment of the comparative costs of commercially available micropublications and paper periodicals clearly depends on many factors: actual numbers of titles, equipment, or centralized versus decentralized microform facilities. This paper has compared many of the potential costs of the two alternative systems. Although various cost factors are sufficiently unclear to discourage conclusions, a number of distinct pluses and minuses of micropublications emerge. On the positive side are the reduction in binding, replacement, and repair costs, and the drastic reduction in storage space. On the negative side are the additional acquisition costs, equipment costs, and potential expenditures for staff assistance. In balance the evidence indicates that substantial savings accrue when current paper periodicals are replaced with commercially available micropublications.

References

1. I prepared an earlier version of this article as a chapter in an M.I.T. staff report. A number of people read and commented on the earlier draft. Among them are Peter Scott of the M.I.T. Microreproduction Laboratory, Susan K. Nutter of the Barker Engineering Library, and Carl Spaulding of the Council on Library Resources. I am indebted to them all for their valuable comments. I also thank David Lewallen of the Dewey Library for his careful reading of my final draft.

2. Norman B. Brown, "Price Indexes for 1975: U.S. Periodicals and Serial Services," *Library Journal* 100 (July 1975): 1291.

3. Franklin Bright, Memo to Technical Services Directors of Large Research Libraries on a Comparative Study of Binding Costs, December 27, 1973, as cited in: Frederick C. Lynden, "Replacement of Hard Copy by Microforms," *Microform Review* 4 (January 1975): 18.

4. This figure may appear high, but the real cost of preparing a volume for binding includes staff wages and benefits, as well as general library overhead. See: John Kountz, "Library Cost Analysis: A Recipe," *Library Journal* 97 (February 1, 1972): 459-464.

5. *Serials in Microform*, 1975 (Ann Arbor, Michigan: Xerox University Microfilms, 1975), p. 209.

6. *Ibid.*, p. 609.

7. William J. Baumol and Matityahu Marcus, *Economics of Academic Libraries* (Washington, D.C.: American Council on Education, 1973), p. 44.

8. *Ibid.*, p. 47.

9. A summary of the major studies on storage costs is listed in: Ralph E. Ellsworth, *The Economics of Book Storage in College and University Libraries* (Metuchen, N.J.: Published by the Association of Research Libraries and the Scarecrow Press, 1969), especially pp. 99-116.

10. Herman H. Fussler and Julian L. Simon, *Patterns in the Use of Books in Large Research Libraries* (Chicago & London: The University of Chicago Press, 1969), p. 140.

11. Jeffrey A. Raffel and Robert Shishko, *Systematic Analysis of University Libraries: An Application of Cost-Benefit Analysis to the M.I.T. Libraries* (Cambridge, Mass.: M.I.T. Press, 1971), p. 13.

12. This type of storage is used in the M.I.T. Microform Center; the figures are derived from actual reel counts of a few sample sections.

13. Keyes D. Metcalf, *Planning Academic and Research Library Buildings* (New York: McGraw Hill, 1965), p. 112.

14. The figure is derived from the moderate-use storage cost of $0.2825 per volume, where 1 volume equals 2/3 journals given in Raffel and Shishko, *Systematic Analysis*, pp. 13-14.

15. The formulae are adapted from Eugene P. Power, "Microfilm as a Substitute for Binding," *American Documentation* 2 (Winter 1951): 34.

16. Ann M. DeVilliers and Barbara Frick Schloman, "Experiences with Scientific Journals on Microfilm in an Academic Reading Room," *Special Libraries* 64 (December 1973): 557.

17. Metcalf, *Planning*, p. 393.

18. Julian L. Simon, "How Many Books Should be Stored Where? An Economic Analysis," *College and Research Libraries*, 28 (March 1967): 97.

19. Judy Fair, "The Microform Reading Room: Part V," *Microform Review* 3 (January 1974): 11.

THE USE OF MICROFILM FOR COMPLETING SETS

by Leonard Jolley, *Librarian, Selly Oak Colleges Library*

There has been plenty of discussion of the technical problems of microfilming, and the potential importance of microfilms to the librarian is generally accepted, but little seems yet to have been written in this country[1] on the practical problems facing the librarian who wishes to make extensive use of microfilms in building up his stock. Microfilm viewers are now to be found in many libraries, but on the whole, microfilms are used in British libraries mainly to satisfy occasional demands, and very few libraries in this country appear to be using microfilms systematically and extensively; an account of one such attempt may therefore be of interest.

The Selly Oak Colleges Library has been forced by circumstances to make considerable use of microfilms. One of its chief objects is to create the only counterpart in this country to the Missionary Research Libraries of the United States. Much of the historical material needed for such a collection has been for years quite unobtainable except for chance good fortune, and the library possessed extensive files of periodicals and reports, all disfigured by vexatious gaps which there seemed no hope of filling. Microfilms were an obvious answer to this need, all the more so as, although this material is essential to the completeness of the collection, it will not be in constant demand, and the question whether microfilms will stand up to the wear and tear of constant use did not arise.

It was found that the amount of photography to be done justified the purchase of a camera as well as a viewer. A reconditioned Graflex Camera and Argus Reader were purchased from Kodak. Improved models of cameras and viewers are now obtainable, but these two have proved very satisfactory. The

Reprinted from *Journal of Documentation*, vol. 4 (1948), pp. 41-4, by permission of the publisher.

camera cost £80, and it has been calculated that, ignoring staff costs, it paid for itself in 2500 feet of film. The camera requires no technical skill to use; almost all the photography has been done by the youngest member of the staff and, apart from initial accidents, there have been no failures. Kodak charges 15s. for processing 100 feet of film, and it is doubtful whether any but the very largest library would find it worth while to do their own processing. In the U.S.A. it is customary to keep the original negative photograph as a master copy and have positives made for use in the viewer. The positive gives a clearer picture, and can always be renewed without fresh photographs having to be taken, but making the positive doubles the cost. We have found the use of the original negative perfectly adequate.

The camera holds 100 feet of film, but it is not necessary to photograph the whole spool of film before sending it to be developed. The film can be torn off whenever required. The camera is supposed to take either about 750 or about 1500 exposures on a film, but we have always had to use the 750-exposure size. This gives a comfortable picture of a two-page opening. At first each separate work was kept on a separate section of film. This involves wasting 30 exposures between each item, adds to the difficulty of storing, and has little advantage, since it seems useless to keep the microfilms in classified order. All films are now photographed straight through, whatever various works are being photographed. This means the reader may have to wind on 80 or 90 feet of film before coming to the material he needs; but it does not take much longer to find a page in 100 feet than in 30 feet of a roll. Many readers are certainly prejudiced against microfilms by the time needed to find a particular item in a roll, and some libraries are now trying to overcome the inconvenience by cutting microfilms into ten-page strips. The advantages of this are discussed by Mr. H.E. Wilson, on pp. 83-4 of *Rapports de la 17me· conférence de la F.I.D.* The Argus Reader could not handle such strips, which, in any case, would appear to justify their cost only if it is known that particular sections of a periodical will be in constant demand.

The films are stored in the tin boxes in which they are sent out by the maker. These boxes are kept in shallow pigeon-holes, and arranged in the numerical order of the film's accession number. Each film is given an accession number which is photographed at the beginning and end, together with the name of the library. The importance of this simple device is obvious, but how obvious can be appreciated only when you have had to deal with an unidentified microfilm. It would be possible to add a contents note at the end of the film; this has not so far been done; a full description of the contents is contained in the Microfilms Accession Register, but it might be useful to repeat it on the film. It would, of course, have to be given at the end of the film, as you do not always know what 100 feet of film will contain when you begin to photograph. The Microfilms Accession Register is kept in a loose-leaf book, ruled into columns. It contains a running number for each film, the date the photograph is made, the date the film is received back, the source from which the material photographed has been received, the contents of the film, and any technical notes on the quality and conditions of the photography. As the cost of processing each film is the same, it need not be recorded, but the accessions number of the film is written on each invoice for processing before it is passed for payment. The catalogue entry contains the statement that a particular work is obtainable on Microfilm No. X. It is a simple matter to pick out the microfilm, and a glance at the register shows approximately in what part of the film the required work is to be found. It has been suggested that each item in a film ought to have a running number, which would also be included in the catalogue entry. This would give some help in locating a particular item, but it would still be necessary to consult the accessions register, unless the frames were numbered, as item (5) might be near the beginning or end of the film. It might seem inviting to number each frame, and so establish the exact position of any item, as 'On Microfilm X, frames y-z'. It would be possible to have consecutive numbers copied on cards and photographed at each exposure, but this would slow up the work of photography far too much. The register is filled up when the photograph is made, and put aside until the processed film is received back. The contents are then checked and initialed as correct. If anything should have failed to be reproduced correctly, it would be done again. It is a rule, though fortunately one which has not so far been needed, never to return an original until the photograph has been checked.

Cataloguing microfilms involved, of course, no new principles, but the actual work of cataloguing direct from microfilms would be difficult and tedious. It has, therefore, seemed quicker to note when photographing all the details needed for making the catalogue entry. The changes in the title-pages of different volumes of periodicals can be more easily noticed in this way, and the size. The catalogue entry is made from these notes. A class number is also added, and the entry in the catalogue is exactly the same as for a book, but contains the note 'Available on microfilm(s) No(s). X'. Most often it is a part of a periodical or a series which is available on the microfilm.

To assist the reader who is working from the shelves, a dummy is put in at the appropriate position, with a label announcing that the work, or parts of the work, are available on microfilms. This does not involve any real waste of space, since one dummy volume usually represents several volumes of the original. In a library where readers do not have access to the shelves dummies would not be needed, but in the Selly Oak Colleges Library the readers work from the shelves more often than from the catalogue. One of the worst disadvantages of microfilms is the impossibility of browsing through them. In the case of periodicals, it is planned to overcome this disadvantage, to some extent, by wherever possible having full-size prints made of the tables of contents and indexes. These will be bound together and placed on the shelves, and the reader will thus be given some opportunity to know whether there is anything to interest him in the part of the periodical which is on the microfilm.

Requests from readers for additions to the microfilm collection are invited and considered along with ordinary book suggestions. Microfilms are available only on application, and must be read in a special room. In the Selly Oak Colleges Library, readers who use microfilms at all use a large number of them, and are normally allowed to take them on and off the microfilm viewer themselves, but a library which did not have the same opportunity of knowing its readers might not be able to permit this.

As has been said, microfilms are being used primarily to fill gaps in the runs of out-of-print and unobtainable periodicals. They will also be used to copy books published in Germany during the war if the originals to copy can be obtained. Only in one case is the possibility of using microfilms when the printed form of the work is available being considered. The Selly Oak Colleges Library receives a large number of the bulletins of news and information which are issued by some societies and governments. Because of their flimsiness and the space they occupy, these have not always been preserved, and yet they contain detailed accounts of day-to-day developments which are of some permanent value. This is probably a case in which microfilms will be made and the originals destroyed. Otherwise, there is no suggestion of using microfilms if books can be obtained. It always takes longer, and is generally less convenient to consult the microfilm.

References

1.   Since this was written, the *Library Association Record* for February 1948 has appeared with 'Microfilms in public libraries. Some notes on procedure from Manchester.' The reader will notice many points of resemblance between the Manchester and the Selly Oak Colleges Library practice.

THE SERIAL MICROFILM PROGRAM AT THE LIBRARY OF CONGRESS*

by Charles G. LaHood, Jr., *Chief Serial Division, The Library of Congress*

The discussion of this topic necessarily includes several important elements: first, the deterioration of the paper on which many serials are published; and second, the matter of storage space. A third factor to be considered, as we shall see later, is acquisition of difficult-to-obtain materials.

Let us briefly discuss the matter of paper deterioration and specifically the deterioration of pulp paper as used by the publishers of newspapers.

The problems of deterioration, as it affects library materials, is, of course, not a new one. The introduction of sulfide paper into the newspaper industry about the year 1870 meant that the problem for those wishing to preserve a newspaper file over an indefinite period of time would sooner or later become so acute as eventually to force a decision on the owner (usually the publisher or library) either to make some effort to extend the useful life of the file, dispose of it altogether, or replace it with some suitable substitute.

The Chief of the Library of Congress Periodical Division, Allan B. Slausen, in his annual report to the Librarian of Congress for the fiscal year ending June 30, 1901, made the following statement:

Wood pulp paper, upon which newspapers are now printed, disintegrates after a few years when exposed to the light, and edges of bound volumes near the windows already begin to show that extra precautions must be taken if

* Paper delivered at the RTSD Serials Section Meeting, Detroit, Michigan, July 7, 1965.

Reprinted by permission of the American Library Association from *Library Resources and Technical Services*, vol. 10, no. 2 (Spring 1966), pp. 241-48.

the files of newspapers are to last beyond one or at the most two decades. Curtains or blinds to the stack windows, I believe, will be found to be a necessity even for the protection of books, but for the newspapers I would recommend, as a special protection that the binder attach to the inside of the covers, canvas flaps which will fold over the edges of the volumes and completely exclude from them the light. This would not add much to the cost of binding, but will add many years to the life of the volume.**

As the problem of deterioration of newsprint became more and more acute (Mr. Slausen's binding flap idea was never adopted) various proposals were offered to resolve or at least mitigate the effects of deterioration: one early proposal recommended the soaking of each newspaper page in a chemical solution, thus effectively lowering the acid content of the paper; another proposal was made to reprint the leading newspapers at half-size, presumably on better quality paper; while yet another called for publishing originally in a rag paper edition.

None of these proposals offered a completely satisfactory solution to the problem—since then (as perhaps now) the soaking procedure was too expensive, while the re-publishing at half-size involved not only appreciable expense but also too much reduction in size of print for practical reader use. The rag paper edition was also expensive and did nothing for retrospective or historical files. A rag paper edition was published for a few titles, notably the *New York Times*, beginning in 1927. However, one could scarcely find a ground-swell for this procedure among newspaper publishers.

It was indeed fortuitous that quite independently of the newspaper preservation problem, the Recordak Corporation had been since about 1927 actively engaged in the microfilming of bank records and other commercial papers. The acceptance of microfilm by the business community led to the application of microfilm to the newsprint deterioration problem. And so it was in 1935 that the Recordak Corporation announced a project to microfilm the *New York Times* for the period 1914-1918. The immediate commercial success of this venture induced Recordak to expand its microfilming of newspapers, first to the remaining back file of the *New York Times*, and later to the current file. Thus was inaugurated a new and highly-succesful application for microfilm. The expansion of the technique to other leading newspapers followed.

By 1939, the Library of Congress had established under the direction of George A. Schwegmann, Jr., its own Photoduplication Service, which included the relatively new practical roll microfilm technique as employed by Recordak. The Service undertook several large newspaper microfilming pro-

** Slausen, Allan B., *Annual Report of Periodical Division to the Librarian of Congress, 1900-1901*. Typescript.

jects, including the filming of such titles as the *Washington Star,* the *Washington Post,* and the *National Intelligencer.*

Although the desirability of substituting 35 mm. roll microfilm for files of newspapers continued to receive acceptance among librarians and newspaper publishers, it was not until the post-World War II period that the microfilming of newspapers on a current subscription basis became commonplace.

Meanwhile, the Library of Congress was experiencing, in addition to deterioration, a second problem in connection with newspaper files. By 1949, just one decade after the move of the Library's bound newspaper collection from the unfavorable physical conditions of the Main Building to air-conditioned facilities in the Annex, the bound newspaper collection had already become so extensive—comprising some 140,000 volumes—that all available shelf space, measuring approximately 18 miles in linear footage, was fully occupied.

With no other shelf space readily available for the Newspaper Collection, the stack area floor space was reluctantly utilized for storage. With the Collection growing at the rate of 3,000 volumes per year, there was, indeed, a critical need to turn more and more to the microfilm approach as the means for mitigating, if not completely solving, the space problem, while at the same time maintaining the long-range preservation requirements of so valuable a library resource.

By the year 1951, the Library had acquired from outside sources and from negative microfilm prepared by its Photoduplication Service, approximately 21,000 reels of positive microfilm. The majority of these reels represented retrospective or historical files. However, these did not necessarily supplant the bound volumes in the Newspaper Collection, so that readers, depending to some degree on their own preference, were served either bound volumes or reels of microfilm.

With the use of microfilm increasing and with space more and more at a premium, the Library adopted the policy which permitted the disposal of current newspaper files at the time microfilm was made available for reader use. By way of exception only a few heavily used titles were bound. Later on, as we shall see, this same rule was applied to retrospective or historical files. Of course, this approach is the key to the ultimate solution of the space problem for the newspaper collection.

As of June 1950, the Library had 88 subscriptions for microfilm—56 for domestic and 32 for foreign titles. Current receipts of newspaper titles, however, exceeded 1,000! While the immediate effect of the 88 microfilm subscriptions was to curtail somewhat the growth of the bound collection, the fact that relatively few newspapers were available on microfilm meant that most titles continued to be bound at the same time microfilms of other titles were being purchased and placed in service. However, additional subscriptions to newspapers on microfilm were placed as they became available. By 1961, although the Library was subscribing to substantially every available microfilm of those newspaper titles which it wished to retain permanently, the number of subscriptions accounted for only one half of the 1,200 domestic and foreign newspaper titles normally retained. The remaining 600 titles were placed, up to the end of 1961, in "permanent" style bindings.

The annual rate of increase in the bound collection at the end of 1960-61 was still a substantial 1,900 volumes. By this date, the bound newspaper collection totalled 160,000 volumes with approximately 20,000 piled on the book-stack floors. The microfilm collection in the meanwhile had increased from 21,000 to 69,000 reels.

The Current Newspaper Microfilm Program

With more funds available in fiscal 1961-62, it became possible to discontinue binding all but a handful of the most important newspaper titles, and to microfilm in our own Photoduplication Service those newspaper titles for which no microfilm subscription was elsewhere available. The number of newspapers microfilmed at the Library approximated 600.

As of January 1962, the Serial Division found itself with a current newspaper microfilming program of rather large proportions. So large, in fact, was the program and so difficult of accomplishment in some respects, that, while on the whole the program has proven successful, there remain certain problem files which as yet have not been microfilmed. The problem I mention here, inherent to the preparation of high quality microfilm, is that of supplying to the microfilming facility a file *ideally in perfect arrangement, and above all as complete as possible.*

Prior to the inception of the in-house microfilming program, when newspapers were prepared for binding, it was possible to proceed with the binding operations even though a file might be incomplete. The shelflist record maintained in the Serial Division indicated the bound holdings and listed in detail the lacking issues. As newspaper receipts were processed, needed issues were found—usually from government transfer—within a one or two year period after binding was complete, but at times as long as five or ten years late. Such needed issues were readily tipped into the appropriate bound volume by a professional bookbinder, and the shelflist was amended.

With microfilm, however, it is not feasible to initiate the photoreproduction process until a newspaper file is complete. The reasons for this are compelling. The cost of filming single issues at a later date, the insertion of these issues in an existing negative microfilm, and the preparation of a new service positive of the entire reel for all regular subscribers of the microfilm—all these add up to a prohibitively expensive procedure. Since the in-house microfilming program includes the more difficult titles from the viewpoint of acquisitions, the Serial Division is faced with the task of securing more than the usual number of missing issues which, for one reason or another, never arrive in the Library. Our first recourse for these missing issues is the publishers themselves; however, because of the delay between publication and claiming, the publishers all too frequently no longer have the required issues available.

Our attempts to solve this problem next shift to the location of a secondary backstop in the form of another library which also acquires a particular foreign newspaper and which is willing to lend or give us such numbers as are needed and available. We have had some success in our endeavor, principally for the countries of Africa; however, there is much yet to be done, else the current filming of many foreign newspapers will have limited value.

Such an ambitious program, you might well ask, must be quite expensive. This I must admit. However, our experience indicates that the binding and storage of newspaper volumes is also expensive. Close analysis of the various processes, however, indicates that the cost of preparing a microfilm negative and service positive, is approximately the same as the cost of binding a three-inch-thick newspaper volume!

At the time funds were furnished for the complete changeover of current newspaper files to microfilm, substantial funds were also allocated for a preservation program of all historical pulp paper volumes in the Newspaper Collection.

This phase of the program—the replacement of bound retrospective files— is in some respects even more critical than the program for current issues, since here we have newsprint which is in a more advanced stage of deterioration. With time running out for many of the files, our goal of replacing all pulp paper means that 125,000 volumes averaging three inches in thickness must be replaced by positive microfilm either from negatives already in existence and available from other sources, or microfilmed in our own Photoduplication Service. The estimate of the pages to be replaced at the beginning of the program approximated a staggering 75,000,000.

Both the current and retrospective segments of the program call for the replacement of newsprint files with a microfilm which is substantially complete insofar as bibliographic integrity is concerned, and which complies with the technical specifications set forth by the American Standards Association, and more particularly ASA Sectional Committee PH-5, chaired by Donald C. Holmes, Chief of the Library's Photoduplication Service, and sponsored by the ALA Resources and Technical Services Division's Copying Methods Section. The obligation for this adherence to standards arises out of a sense of duty to future generations of researchers and a need to help maintain a high standard, which we trust will eventually, if not now, benefit the resource capabilities of the entire library system in the United States. The caliber of microfilm we are striving to purchase or prepare is difficult and expensive to produce, not only at the Library of Congress, but by everyone who would be a producer of archival quality microfilm.

You may recall how earlier I stated that the production costs of microfilm substantially equalled that of binding. I did not mention at that time the cost factor of preparing the files before they ever reach the microfilm camera.

In managing the preservation program, one of the first tasks the Serial Division undertook was the formulation of the requirements necessary for producing high quality microfilm and the procedures necessary for preparing the best possible file prior to the actual microfilming process. Early in the program we learned that the shelflist record of our newspaper holdings did not adequately reflect the information required for preparing a master microfilm negative. The record of missing issues, on close scrutiny, did not always prove accurate: issues were at times bound out of order, and, occasionally, the issue of an entirely-different newspaper title appeared in the wrong file. In other words, we had to correct the errors made out of human frailty, and, in addition, update the file to reflect the effects of use, such as mutilation, mostly, I am sure, of an accidental nature, but nonetheless present.

Once the new record is established, the volumes are sent to the Government Printing Office Bindery, where newspaper bindings are cut away from the newsprint. The cutting is done with extreme care so as not to lose any text, and the newsprint volume is reduced to a stack of loose sheets which are held between the bindings. On return to the Library, based on the newly established collation record, the misfiled issues, sections, or pages, are inserted in proper sequence. The next task is to attempt to secure the needed portions of the newspaper file which might be available from other repositories.

In practice, we have had difficulty in achieving the part of our objective concerned with the acquisition of missing portions of the files. For domestic newspapers, we find that the Library which owns a particular newspaper file may not have an adequate microfilming facility, or, if it does, is unwilling to permit the volume to be prepared for microfilming in such a manner as to permit the photocopying of the entire page. For foreign newspapers, we are hampered by the lack of a comprehensive union list. In some instances, therefore, we find ourselves microfilming the Library holdings, and including in the film a record of missing mutilated issues or pages.

Where a negative microfilm is already in existence, we are acquiring positive microfilm only. The problem here, we find, is the uneven quality of the negatives in existence. The problems generally involve the use of tightly bound volumes in the production of the negative and the resulting loss of a portion of the text, the use of a very poor file, and technical problems resulting in poor lighting or poor lens focus.

In our effort to secure high quality microfilm, the Library published in 1964 *Specifications for Library of Congress Microfilming*, by Stephen R. Salmon, which sets forth the "conditions under which microfilm would be considered for addition to the permanent collections of the Library before purchase of a microfilm is consummated."* In pursuing this end, the Library requires the supplier to furnish sample rolls of each file. The samples should be representative of the general quality of the file insofar as possible. On the basis of favorable testing results and assuming the samples are indeed respesentative, a purchase order is placed for the entire run needed to replace the Library's own pulp file. Receipt of the positive microfilm in the Serial Division Collection is the signal for discarding the pulp file. Because this latter procedure is irreversible and because in some instances the Library of Congress files are the last ones available, the necessity for the cautious approach is obvious. Since 1962 this program has resulted in the replacement of approximately 25,000 bound volumes by microfilm, leaving to be replaced in future years approximately 100,000 volumes. We have, in effect, completed approximately 20 percent of our objective.

As of June 30, 1965, the microfilm collection totalled some 110,000 reels, and grows by approximately 10,000 reels per year.

The Library has not developed as comprehensive a program for the microreproduction of other types of serial publications—namely, periodicals and government serials. To date the microfilming of these types has been restricted to newspaper format pulp periodicals and selected government serials, published on relatively poor quality sulfide paper.

Of these two groups I will first discuss briefly the periodicals. The effort here, as for newspapers, is to replace the titles, of which the Library receives some 500, published in newspaper format and on poor quality paper. As with the newspapers, our policy is to acquire as many microfilm subscriptions as are available from other sources. At the present time the Library acquires 150 titles on microfilm by subscription, of which 20 are microfilmed by the Photoduplication Service. Since the problem of acquisition for these titles is similar to that of newspapers, there is no need to present further details.

The final category worthy of mention is that of official government serials. Our effort in this area has been limited to some significant U.S. non-GPO imprints which are difficult to acquire in complete sets, even at the Library of Congress. These are, for the most part, the various consular press summaries and press release series.

* Salmon, Stephen R. *Specifications for Library of Congress Microfilming*. Washington, U.S. Government Printing Office, 1964. (Available from Supt. of Docs.)

At the present time there are microfilmed on a continuing basis some sixteen series. They are the four currently published series of the U.S. Consulate General in Hong Kong, the three series published by the U.S. Embassy in Tokyo, the U.S. Department of State Press Release series, the U.S. Mission to the United Nations Press Release series, and a few others.

Among the complete projects are the Joint Press Reading Service, 1944-1956, published in Moscow by the Embassies of the U.S., Great Britain, Canada, and Australia, and a recently completed project for the Press Summaries of the U.S. Consulate Offices and U.S. Information Services in China during the period 1944-1950. Positive microfilms of all these series are available from the Photoduplication Service.

I could not complete this part of the presentation without mentioning by name Donald F. Wisdom, Head of the Serial Division's Government Publication Section, who has labored most diligently in the preparation and completion of all these files. Consistent with our objective to produce the highest quality library resource, he has spent many hours in contacting Washington area libraries, research libraries which are known to have an area interest for a particular title, and, as a final effort, placing a location request in the *Weekly List of Unlocated Research Material* published by the Union Catalog Division. All these efforts generally result in locating items which may be unique in the United States.

Conclusion

In concluding my remarks, I wish to make a special request to the serial librarians. I would ask for their cooperation in helping us in our task of preserving as complete a record on microfilm as possible of materials included in the current microfilming program, and, wherever possible, in our effort to microfilm the historical files. For the current program we have prepared a list of the titles filmed at the Library. This list is available in limited quantity for those willing to check their newspaper receipts by title and to inform us of their willingness to cooperate by lending needed issues. For the retrospective program we would ask in general that we have your willingness to support the program whenever the opportunity arises.

Finally, I wish to take the opportunity to extend a word of appreciation to those libraries who have materially assisted us in completing many files. This spirit of cooperation is rewarded by the enrichment of our library resources for the benefit of all.

III ■ SPECIFIC MICROFORM APPLICATIONS: CASE STUDIES

INTRODUCTION

How does a microform collection for serials work? What are its specific problems? What old problems have been avoided? What new ones have been added? How does one avoid these? Or are some problems intrinsic to the medium or the nature of serials format and therefore can never be avoided, but perhaps sometimes solved?

A spectrum of library applications is here considered. In each application, there are separate and unique problems encountered. There are also some general problems solved; these run as a thread throughout the discussions: the central issues of acquisitions, binding, storage and access.

It had been estimated in 1970 that the average cost per year, per volume of a periodical, for binding was $6.00.[1] Since then the cost has been set as being somewhere between $8.00 and $10.00. A Northeastern University study (*Suburban Campus Library Cost Comparison Study*, 1961) indicated then that the cost for binding 100 periodicals ($828.00) was 25 percent more than the cost for these same 100 periodicals in microform. Likewise, it has been estimated that the storage costs for bound periodicals will in the near future equal (if not exceed) the initial acquisition costs. By choosing microforms, savings can be accomplished in initial acquisitions, binding, shelving and storage. However, costly mistakes can only be avoided if foresight is planned and conversion priorities are clearly thought out and set forth.

The provision of access to microform material is paramount. As Frances Spigai has referred to microforms, they are an "invisible medium."[2] Without proper bibliographic control and thorough indexing, microforms are useless in the original sense of the word; they literally *cannot* be put to use. Without these controls, there is only random picking and hopeful hunches. This certainly should not be the case. The contrast is only all too glaring between the sophisticated technique of microforms and the primitive condition of the lack of bibliographic descriptions and indexed access points. Care must be taken to provide for both of these.

References

1. Helen W. Tuttle, "Price Indexes for 1970," *Library Journal*, vol. 95, no. 13 (July 1970), p. 2428
2. Frances G. Spigai, *The Invisible Medium: State of the Art of Microform* (Stanford: ERIC Clearinghouse on Media and Technology, 1973).

Additional Readings

Basile, V.A. and R.W. Smith. "Evolving the 90% Pharmaceutical Library." *Special Libraries*, vol. 61, February 1970, pp. 81-86.

Bloch, Gail, *et. al. "Two Studies on the Effect of Film Polarity on Patent Examiner's Performance."* Washington, DC: National Bureau of Standards, 1969.

Burchinal, Lee G. "Uses of Microfilm in Educational Institutions." *Journal of Micrographics*, vol. 7, 1974, pp. 107-112.

Central State University. [Edmond, Oklahoma]. *The Library . . . Where Microfilm Is a Working Reality.* [Pamphlet]. n.p., n.d.

Curtis, Ron. "The Central State University Story: The Microfilm Decision."*Microform Review*, vol. 3, no. 1, January 1974, pp. 23-24.

Daghita, Joan M. "A Core Collection of Journals on Microfilm in a Community Teaching Hospital Library." Medical Librarians Association, *Bulletin*, vol. 64, no. 2, April 1976, pp. 240-241.

Dessauer, John P. "Library Acquisitions: A Look into the Future." *Publisher's Weekly*, vol. 207, no. 24, June 16, 1975, pp. 55-68.

Dodson, Suzanne. "The University of British Columbia Library's Guide to Large Collections in Microform. One Attempt to Minimize a Major Problem." *Microform Review*, vol. 1, April 1972, pp. 113-117.

Duncan, Virginia L. and Francis E. Parsons. "Use of Microfilm in an Industrial Research Library." *Special Libraries*, vol. 61, July/August 1970, pp. 288-290.

Erbes, Raymond G. "Microfilm in the High School Library." *Wilson Library Bulletin*, December 1958, pp. 302-303.

Guilfoyle, Marvin C. *Microform Centralization Project: A Survey of Current Practice and Possible Application in Bizzell Library.* 1976. ERIC Document 122 785.

Heim, Kathleen M. "The Role of Microforms in the Small College Library." *Microform Review*, vol. 3, no. 4, October 1974, pp. 254-259.

Judisch, J.M. "The Effect of Positive-Negative Microforms and Front-Rear Projection on Reading Speed and Comprehension." National Micrographics Association, *Journal*, vol. 2, Winter 1968/9, pp. 58-61.

Oliva, John J. "Microfilm Cartridge System at Prince George's Community College." *Journal of Micrographics*, vol. 6, November 1972, pp. 89-92.

Rogers, JoAnn V. *Microforms for Kentucky Public Libraries*. 1975. ERIC Document 119 654.

Staite, Keith D. "Microforms in a College Library." *Microdoc*, vol. 15, no. 4, 1976, pp. 119-128.

Thomae, Henrietta and W.T. Johnston. "A Glance at Junior College Libraries." *The Junior College Journal*, vol. 29, 1958, pp. 195-202.

Weil, B.H. "Esso Research Experiences with *Chemical Abstracts* on Microfilm." *Journal of Chemical Documentation*, vol. 5, November 1965, pp. 193-200.

CONVERSION OF THE PERIODICAL COLLECTION IN A TEACHING HOSPITAL LIBRARY TO MICROFILM FORMAT*

by **Esther R. Meiboom,** *Librarian, Martland Hospital Library, College of Medicine and Dentistry of New Jersey, Newark, New Jersey*

The use of microfilm for journal backfiles as a substitute for bound hard copy originals has become practical during the last decade. Although the microfilm medium has been available commercially since the 1940s, it has been used primarily for archival materials, out-of-print periodicals, or to replace volumes with deteriorating paper. The use of microfilm for active collections had to await advances in micrographics technology. The introduction of convenient formats and the availability of fast, dry copying equipment stimulated the acquisition of microfilm for library collections.

There are few reports in the literature on file conversion to microfilm. DeVilliers and Schloman[1] describe their experiences at the Massachusetts Institute of Technology Ford Reading Room, which maintains a core collection of one hundred chemistry and biology journals. Seventy of the journal titles are available in 16mm microfilm cartridge format: thirty titles are maintained in hard copy. DeVilliers and Schloman report satisfactory acceptance of microfilm by users, but stress the need for improvements both in film quality and reader-printer machines. Oliva[2] discusses the adoption of the Information

*Supported by National Institutes of Health Grant No. 1 G08 LM 02228-01 from the National Library of Medicine.

Reprinted from the *Bulletin of the Medical Library Association*, vol. 64, no. 1 (January 1976), pp. 36-40, by permission of the publisher.

Design (ID) microfilm system for back volumes of journals and newspapers in the Library of Prince George's Community College. He ascribes the success of the system to the format. The ID cartridges used with 35mm and 16mm film are easy to handle and are readily accepted by students. Microfilm in roll format, previously acquired by the library, was difficult to thread and presented problems in winding, fingertip smudging, and placement after use in the wrong boxes; in short, the roll format was disliked by users. A description of the use of microfilm cartridges at the Monmouth Medical Center Library, Long Branch, New Jersey, was presented by Joan Daghita at the 1974 annual meeting of the Medical Library Association in San Antonio, Texas. The Monmouth library converted seventy-five periodical backfile titles to 16mm microfilm cartridges in 1971. One 3M model 400 reader and one reader-printer were made available to users. The prints produced by the 3M 400 printer are rather expensive (11 cents per page), tend to curl up, and fade.

Until the present time the use of microfilm for journal backfiles has been much more prevalent in industry research libraries than in any other type of library. These libraries share a common problem of lack of space. Discussions of microfilm use in industrial libraries have been published by Weil,[3-5] Starker,[6] Kaback,[7] Duncan,[8] and others. All these authors report satisfaction with 16mm microfilm cartridges. User reaction is favorable to the primary and secondary journals of the American Chemical Society available in this format, and most readers prefer the microfilm edition of *Chemical Abstracts* to conduct literature searches. A limited use of microfilm in the Library of the College of Medicine and Dentistry of New Jersey is described by Basile and Kapadia.[9] For reasons of economy this library uses microfilm as substitute for hard copy journals, for seldom used titles and to replace missing volumes.

Martland Hospital and the Library

Martland Hospital is the 600-bed teaching hospital of the College of Medicine and Dentistry of New Jersey, located in Newark. It serves as a teaching and training center for 280 third- and fourth-year medical students, 280 interns and residents, and allied health and nursing students. The hospital also serves as the center for community health services for Newark.

The Martland Hospital Library is a branch of the Library of the College of Medicine and Dentistry of New Jersey (CMDNJ). Situated on the first floor of the hospital, the library is about four blocks away from the CMDNJ. By virtue of its location and limited resources, the most important function of the branch library is to provide ready reference material in clinical medicine for students and staff working in the hospital. The library also serves as an access point to the collection and services available in the central library. To fulfill these functions, the library maintains a collection of 2,200 recent textbooks and monographs, a reasonably good coverage of reference material, and subscribes to 160 periodical titles, maintaining a ten-year run of backfile volumes. The collection duplicates holdings of the CMDNJ Library.

During the past few years the library's clientele has grown steadily due to the expansion of the hospital's educational programs and increases in the number of students and house-staff. When library shelves filled up and the lack of seating space became critical, we weeded the book collection, retaining only titles with an imprint date of the last eight years. A survey of periodical usage was conducted in the hope that little-used journals could be eliminated. However, these attempts did not increase available stack space appreciably. Because of general space shortages in the hospital, any expansion of storage space was out of the question.[10] We decided that the best solution to the problem would be to convert to microfilm.

General Considerations

In mapping out a program for the conversion, the following guidelines were adopted: current hard copy subscriptions to periodicals would be continued; microfilm backfiles would be acquired for all periodicals if they were commercially available in a satisfactory format. For the titles available on microfilm, binding would be discontinued for their hard copy counterparts and the printed issues would be offered to other libraries through the MLA Exchange or the U.S. Book Exchange.

Reports in the literature as well as personal inquiries we made at several libraries indicated that much of the dissatisfaction expressed by microfilm users is due to the discomfort and eye strain from reading a screen-projected image. Although a reader is adequate for fast perusal of a paper, more thorough study requires a print. Accordingly, we decided that a sufficient number of reader-printers should be made available. High quality and low cost of prints were essential requirements of the equipment to be selected. The library already had a policy by which the hospital staff could charge copying costs to their departments. However, we expected the amount and cost of printing to increase appreciably with the introduction of microfilm. We decided that the library's policy of open shelving would apply to the microfilm file as well as other materials. The creation of a comfortable microfilm reading area would be necessary. Some of the requirements for a reading area have been discussed by Holmes,[11] Fair,[12] and Weber.[13]

Implementation

Microfilm: Because custom filming is prohibitively expensive, we decided to purchase commercially available microfilm only. Periodicals are available in a variety of different microform formats: 35mm film or 16mm film in rolls, various cartridges, casettes, or microfiche. We chose 16mm microfilm in cartridges with negative polarity. This relatively new format has been adopted after lengthy experimentation by the American Chemical Society and the American Institute of Physics for all their primary and secondary journals. Many people feel that this format will be most widely used for scientific journals in the future. The 16mm film affords excellent resolution while the cartridge insures integrity of the film and ease of use. The negative polarity film reverses, in the 3M reader-printer we selected, so that positive polarity prints can be obtained. Studies of the effect of film polarity on reading speed and comprehension have shown that subjects perform better when reading positive polarity material.[14-15]

Of the 160 journal titles held by the library, 118 are curently available in 16mm microfilm: 103 from University Microfilms and 15 from Williams & Wilkins. About 70 percent of these titles have files dating back to 1965. We purchased 1,018 microfilm cartridges for our initial conversion to the new format, withdrew 1,300 periodical volumes, and were able to remove twelve stack sections of shelving.

Readers and Reader-Printers: Purchase of equipment has to be recognized as a long-term commitment because of substantial investment costs and the fact that cartridges produced by different companies are not yet compatible. The choice of specific readers and reader-printers inevitably involves a fair amount of guesswork. Our choice was based on information obtained from a number of users, equipment manufacturers, and published reports.[16-21]

Two reader-printers, 3M model 500 C, were considered necessary to satisfy expected demand; the second machine would assure continuity of service in case the first machine broke down. In addition we acquired one reader, 3M COR 701. This machine can be used to read both microfilm and microfiche.

Storage. The microfilm cartridges are stored in Princeton micro-shelves housed on standard shelving, side by side with hard copy volumes. One location for both forms minimizes patron inconvenience and allows free access to materials. This arrangement requires more shelf space than carousels and cabinets and provides less protection for film than the latter; however, we considered this method of handling adequate, because the library has no archival role.

Environmental Condition: To insure that microfilm users not be disturbed by other library patrons, we set up an area separated by book stacks from the rest of the library. Three study stations consisting of portable cubicles (manufactured by Herman Miller) were placed along a wall away from windows. Each cubicle encompasses a floor space area of twenty-four square feet and contains a shelf 30″ wide and 48″ long with adjustable height. A free-standing table which can be moved to either side of the reader for left-handed or right-handed people, and a swivel chair are contained in each cubicle. The reader and reader-printer are situated on a turntable which allows readers to view the screen from an adjustable angle and facilitates insertion of print paper. We removed ceiling lights in this area and placed a tensor lamp in each cubicle. Two window air conditioners in the library provide humidity and temperature control.

Program Costs

The initial costs of the program amounted to about $23,000. We spent a little more than half this sum, $14,000, on microfilm cartridges for 118 periodical titles dating back an average of eight years. The cost of the two reader-printers, one reader, and accessories was $7,500. The remaining $1,500 was spent on study stations and micro-shelves.

Recurring yearly costs can only be estimated at this time. Based on 1974 prices, the cost of microfilm for 118 titles is $1,850. Paper for the reader-printers is estimated at $1,000 for 17,000 pages. Finally, a service contract for the machines costs $525.

The above costs are higher than those for the maintenance of equivalent hard-copy volumes of periodicals. Binding of these volumes would amount to about $800 for 118 titles at $5.25 per volume. The cost of the print paper for the Underwood-Olivetti photocopying machine used for hard copy material is only half of that used in the 3M reader-printer for microform material. ·

The increased costs are largely offset by "invisible" savings in storage space. A 1966 report by the Library Study Committee of the Association of American Medical Colleges[22] estimated the cost of storing one volume on a library shelf at $1.00 per year. Today, this cost should be at least 50 percent higher. We withdrew over 1,300 volumes from the library, resulting in space savings of approximately $2,000, roughly equivalent to the increased operating costs.

User Reaction

Users' acceptance of microfilm has been mixed. Staff members who can charge copying costs to their departments almost always copy an article they need. Because printing from microfilm is more convenient and faster than from a bound volume, the staff consider the microfilm an improvement. Students are charged $0.05 per print. In order to save expenses, they may attempt to study a lengthy article at the screen. We receive expressions of dissatisfaction from students because of the vertical position of the screen and the rigid position the user has to maintain.

Stevens[23] has suggested that prolonged reading could be made more comfortable by a better engineered machine with a tilting screen and a button to automatically change lenses. A chair with a headrest, designed specifically for screen reading, might also help.

Limitations and Problems

Although the conversion to microfilm has been a success, we have encountered a number of problems. One well-known fact is that x-rays and microscopic illustrations do not reproduce well on microfilm. High quality text reproduction requires high contrast film, which is unsuitable for halftones. Use of two different films is impractical because the required splicing would be much too costly. Therefore, we cancelled microfilm subscriptions to all radiology and pathology journals and returned the hard copy volumes to the shelves. Although other journals occasionally contain halftone illustrations, we have had no serious complaints about them. Apparently an occasional poor half-tone is not a major problem. Publishers are aware of this problem and are experimenting with a new process which, from samples we have seen, shows significant improvement. Publishers have assured us that they are committed to finding a solution within a year or two.

Probably the main reason that advertisements are reproduced in microfilm editions as they appear in original journals is the publisher's desire for routine processing. Because advertisement pages are not numbered consecutively within the text, they hinder searching for a specific page. The removal of advertisements which are not located on the same page with text would be desirable.

The 3M cartridges are not suitable for film lengths of less than fifty feet; otherwise the leader buckles on rewinding. This could probably be corrected by a slight change in cartridge design. At present we solve this problem by splicing two or three volumes of a title together into a single cartridge, or by adding filler to single volumes.

Sometimes a page will not focus evenly on the screen. This can be corrected by rewinding the film and returning to the desired page. But frequently the rewinding has to be repeated several times until even focus is achieved.

A desirable machine feature would be an interlock preventing removal of a cartridge when the film is not completely rewound. At present, inexperienced users too often forget to rewind a film before cartridge removal. Manual respooling then becomes necessary, and sometimes a film is damaged.

Poor product quality control also causes some problems. Since the beginning of the project, forty-seven cartridges have had to be returned for replacement because of missing sprockets; sixteen rolls of print paper were not coated evenly and parts of them did not print. Four microfilms had no index, five were lacking supplementary material, and three microfilms, presumably copied from library volumes with very narrow margins, had the first letters of the lines cut off. All these defects are, on the whole, comparable to those occurring in bound volumes. The companies we deal with have established reputations and readily exchange faulty materials. Obviously a good, generally adopted set of standards would be highly desirable, but no such set of standards is yet available. The National Microfilm Association is presently revising the ANSI PH 5 standards. The Association of Research Libraries and various groups within the American Library Association are cooperating with the PH 5 Committee to assure that improved standards take library users' needs into consideration.

Conclusion

On balance we feel that the conversion of journal backfiles to microfilm has been a success. We have achieved our main goal of significant space savings. Secondary benefits include better integrity of the collection. We have no problem collecting a complete set of journal issues for binding, and journal issues are no longer unavailable while at the bindery. No volumes are being stolen or defaced. In addition, cartridges are easier to handle than bound volumes.

The major negative aspect of microfilm use is the pronounced dislike of many patrons who must use the reader for an appreciable length of time. This difficulty can be remedied by a liberal printing policy, which unavoidably increases costs. We feel that such a policy is essential for success. Without it, conversion of periodicals to microfilm in a hospital library can be justified only where lack of space leaves no alternative.

Acknowledgements

I am grateful to M. Bahia for her help in implementation of the project and to Philip Rosenstein and Victor Basile for suggestions.

References

1. DeVilliers, A. M., and Schloman, B. F. Experiences with scientific journals on microfilm in an academic reading room. Spec. Libr. 64: 555-560, Dec. 1973.

2. Oliva, John J. Microfilm cartridge system at Prince George's Community College. J. Micrographics 6: 89-92, Nov. 1972.

3. Weil, B. H. Esso research experiences with Chemical Abstracts on microfilm. J. Chem. Doc. 5: 193-200, Nov. 1965.

4. Weil, B. H. Revising the publication process. Science 169: 631, 14 Aug, 1970.

5. Weil, B. H. Document access. J. Chem. Doc. 11: 178-185. Aug. 1971.

6. Starker, Lee N. User experiences with primary journals on 16mm microfilm. J. Chem. Doc. 10: 5-6, Feb. 1970.

7. Kaback, Stuart M. User benefits from secondary journal on microfilm. J. Chem. Doc. 10: 7-9. Feb 1970.

8. Duncan, Virginia L., and Parsons, Frances E. Use of microfilm in an industrial research library. Spec. Libr. 61: 288-290. July/Aug. 1970.

9. Basile, V. A. and Kapadia, S. Microform in a Medical Library Environment. May 1973. (ERIC Pub. ED 097-876).

10. Basile, V. A. and Smith, R. W. Evolving the 90% pharmaceutical library. Spec. Libr. 61: 81-86. Feb. 1970.

11. Holmes, Donald C. Determination of environmental conditions required in a library for effective utilization of microforms. Washington, D.C., Association of Research Libraries, 1970. p. 1-44, and appendices B.C. and D. (ERIC Pub. ED 046-403).

12. Fair, J. The microform reading room. Part IV. Microform Rev. 2: 168-171, July 1973.

13. Weber, D. C. Design for a microtext reading room. UNESCO Bull. Libr. 20: 303-308, Nov./Dec. 1966.

14. Bloch, Gail [and others]. Two studies on the effect of film polarity on patent examiner's performance. Study no. 1: Simulated search. Study no. 2: Ability to discern fine detail. Washington. National Bureau of Standards. 1969.

15. Judisch, J. M. The effect of positive-negative microforms and front-rear projection on reading speed and comprehension. N.M.A.J. 2: 58-61. Winter 1968-69.

16. Microform reader/printers for libraries. Libr. Technology Reports, July 1972.

17. Microform readers for libraries. Libr. Technology Reports. Nov. 1973.

18. William R. Hawken Associates. 3M 500 series reader/printers. Libr. Technology Reports, March 1973.

19. Checklist for selecting microfilm readers. Audio-visual Instruction 18: 36, Feb. 1973.

20. How to select a microform reader or reader-printer. Silver Spring, Md., National Microfilm Association, 1974, p. 12-16.

21. Ballou, Hubbard W., ed. Guide to Microreproduction Equipment, 5th ed. Supp.: Readers, Reader-printers. Silver Spring, Md., National Microfilm Association, 1972.

22. Association of American Medical Colleges. Library Study Committee. The health sciences library: its role in education for the health professions: report to the National Library of Medicine, J. Med. Educ. 42 (No. 8. Pt. 2): 1-63, Aug. 1967.

23. Stevens, Roland E. The microform revolution. Libr. Trends 19: 379-395, Jan. 1971.

MIXED MEDIA FOR A SERIAL SYSTEM: HARDCOPY, MICROFORM, AND CRT'S

by **Susan K. Martin,** *University of California, Berkeley, California*

After more than a decade of conversion of bibliographic records into machine-readable form, the libraries of the United States have in their possession a formidable number of bits and bytes representing an only slightly less formidable number of bibliographic entities. An educated guess would place that formidable number somewhere above four million records; the quantity of unique records remains unknown. The largest group of machine-readable information is probably the data base held by the Ohio College Library Center, which added its millionth record in August 1974. The OCLC system is an on-line system, of which the principal output product is catalog card sets. [1]

Institutions with growing data bases and without on-line systems are being forced to look carefully at the quantity and type of products that are to be derived from these data bases. Ten years ago, line printer output was most acceptable; indeed, it was often an improvement over the previous manual system. However, two major justifications for machine-readable data bases are that: (1) data would be able to be distributed widely to points which earlier had no access to central files, and (2) records which in a manual system could be accessed by only one data element could now be sorted in a variety of ways for increased access by different user groups. In order to fulfill these promises, much output is required. The larger the data base, the more expensive and unwieldy become the computer processing and printing operations, especially at computer centers which penalize heavy I/O operations.

Libraries have attempted to solve this problem in a variety of ways, in an

Reprinted from *Information Roundup* (Washington, D.C.: American Society for Information Science, 1975), pp. 1-8, by permission of the publisher.

effort to keep down costs while providing increased access. The book catalog, either from line printer copy or photocomposed, is a well-used path. However, the market for book catalogs is limited, and production costs are soaring even above the rate of inflation. Microform bibliographic tools are used at a number of locations, such as the Georgia Institute of Technology, Wayne State University, and Yale University.[2-4] This approach requires an investment in microform readers and the acceptance of the users, together with the not-always-easy decision to use microfiche vs. microfilm. Minicomputers and large on-line systems have their own associated development and hardware costs; in addition, use of these devices in public service areas has been attempted only in small libraries or on an experimental basis.

This paper will describe the effort of the General Library at the University of California, Berkeley, to resolve some of the problems outlined above.

Data Base

Nature of File and Input

Since 1970, a conversion task has been under way at UC Berkeley, with the goal of obtaining in machine-readable form the basic bibliographic and payment data of all serial titles.[5] "Serial" is defined broadly; the conversion has included periodicals, newspapers, monographic series, annuals, regular and irregular serials, and some works-in-part. By summer 1974, 150,000 titles were in the data base; these included all currently-received titles, all inactive and active document serial titles, and the titles held by several special libraries located on the campus but not organizationally part of the General Library. The Library is continuing to convert the inactive titles held by the General Library (estimated at 80-100,000 titles), a task which is estimated to be completed in Fall 1975.

The retrospective conversion task has been and continues to be performed by keyboarding the fixed and variable information on IBM Selectric typewriters equipped with optical scanning font type balls. The sheets of paper thus generated are sent to a service bureau to be read onto magnetic tape, from which the master file is updated. New titles, corrections, and lines of payment information were, until recently, coded on worksheets by members of the Serials Department; the worksheets were then sent to the Campus Computing Center, which is a keypunching service bureau.

The file is in a MARC-like format (UCB MARC). The leader and dictionary follow MARC conventions. The 008 field has been expanded to accommodate local requirements, and thus far no tracings have been included in the file.

However, the software is generalized, and a proposal under consideration calls for upgrading the file by adding the missing information.

Usage of the Serials Data Base

The data base described above serves three major functions:

(1) public service;
(2) payment control; and
(3) collection development.

Service units throughout the library receive copies of the key word index, plus quarterly listings of the holdings of their units. The Payments Division of the Serials Department uses the data base to record payment, to therefore avoid duplicate payments, and to facilitate the claiming and cancellation procedures. The book selectors (six in the Main Library, plus all branch librarians) are able to obtain lists of the serials for which they are responsible. The present inflation rate has combined with a steady-state budget to force upon us a formal program of de-selection of serials for cancellation or potential cancellation. A cancellation procedure has been built into the system, providing those responsible for serial funds with more information and control than were available in the past.

Output Products

To serve these public and technical service needs, the Berkeley Library has evolved a system which takes advantage of several existing technologies.

Key Word Index

To facilitate public service, the library has published two photocomposed editions of a key word index, giving access by key words to all titles in the data base.[6] The 1973 edition, reflecting a file of 50,000 titles, had 147,000 access points and was a three-volume set. The 1974 edition has 150,000 titles, 750,000 access points, and is a ten-volume set. It is clear that the Library cannot afford to keep meeting its data base in this way. Although photocomposition costs are not unreasonable, the rising paper costs have kept publication costs high. A full key word index in hard copy is not foreseen as a real possibility for the future, unless circumstances change radically.

Printed Lists

Once every quarter, each branch and public service point receives a printout of its titles; arranged by vendor and alphabetically by main entry within vendor. The size of this list is second only to the master edit list, which is printed quarterly in two segments: documents and non-documents.

Computer-printed products also form the basis of the support given to fund managers. Lists of titles within fund, giving payment histories, are printed at intervals, together with management reports which indicate the progress of each fund during the current fiscal year. Special lists by call number, by branch library, by language, etc. are produced on demand.

Microfiche Indexes

Access to the payment printout (by vendor and title), although usually straight-forward, is sometimes fraught with "snags." Until spring 1974, alphabetic and order number indexes to this large printout were printed on the computer. The generation of these index files and their subsequent printing were quite costly; therefore, the indexes were produced only three or four times a year. They gradually became asynchronous to the payment printout, which is produced monthly.

In spring 1974, the library purchased for each public service unit a micro-fiche reader, to be used for a COM file of in-process items. Since the readers were available, an experimental run was arranged to produce the two payment indexes on COM fiche. The resulting files, at 48X reduction, are eight fiche (order number) and sixteen fiche (alphabetic). The pilot run was successful, and the indexes are being used not only by the Payment Division, but also by other areas of the library in increasing numbers.

CRT Input and Edit

In an effort to obviate the manual coding followed by keypunching which was necessary to update the file, the Library obtained a Datapoint 2200 mini-computer in summer 1974. It is being used as an input and edit device for invoice information; the cassettes are copied onto the Datapoint's large tape drive, which then interfaces with the host IBM 360/65 computer. In the coming months, additions to the file will also be keyed directly to cassette, with some editing functions carried out by the Datapoint. (Retrospective conversion will continue to be typed for optical scanning). The servoprinter of the Datapoint prints out audit lists of keyed invoices for immediate checking for errors and problems, or for an audit trail to solve problems which crop up later.

Discussion

The gradual adoption of multiple forms of computer output from the serials data base has allowed increasing participation of the library staff in the selection and evaluation of these tools. Both technical service and public service staffs are involved in the decision-making process, and almost all members of the library staff use one or more of the output products on a fairly regular basis. The staff of the Serials Department has been most heavily involved and continue to consult with the Systems Office regarding desirable changes or new services. Since the acquisition of the Datapoint 2200, the clerical staff which had been coding new data or corrections manually began to enter these data directly on the CRT. There is widespread recognition of the potential benefits of automating these processes, and the staff on the whole has been very receptive to change. "Everything on-line" is the ideal, however, and it is difficult for those working with the outputs of the data base to make decisions regarding the acceptance of the interim products in the form of hard copy or microform. The key word index is without doubt the most heavily used product of the serials data base, and the staff informs us not only of its immense utility but of its shortcomings.

Equipment Implications

Obviously, the decision to create a line printer or photocomposed product is not a difficult one. The commitments and costs of such a decision lie totally in the cost of producing the hard copy itself, and have no further ramification. It must be ascertained that the system outputs can be contained within the budget provided for the system. When considering other forms of outputs, however, complications are introduced. Should microform be used? If so, will it be microfilm or microfiche? We select microform knowing full well that the economic feasibility of eliminating all batch forms of data representation and going to an on-line system may be within our reach in five to ten years. Therefore, any investment in microform readers will have to be written off.

Having selected one of the microforms, we must then select reduction ratios. There has been no standard until last year when the government adopted 48X for the reduction ratio for computer output microform, and 24X for text reduction. As mentioned earlier, a decision had already been made at Berkeley to produce an in-process list in microfiche. Therefore, the production of microfiche indexes to the serials data base was preordained. Had we begun use of computer output microform with the existing serials data base, however, the decision would have been more difficult. The file is large and could easily fit on one or more of the automatic microfilm readers which hold 25,000 or more frames.

With a large number of microfiche readers in the library, the decision about whether to publish the next key word index in microfilm or microfiche has been made for the library. It would be microfiche, and it would be a file of a least 70 fiche. Bearing in mind the factors of cost, anticipated lifespan, ease of use, and size of file, Berkeley purchased 35 Datagraphix 1400 microfiche readers, which are relatively cheap and of good quality. The readers are ¾ size, with a 48X reduction ratio. It is quite likely that for units using microfiche most heavily, additional readers will be obtained which are full-sized rather than ¾ size and of sturdier construction.

Computer Implications

As is the case with many academic libraries, the Berkeley Library is expected to use the university's computing centers. The system described above forces us to stray from this path for two reasons. Firstly, a commercial computer output microform service bureau is used to produce the microfiche, and secondly, the Datapoint 2200 was purchased to input the bibliographic and invoice data, thereby creating an in-house computing facility. Fortunately, the Library has encountered no problems in straying from the university computing center. Our system development appears to be typical of administrative system developments elsewhere in the university. A few months ago, the Northern Regional University Computing Center set up a blanket arrangement with Zytron, the company which produces our microfiche, and another blanket arrangement with the Datapoint Company. These developments have made our life much easier.

The use of several computing facilities to support a single application without telecommunications does, however, hamper the turnaround time of these products. There is the additional labor of determining the compatibility of machine-readable character representation from one system to another. Fortunately, we have had much assistance from Zytron with the COM production, and Datapoint has been helpful in solving some of the problems of the interface between the Datapoint and the IBM 360. The current small fly in the ointment is that the computer center changed from 7-track to 9-track drives on very short notice. A 9-track drive has been ordered from Datapoint for the minicomputer, but in the meantime, we must send our 7-track drives to the campus computing (a CDC 6400) to have the tapes converted to punched cards, rather than having tapes sent immediately to the administrative data processing center for input to our programs. The reallocation of computing service requirements has meant a reallocation of expenditures generally favorable to the library.

Budgetary Implications

It is still early to measure the full impact of Berkeley's serials system on the library's budget. The serials key word index and other tools which are most widely distributed in the library are added tools, not replacing any earlier file or function. No effort has been made to measure the benefits accrued by the introduction of these products into the various line operations of the library. While such measurement would be possible, it is generally accepted that the key word index and the other products of the data base are valuable tools, and no request has yet been forthcoming to justify the existence of the system by means of a cost benefit study.

It is in the area of serial payment approval where the system has been felt most tangibly. Two years ago, this division had a staff complement of 8 FTE. As of March 1975, the staff was down to 4 FTE, and it is entirely possible that the operation can be handled by 3 people. The introduction of automatic production of claims letters and catalog card sets may have a similar effect in the library's Periodical Room and Serial Cataloging Division, respectively. These applications will be initiated over a period of the next six months to a year, and any effect from them will not be felt for at least a year to two years.

While the staff in the Payment Division has decreased, there has been an increase in staff elsewhere. A new position was created to coordinate the serials data base. This is a technical processing rather than a systems position, held by a librarian who has one non-professional assistant. Exclusive of production of the key word index, the serial system computer costs are between

$14,000 and $15,000 a year. By using microfiche indexes, we have been able to cut the cost of index production from $300 to $100 a run. By far the major part of the $100 cost is sorting the file and creating a print tape. By using a minicomputer for data entry, we are able to avoid the $3600 annual cost for keypunching. This alone would allow the minicomputer to pay for itself in less than four years. But in addition, one entire step in the process of handling the invoice data has been eliminated, an item which has not at this point been costed out completely. It is estimated to be in the order of $2500 annually.

The question concerns the cost-benefits of those tools which were not available before and are now available and heavily used by members of the staff (such as the Collection Development Office and the branch librarians). Each situation is different and would require individual study. How many questions can branch librarians now answer within their own unit rather than calling the Main Library, because the key word index is available to them? In these times of crises with the book budget, how would book selectors evaluate and cancel or retain serial titles, were it not possible to produce lists of titles ordered under each selector's fund? How much time is saved by the Serials Department because check-in cards and New Serial Titles reporting slips are now produced automatically for each new title rather than requiring additional keyboarding?

Conclusion

The system has evolved gradually without any prior master plan. It is not the intent of this paper to tell you, penny for penny, the benefits and trade-offs that occur in the implementation of a system with a variety of forms of outputs. The economic realities of our situation have forced us to be flexible and relatively imaginative in attempting to maintain our serials data base as a useful and viable tool of the library. The resulting system, while by no means perfect, has a good deal of utility, is economical, and will not be a burden to the more advanced technologies.

References

1. KILGOUR, FREDERICK G.; LONG, PHILIP L.; LANDGRAF, ALAN L.; WYCKOFF, JOHN A. "The Shared Cataloging System of the Ohio College Library Center." Journal of Library Automation, 5:3 (September 1972) 157-183.

2. ROBERTS, EDWARD G.; KENNEDY, JOHN P. "The Georgia Tech Library's Microfiche Catalog." Journal of Micrographics, 6:6 (July 1973) 245-251.

3. SAFFADY, WILLIAM. "A Computer Output Microfilm Serials List for Patron Use." Journal of Library Automation, 7:4 (December 1974) 263-266.

4. UNGERLEIDER, S. LESTER. Study of Usability of Computer Output Microfilm in the Technical Processing Area of Yale University Library. Yale University Library, New Haven, Conn., 1971, paging varies. (unpublished report).

5. SILBERSTEIN, STEPHEN M. "Computerized Serial Processing System at the University of California at Berkeley." In preparation.

6. CRAWFORD, WALT. "Building a Serials Key Word Index." In preparation.

MICROREPRODUCTIONS OF PERIODICALS
IN A SMALL UNIVERSITY LIBRARY

by **Stephen Ford,** *Chief, Serials Division, Southern Illinois University Libraries, Carbondale, Illinois*

This library receives about 160 periodical titles on microfilm and microcard annually. We have been moved to this program by the now well-known arguments in favor of film as a medium of preservation of certain library materials. The space problem has been a decisive factor in this rapidly expanding institution where we receive 1,450 periodical titles annually and bind something over 900 of them. We find certain other advantages to this program which are not as tangible as the cost of storage: we need not be overly concerned about missing issues for those titles received in microform; the problem of out-of-print back issues is solved; and, with one exception, there are no periods when a volume is unavailable to our students and faculty because it is in the bindery; the exception is the case of issues missing in the sometimes lengthy interval preceding receipt of the microreproduced copy. In addition, the high cost of gathering and preparing a volume for the bindery is eliminated.

However, the blessings of microreproduced periodicals are not unmixed. Fundamentally, film and microcards are not as convenient as the physical volume, for the intermediary of magnified projection is a handicap to the patron and to the librarian who must instruct and supervise him, and the use of film is, without equivocation, tiring for the user. Periodical volumes published in the last three to five years receive the highest use and therefore represent the greatest inconvenience if they are available only in microreproduction, except

Reprinted from *Serials Slants*, vol. 5 (1954), pp. 62-65, by permission of the publisher.

in the case of missing issues which are out-of-print, whereby the micro-reproduction immediately becomes a very real asset. We retain these unbound volumes for several years, but it is obvious that the storage and maintenance, unbound, of a periodical like *Business Week* is almost a physical impossibility. Therefore, we have found it necessary to bind 33 of the 160 titles received in microreproduction. They are bound in an inexpensive commercial binding, and we are experimenting to find a cheaper temporary but satisfactory binding which will justify this obvious expensive method. In short, we prefer micro-reproductions of periodicals only when their high-use period is ended.

The cost of binding and the cost of purchasing periodicals on film and microcards is approximately the same, and, when the cost of gathering and preparing volumes for binding is compared with the cost of placing standing orders for microreproductions, the latter is definitely cheaper. Microreproductions may seem, on superficial examination, more expensive than binding. For instance, the *Oil and Gas Journal* annually costs approximately $35.00 on microfilm and $20.00 bound. However, closer examination indicates that there are many instances where microfilm is cheaper than binding. As an example, *College English* annually costs approximately $1.70 on film and $2.17 bound. In a cost comparison, we find that 33 periodical titles chosen at random cost, annually, $129.45 on film and $116.81 bound. Comparative storage costs have been adequately discussed elsewhere and we capitulate to the arguments in favor of microreproductions. Microfilm storage cabinets are more elaborate and expensive than necessary for the adequate preservation of the film. Micro-readers are expensive to purchcase and maintain; they must be had in quantity; they will have to be replaced periodically; and they occupy valuable space in the library. However, the combined expenses are not as great as the expense required to house bound volumes.[1]

Certain economies may be effected to reduce microreproduction costs: the storage cabinets recommended for film are probably unnecessary for humidity control in most libraries and a cheaper means of storage might be devised locally; many librarians do not splice together volumes of each periodical title on film when, with a relatively reasonable investment in a splicing machine (about $35.00), three or four volumes of some periodical titles received in as many film boxes can be combined in one box on one reel. In a sampling of 72 boxes of microfilm containing about 2,740 feet, we discovered that the same footage, if spliced, could be contained in approximately 40 boxes, which would in effect be a saving of almost 45 percent of the housing space plus the cost of splicing. Probably no volumes less than five years old should be spliced since they become increasingly difficult to use in that form.

In binding the recent volumes of periodicals for temporary use, economy methods can be utilized internally, but it is unfortunate that most commercial binderies refuse to offer cheap temporary binding which could be used for this purpose. Of five binders sampled in the Middle West, only one offers an economy binding which can be considered reasonable enough for the temporary binding of periodicals also received in microreproduction. Prices on this binding range from $1.25 for an eight inch periodical to $1.90 for a thirteen inch periodical. We have experimented with the new plastic adhesive applied to the backs of periodicals and find them suitable for small, light weight periodicals of several issues. At the present, we are beginning experimentation with a combination of a plastic adhesive and a simple case binder. Purchasing the binder and the adhesive from a library supplies house and having the work done in the library by students should produce a suitable temporary binding for approximately $.57 per volume, including lettering.

Our five microreaders are heavily used, which seems to lead to the conclusion that microreproduced periodicals are likewise in great use. However, close observation indicates that patrons are most frequently using recent newspapers on film, which are preserved only in that form. Microreproduced periodicals are not in great demand since we retain the periodical in original form from three to five years and patrons usually prefer to use that more conventional and sympathetic medium. Perhaps reader acceptance cannot be evaluated until that time in the future when periodicals are available only in microreproducion. Our portable microfilm reader, for home and office loan, has been utilized to good degree, which helps to overcome the objection that microfilm cannot be circulated.

No periodical is ever purchased in microreproduction without the approval of the university department which originally requested the periodical; therefore we have little faculty resistance to this new form once it is in the library. The problem of gaining faculty acceptance of microreproduction is deserving of closer examination and cooperative comparison among libraries. Faculty responses are often related to librarians' responses. If a staff is enthusiastic about microreproductions, it is likely that the faculty will react similarly. Periodicals in the field of art and home economics are notably unsuitable for microreproduction and periodicals in certain other subject fields do not always lend themselves to the medium where maps, diagrams and charts are included. The following chart attempts to evaluate faculty and library staff response to the microfilms of periodicals available from University Microfilms, Ann Arbor, Michigan. Obviously, certain departments are enthusiastic about the medium and others react unfavorably. Another conclusion which may be drawn from this analysis is that not enough periodical titles are available on film. [The following chart is certainly not, by any means, an accurate indication of the present state of availability, but rather serves as an indication of what had been available in 1954, the date when this article was written. Ed.]

AN ANALYSIS OF PERIODICALS RECEIVED
IN THIS LIBRARY, BY SUBJECT

	Available on film	Received on film
Agriculture	16	14
Art	11	6
Audio-Visual	5	4
Aviation	2	2
Biological Sciences	21	5
Business	18	9
Chemistry	5	5
Current Events	4	2
Economics	6	2
Education	29	14
English	14	10
Foreign Govt. Pubns.	0	0
Foreign Language	4	2
General	13	5
Geography-Geology	13	8
Government	9	0
Health-Medicine	22	14
Higher Education	5	2
History	8	6
Home Economics	12	2
Industrial Education	8	3
International Relations	3	1
Journalism	4	1
Labor	1	0
Library	7	4
Mathematics	3	0
Music	3	3
Philosophy	4	3
Physical Education	3	3
Physics-Astronomy	16	8
Psychology	9	5
Religion	4	2
Science	3	1
Sociology-Anthropology	13	9
Special Education	3	2
Speech-Dramatics	2	0
	297	152

In the small university library the immediate large program of microreproduction has advantages and disadvantages which are about in balance. Judgment of the real advantages of such a program must anticipate the period beginning ten or fifteen years hence when little-used periodicals will be readily available, without expensive storage problems. We do not regard our program for microreproductions as expensive and we otherwise justify our program on the bases of service to our library users and the necessity of keeping our library within manageable limits, not overwhelmed by periodical storage problems now and in the future.

References

1. *see* "Microfilm as a Substitute for Binding," by E.B. Power, American Documentation, 1951.

MICROFORMS AT TEXAS A&M UNIVERSITY

by **Henry L. Alsmeyer, Jr.**, *Associate Director of Libraries, Texas A&M University, and* **Tawana P. West**, *former Microtext Librarian, Texas A&M University*

Texas A&M University (TAMU), the oldest public institution of higher education in the state, is preparing to observe its centennial. Among the members of the Association of Research Libraries, the TAMU libraries now rank forty-fifth in the number of microform units held. TAMU reported approximately 600,000 physical units of microforms and more than 800,000 printed volumes as of August 31, 1973.* Most of the microforms are held in the documents division of the university library. The quantity of microforms and the situation concerning them generally differ greatly from the 1960s and early 1970s.

The growth of the collection has been from the approximately 40,000 microform units held in the fall of 1964. Equipment has increased to twenty-two readers from the four available before 1968. In September 1972, the services of one professional librarian became available full-time in the microtext center. At the same time, a full-time staff member also was added for staffing of the center, which holds materials in microfilm, microfiche, Microprint and microcard.

Patrons of the TAMU libraries have access within seventy-two hours or so to the thousands of microforms held by The Center for Research Libraries (CRI), in addition to the materials available from other libraries through the active

*Editor's Note: The methods of counting hard-copy volumes and their "equivalent" in microforms are not at this time comparable. However, it is hoped that forthcoming revisions in the counting method will soon resolve this undesirable ambiguity. See also John Berry's "Microform Volume Equivalency Question" in *Micropublisher* 13 (January - February 1974): 8.

Reprinted from *Microform Review*, vol. 3, no. 4, (October 1974), pp. 260-262. ©1974 by Microform Review Inc.

interlibrary services department. Format is not considered a barrier to either lending or borrowing. The interlibrary services department head estimated early in 1974 that roughly 7 percent of the total transactions—lending and borrowing—involved microforms. TAMU was the first southwestern institution to join the CRL and actively supports this cooperative program involving research materials in both print and microformats.

The university library is housed in a four-story building, with the documents division occupying much of the second floor and the special collections area and the microtext center occupying a considerable portion of the third floor. The Readex Microprint series makes available nondepository government publications. Technical reports available on microfiche supplement the collection of U.S. goverment publications.

Several statistics provide insights into microtext center activities during 1972-1973, the first year of full-time staffing by a professional librarian. The record shows that 17,269 pieces of microform were refiled after use, that information about the collection was given individually to 1,466 patrons, and that assistance with the equipment was given to 1,112 users. The staff made more than 8,000 hard copies for patrons on a reader-printer. Machine maintenance was necessary in 301 cases (many of these involved only the replacement of light bulbs). Dozens of students visited the area during tours of the library. This was the first year that such statistics were kept; however, there is no doubt that the level of usage is growing for microtext material, as well as for more traditional materials.

One source of complaints by patrons—and augmented by librarians—is that due to present usage levels and the costs of making available a reader-printer for micro-opaques, copies cannot be made from the microcards and prints, which include such important materials as the *British Parliamentary History* and *Early American Imprints*.

The collection is planned to meet the needs of students ranging in academic levels from freshman through graduate studies, as well as faculty. Professors in several colleges of the university routinely send their students into the area for research. Accounting students, for example, use specialized reports filed with the Securities and Exchange Commission and made available on microfiche. Education students like the practically complete holdings of ERIC materials augmented in fall 1973 by computerized searches requested through the microtext center on a trial basis and funded experimentally. A freshman reading last year's newspaper accounts of his high-school athletic experiences, the graduate student reading newspaper files dating to Texas' early days as a republic, and a professor examining foreign archival materials on film illustrate the usage patterns.

Patrons find the collection available slightly more than a hundred hours weekly with a library staff member on duty for fifty-seven of these hours.

Additional hours of staffing may be provided in the future, but the present schedule of full staffing (8 A.M.-9 P.M. Monday through Thursday and 8 A.M.-5 P.M. Friday) is believed to meet major needs. When the center is not under full staffing, users may obtain assistance from library staff at adjacent service points. The serious researchers who use the collection during the weekend hours are generally self-sufficient. Night staffing is provided through the cooperation of the special collections faculty and staff. The assistant director for special collections is the immediate supervisor of the microtext center and is among the TAMU librarians most knowlegeable concerning micrographics in general.

The daytime staffing of the center is budgeted for a professionally educated librarian and a clerical assistant. The center is no stepchild; the TAMU libraries administration believes in staffing with the best qualified people.

The professional development of TAMU librarians is encouraged in several ways, including attendance at national meetings. Information, insights and personal contacts gained through participation in the microforms group of the 1972 American Library Association preconference and the NMA-sponsored Micrographics Seminar for Librarians held in Houston early in 1974 have been particularly valuable. Different librarians represented TAMU at these two sessions, and each returned with a firm belief that TAMU's handling of microforms compares quite favorably with that on many other campuses. The encouragement of professional reading, including the regular routing of *Microform Review* and other journals and newsletters devoted to micrographics, is another method of keeping TAMU librarians well informed on developments and materials in this field. The program of university library lectures brings to the campus outstanding persons who lecture upon varied topics of professional interest.

Librarians participate actively in the collection-building process for both microforms and hard-copy materials. The commitment to buying microforms is reflected through the statistics of recent years. A general rule in the TAMU libraries is to buy microform if the desired materials are available in that format and acceptable to the faculty. The ready availability of materials in microform and the economics of both acquisition and storage are argued as positive factors. Significant problems of acceptability involve materials that include numerous scientific illustrations or superscripts in formulas. This view of scientists in the biological sciences and mathematicians has been significant. The collection thus is weak in scientific publications. The rate of annual acquisitions since 1965-1966 has fluctuated considerably to reflect the changing budgetary situation. This rate has varied from a low of 11,155 pieces added in 1966-67 to a high of 105,153 pieces added in 1969-1970. For 1972-1973, the figure is 62,264.

Acquisitions planned for calendar 1974 include the first portion of the

Goldsmiths'-Kress Library of Economic Literature and the presidential papers of William Howard Taft; recent additions have included the Sabin bibliography and the Carnegie-Myrdal study of the Negro in America. The additions go into the cabinets or shelving alongside such varied materials as magazines such as *Time* and *Playboy*, archival materials such as church records and presidential papers, a set of rare books in accounting, and a drama series. A relatively small amount of materials is available in color. The set of *British Parliamentary History* (Hansard's) was obtained as the result of a successful proposal to a Dallas foundation for funding.

The collection includes 171 newspaper titles; however, holdings are incomplete for some of these. These papers range in time from the *Boston News-Letter* (1704-1776) through the recent issues of state and national newspapers. A number of newspaper indexes formerly separated by some distance from the microfilm cabinets were moved into the area when the microtext center was established. The indexes now available include those of *The Christian Science Monitor*, *The National Observer*, the *Newspaper (4 and 1) Index*, *The New York Times*, *The Times* (of London), and *The Wall Street Journal*. Also available conveniently are the printed bibliographies necessary for using such major series as *Early American Imprints* and the ERIC system's *Research in Education*.

TAMU librarians use a simple classification scheme to differentiate the several broad original formats of the materials. For example, *The New York Times* is classified as "N" for newspaper and has been assigned number 424 in the sequential numbering for newspapers. The type of microform is indicated over the classification letter, forming the call number. Thus the call number for *The New York Times* is "MICROFILM-N-425." The cataloged microtext material, which now includes most of the newspapers and serials titles, is given complete descriptive cataloging and appropriate subject headings. The cataloged materials are reflected in the public catalog; all newspaper and serial titles, whether cataloged or not, appear in the computerized serials printout with location of materials; and a card index guide in the microtext center locates all holdings in that area. Additionally, the printed bibliographies used as the basis for certain major micropublishing projects such as *Early American Imprints* provide access for items not individually cataloged.

Anyone who has used a microform collection housed in unpleasant surroundings will appreciate the facilities of the microtext center. The original reading room provided in the university library building measures twenty-five by twenty-two feet (550 square feet) and remains in use as a reading room. A rheostat was provided as original equipment of the room, so that readers may control lighting from total darkness through normal room lighting. The architect—apparently for reasons relating to external appearance—placed a three by eight foot window in this room. The window in a corner of the room has been the source of complaints and now is covered with paper to reduce the incoming light. The expansion of the microtext area involved relinquishing the use of eighteen by twenty-two foot (396 square feet) room used originally to house the cabinets containing microforms and gaining the use of 1,935 square feet of new, carpeted space. This new space, almost squarish with more than forty feet in each direction, houses the desks of the librarian and the clerical assistant, all of the collection in both metal filing cabinets and built-in wall shelving, index tables, and seven readers. There is space for additional readers. In this area, normal room lighting is constant. Users have not commented adversely upon reading in this normal lighting chiefly due to the use in this area of nonglare screens.

The strongly positive attitude toward microforms at TAMU results in the firm commitment by librarians of funds, space, and staffing to make materials available through microphotography in a modern, pleasant microtext center. Students and many faculty and staff accept casually the fact that their information needs are met by materials produced through filming processes. The microtext center, like practically all of the other collections areas, is on a self-serve basis, but librarians are conveniently available. This combination of commitment, collections, staffing, facilities has resulted in a major expansion of the microforms areas, although the university's new library building was occupied only in the summer of 1968.

WE CHOSE MICROFILM

by **Frances L. Meals,** *Librarian, Colby Junior College, New London, N.H. and* **Walter T. Johnson,** *Librarian, Abraham Baldwin College, Tifton, Ga.*

In a survey made of a selected group of junior colleges in 1958,[1] it was discovered that only two of the seventy-nine libraries surveyed were using microfilm to any extent as a means of preserving periodicals. This survey did reveal much interest in periodicals on microfilm by librarians who would like to use microfilm or who were considering using it.

Because of this interest the librarians of the two junior college libraries—Abraham Baldwin and Colby—using microfilm to preserve periodicals felt that their experience with this medium might be of value to others.

Colby Junior College began using microfilm in 1952 and Abraham Baldwin College began in 1956. Each receives twenty-eight titles on microfilm and both purchase the completed films from commercial suppliers rather than attempting to process their own.

Baldwin's back periodical file was in very poor shape in 1955. Few items had been bound professionally and back periodicals were kept in home-made binders, in pamphlet boxes, or just tied up. That a binding program needed to be started was increasingly evident, but since the Baldwin Library was in need of space, there was no room to store the bound items properly. In going through the periodicals selected for possible binding, Baldwin discovered that there were many missing issues which would have to be replaced and thus add to the binding expense.

Colby had a back file of bound periodicals and had moved into a new building in 1950 so that space was not a problem, although the cost of building

Reprinted from *College and Research Libraries*, May 1960, pp. 223-226, 228 by permission of the publisher.

had made Colby well aware of the need to conserve space. Colby was bothered by the proverbial missing issues at binding time and had also had the sad experience of some articles being clipped from volumes already bound.

Thus the problem of space led both Colby and Baldwin to consider microfilm, and that was the primary reason that both chose to preserve back issues of periodicals on microfilm.

The space-saving possibilities of microfilm in actual practice come as something of a shock even after one has seen the promotion pictures of a bound periodical together with a reel of microfilm of the same volume showing the reduction in size. A nine-drawer microfilm cabinet using 16.2 cubic feet of space will hold 540 reels of microfilm or some 725 periodical volumes, since many titles come in two volumes, or twelve months of issues, to the reel. Regular ten-inch double-faced stack shelving would require half as much space to hold the same number of volumes. On a square footage basis the difference is not so great.

The missing and mutilated issues problem was the second reason that both elected to use microfilm. Since the microfilm is supplied in finished form by a commercial firm, one does not have the problem of finding a missing issue to complete a volume. To date, neither has had an article clipped from a reel of microfilm, and this seems to be a rather remote possibility since the student does not possess a film reader.

Colby and Baldwin both considered the cost of microfilm versus binding. Microfilm runs about one-fourth cent per page; therefore, the thicker the magazine, the higher the cost. Binding is generally priced according to the height of the magazine with the taller ones costing the most to bind. Table 1

Table 1. Comparison of Binding and Microfilm Costs

Periodical	Issued	12 Months bound as	12 Months filmed as	Binding Cost for one year*	Microfilm Cost for one year†
Reader's Digest	Monthly	2vols.	1 reel	$ 6.58	$ 7.45
Science Digest	Monthly	2 vols.	1 reel	6.58	3.50
Changing Times	Monthly	1 vol.	1 reel	3.59	2.00
U.S. News and World Report	Weekly	4 vols.	2 reels	15.36	21.08
House and Garden	Monthly	2 vols.	1 reel	8.26	6.97
Total				$40.37	$41.00

* Average of prices of three binderies (excluding transportation charges).
† Average of three years 1955 through 1957 (including postage charges).

gives a rough comparison of binding and microfilm costs for five magazine of various thicknesses and height. This comparison indicates that binding is slightly cheaper. In actual practice, Baldwin and Colby have found that the base price of binding and microfilm for the number of titles each receives works out about the same, with microfilm being slightly cheaper. The extras—to borrow an automotive term—are what make the difference. No extras are involved with microfilm except writing and mailing the order, and a one-time standing order can be made. Binding involves several extras: periodicals must be collated and tied; missing and mutilated issues must be secured through purchase or exchange; periodicals must be packed for shipment to the bindery and unpacked on return; and transportation must be paid on smaller shipments. These extras cost in staff time if not money.

The biggest drawback Baldwin and Colby faced in starting a microfilm program was the initial cost. Microfilm readers run from $125 up, with $350 being the price of one of the better ones. Humidified storage cabinets start at $186, although less adequate storage boxes for a few reels of film can be purchased for a few dollars. One might figure an initial outlay of $500 for one reader and one humidified storage cabinet. At Baldwin the space-saving feature was used in presenting the budget request for the extra $500 necessary to cover the initial equipment cost.

Baldwin's need for a larger library building is acute. In 1952 part of the workroom was given over to periodical storage and in 1954 a small nook was re-partitioned from reading room area to periodical storage area. It was correctly anticipated that microfilm would prevent the necessity of borrowing periodical storage area from another floor area for several years. Of course, the point was made to the librarian that an eventual new building would solve space problems. To answer this argument against the high cost of microfilm equipment one can present figures on space costs. 40.5 square feet of floor space for the storage of bound periodicals will cost at least $445.50 if one uses the low building cost of eleven dollars per square foot. To this must be added about $175 for nine feet of double-faced ten inch library-type shelving. Compared with this, the space for the microfilm storage cabinet will cost $97.57 at eleven dollars a square foot, but the space above the fifty-inch high microfilm cabinet can be used for some storage. Adding $500 initial equipment outlay to this gives a figure of $597.57 for microfilm storage, compared to $620.50 for conventional storage. If the cost of the film reader is omitted, the cost of comparable microfilm storage drops to $283.57. One might even go so far as to add something for heating, cooling, lighting, and maintaining the large space required for conventional periodical storage. Consequently, microfilm either means less space needed in a new building or more space for other purposes.

Baldwin and Colby each elected to secure twenty-eight titles on microfilm although each takes many more periodicals than this. The selection was made on the basis of whether or not the publication was indexed in the *Readers' Guide* and how frequently back issues were called for in the library. There is little similarity between the microfilm lists of the two libraries. Colby also receives the *New York Times* on microfilm. Since Baldwin had only a small collection of bound periodicals, it has purchased many back reels to try to complete certain holdings from 1950 on.

In selecting equipment, both chose nine drawer humidified film cabinets which are filing-cabinet height. A six-drawer cabinet, which is table-top height and so permits the film reader to be placed on top, is available, but the nine-drawer cabinet provides more storage space per dollar of cost.

Colby elected to purchase one of the more expensive readers (about $350 list). Baldwin chose to buy two cheaper film readers (about $125 each) in order to accommodate two users at once. Baldwin feels that in selecting two of the cheaper readers instead of one more expensive reader it erred because expensive readers have more refinements which make them easier to use and less likely to scratch film and they also offer slightly greater magnification. The two readers have prevented waiting at times, but Baldwin could easily have gotten by with one reader about 90 percent of the time, although the second reader is currently receiving much more usage. Colby presently feels the need for a second reader. Both discovered that the readers may be placed anywhere in the library, although the best location is a spot where the room light is about the same brightness as the light projected by the reader and the user does not look up from the reader to face a window.

Colby plans to revamp its serial cataloging and so has not yet listed its microfilm holdings in its public catalog. Baldwin lists its periodical holdings on cards in a catalog drawer marked "Periodicals." To list periodicals held, Baldwin uses a card bearing volume numbers and the notation "Library has those volumes which are dated." On the card in call number position the symbol PB is used to indicate "Periodicals Bound" and PMF is used to indicate "Periodicals on Microfilm." Where both bound and microfilm volumes of a title are held, two cards are used with PB items on one and PMF items on the second. This works well for Baldwin since all bound volumes are older than the microfilmed issues.

Colby follows its open-shelf policy in connection with its microfilm holdings, and a student may go directly to the file, select the film she needs, and use the reader. Because of its building arrangement and the location of its microfilm storage, Baldwin does not apply its open stack policy to microfilm, and the students must ask the librarian for film. At Baldwin, in the event the readers are in use, the student fills a request card and is scheduled to use the reader at another time convenient to him. Both Colby and Baldwin instruct the student in how to use the film reader for the first time and check on his next use to see that he is doing it correctly. Neither attempts to give group instruction in the use of the reader.

The disadvantages of microfilm appear to be few. Perhaps the complaint most often heard is made by those looking for articles on interior decoration, clothing design, travel, etc., for microfilm is black and white and thus color is lost. [Now color microfilm is available. Ed.] Not all periodicals are availalble on microfilm from commercial suppliers, but 78 percent of the titles indexed in *Readers' Guide to Periodical Literature* can be obtained on microfilm, and Baldwin and Colby have found this sufficient for their needs.

Microfilm is usually supplied anywhere from several weeks to several months after the periodical year is complete. Since the paper issues are not sent away for processing as in binding, the library always has a complete file available for use. Both Colby and Baldwin libraries dispose of the magazines which have been replaced by microfilm.

In comparing notes, Colby and Baldwin agree on the advantages and disadvantages of microfilm except for one item. Colby feels that films are easier to use since one does not have to handle weighty volumes of periodicals. Baldwin considers bound volumes easier to use since the librarian does not have to give instructions in the film reader operation and since a page is easier to find than a frame of microfilm. To see the frame-finding problem, one must realize that microfilm is stored on hundred-foot reels which accommodate twelve issues of monthly magazines, and in using microfilm one always starts at the front of the reel. For example, if the November issue is wanted, one must reel through January, February, March, etc., to reach November. The experienced microfilm reader soon learns to "watch for the cover," which is a single page frame causing a light flick and enabling one to count months while winding film at a rapid rate, and so find the right month with a minimum of time; but frequently the beginning microfilm user complains that it takes him several minutes to find the right frame. However, Baldwin considers this a minor complaint.

One unexpected advantage that came to Baldwin and Colby from their microfilm programs is that both are able to provide microfilm readers for faculty and non-college personnel borrowing or buying materials in connection with research or graduate study. Colby feels that this has made many off-campus people friends of its library.

The librarians of Baldwin and Colby are pleased with the space and money-saving features of microfilm and consider it an excellent solution to many problems involved in keeping and in using back issues of periodicals, especially in the small library which is limited in space, staff, and funds. Most students are intrigued by microfilm and delight in finding opportunities to use it.

References

1. Henrietta Thomae and W. T. Johnston. "A Survey of a Selected Group of Junior College Libraries" (Mimeographed, 1958). Partially published as "A Glance at Junior College Libraries," *The Junior College Journal*, XXIX (1958), 195-202.

A MATTER OF MICROFILM

by **Emma Ruth Christine**, *Resource Teacher, Henry M. Gunn Senior High School, Palo Alto, California*

Once just a title of a file in my desk, the microfilm program in the Palo Alto Senior High Library became a reality through determination, careful planning, and a cooperative administration willing to gamble on a new idea!

After learning about microfilm during a graduate class in librarianship, the librarian dispatched a letter to University Microfilms, Inc. of Ann Arbor, Michigan for more information. A lengthy letter returned, outlining possible uses, expenses involved, necessary equipment, and a general willingness to help get the program started. After studying the catalog of prices and publications available and comparing these to the school curriculum, it was decided that rather than set up an across-the-board back file of magazines, as is the usual approach, a core collection of microfilms augmenting those areas of the curriculum in which book materials were either scarce or inadequate would be established. A gift of $600 from the senior class enabled us to purchase three portable readers. Initial purchases of film were *Business Week* for the depression era of 1929-1933, *The Nation* for the pre-war and war period of 1913-1919 and also for the stock market crash period of 1929-1930, and *The New Republic* for the period of the European war, 1914-1919. Later on in the first year, some early English literary periodicals were purchased for use by our advanced placement students. Since these same subject areas are regularly included in the curriculum, there will always be a need for these films, something that is not always true of all back issues of all magazines. After a period of orientation, teachers in fields covered by the collection became very interested, especially when they discovered that using the readers appealed to the low range student who enjoyed studying something other than a textbook, and to

Reprinted from *School Libraries*, vol. 16 (Winter 1967), pp. 29-33, by permission of the publisher.

the high range student who thrilled at using original source material. After the initial breakthrough, regular use of the microfilm was incorporated into lesson planning and assignments.

With that background experience, the Resource Center of the district's newest high school was opened on the same principles of orientation. Two readers were purchased, with plans to add others. In the Listening Center which also housed phonographs with headsets, filmstrip and slide projectors, a special area was established to house the readers. Since the readers project onto a wall surface as well as onto a total surface, it is possible for a small class group to view a microfilmed article.

The beginning collection at the new school included the titles previously mentioned, plus coverage of the pre-war and war years of World War II in *Time* and *Newsweek*. The Civil War period is amply represented by editions of the Atlanta, Georgia, *Southern Confederacy* from 1861 through 1865, and the Freeport, Illinois, *Weekly Bulletin* for the latter part of the war, Lincoln's assassination, and the events immediately following. The eastern seaboard's part in the war, as well as metropolitan news of a completely different nature than that reflected in the midwestern paper or the southern one, is covered in Frank Leslie's *Illustrated Newspaper*, one of America's major early publications. For a swing to the far west and its historic past, the Marysville (Calif.) *Herald Weekly* for the years 1850 to 1858 and the Oroville (Calif.) *Butte Democrat* for the next span of years, 1859 into 1862, were purchased. The *Oregonian Weekly*, published in Portland, is on file for the years 1855 through 1862. Of course, there are many other areas of use and interest latent in these films besides the strictly historical ones. The cultural and economic progress of America is also written in these pages, as well as personalities who made events, advertisements of technological advances as they came along, opinions and editorials on ethical questions of the day, personal accounts of pioneers, and many other fine possibilities.

In order to inform students and staff of the microfilm holdings and to make them seem an ordinary instrument of research rather than a gimmick, the microfilms are listed in the card catalog under such subject headings as MICROFILMS and PERIODICALS and NEWSPAPERS, plus any subject areas to which they refer, such as UNITED STATES - HISTORY - CIVIL WAR - SOURCES or UNITED STATES - SOCIAL LIFE AND CUSTOMS or THE WEST - DISCOVERY AND EXPLORATION. In this fashion, the student is led to a new source of information and becomes accustomed to getting as much from it as he would from the more traditional approach via books.

Students are given individual instruction in the use of the microfilm machines, with special attention given to the threading procedure. It is very simple, but must be done correctly in order to avoid scratching the film. After this instruction, students operate the machines themselves. The films are stored in clearly-labeled boxes accessible to students.

The purchase of two readers, one to be permanently in the library or listening center, and one to be circulated to departments on demand, would be an adequate beginning for a small high school collection, with additional readers added as need demands. This would mean an initial expenditure of about $400 for machines. A core collection similar to the one outlined would cost about $400, depending upon the periodicals chosen. A note of caution must be raised here: The periodical budget of the school library must be enlarged to accommodate purchases of microfilms with no reduction in the number of current issues purchased, as the microfilm collection is an addition to, not a substitute for, regularly received materials. Another factor to be considered is that in order to purchase current issues of a magazine on microfilm, the current paper issue must also be purchased. If issues are bought on the selective coverage idea, however, this problem does not arise.

The use of periodicals fluctuates according to the emphasis teachers place upon this type of research. In most cases, however, there is enough demand for periodicals to cause quite a problem, both for the school library, and the public library. It is a wide-spread complaint among public librarians that the demands for their services by high school students needing periodicals takes entirely too much of their time. Perhaps a wider use of microfilm in the school library would help alleviate this situation.

Besides the obvious advantages of solving the vast amount of storage problems created by back issues, the life of the materials is also lengthened due to its microfilmed format. Pages are not lost or torn out, nor do rolls of film vanish mysteriously into someone's notebook, at least not yet! The wear and tear on a periodical is also gone, as is the binding expense if that has been the previous way of preserving materials.

Our next move is the purchase of a reader-printer, which will enable us to reproduce numerous copies of certain pages, maps, photographs, or other microfilmed materials in our historical collection. Being able to hand a copy of such material to a student would surely add a dimension to his learning.

These considerations and practices which we used in beginning two collections of microfilm may be of some assistance to others attempting such a program. In order to make it succeed, there must always be a willingness on the part of teachers to use and to assign students to use machines and films; and adequate periodical budget to cover the additional expenses of materials; a large enough library staff to instruct users (student assistants serve well here); and an eagerness on the part of the librarian to take advantage of a technological advance in the presentation of materials. When these are present, the results are well worth the amount of additional planning time required of the library staff.

THE IMPACT OF MICROFORMS UPON JOURNAL FORMAT

INTRODUCTION

Are microforms the shape of the journal literature of the future? The twin factors of decreasing circulation and increasing subscription costs both point to the need for microforms as a viable alternative to hard copy for journal publishing. Simultaneous publications of journals in both hard copy and microform indicate this growing trend. To cite one specific example, the Chemical Society of Great Britain and the American Chemical Society produce "synopsis journals," wherein the abstracts of articles appear in hard copy and the texts of the articles themselves appear on microfiche. From the economic point of view, this goes far to keeping production costs low since the microfiche segment can make use of directly photographed typewritten pages, while the abstracts are the only section incurring typesetting costs. This also permits something that is not usually associated with microforms and remains a generally strong point in favor of hard copy: *browsing*. The reader can still skim through the abstracts to alight upon what interests him; in fact, browsing has been facilitated in that only the abstracts remain to be gone through, not the entirety of the text pages. [Of course, it can be argued that any journal providing initial abstracts serves this need.] However, these abstracts are composed of 1,000 word *précis*. Also, the number of microform frames has likewise been limited to only those of direct interest. This process provides both bibliographic access and indexing information, and must be considered a sizable boon to the librarian.

In this era of proliferation of journals and serials, there is a real danger that a library be swamped by subscription items (if it could afford to maintain these subscriptions!) No more space, no more money—both are sobering facts to a serials librarian. Microforms perhaps can relieve both these ailments, or at least go a long ways in alleviating them. The economics of journal publishing present their own strictures. Either raise the price of a subscription in the face of diminishing standing orders, or publish in microform for a select audience and maintain a reasonable price. Rather than being faced with the total absence of a needed journal, there would be few interested readers who would not accept microforms. In this instance, the issue is *in lieu* of *nothing*. Witness, for example, the *Journal* of the Association for Computational Linguistics which is only available in microform.

From the journal publisher's point of view, fulfillment and storage costs can be decreased by the adoption of microforms. Editorial costs remain (or are perhaps higher); printing costs decline. Microforms might prove the only viable route for specialist journals in the future.

Additional Readings

Bilboul, Roger. "The Economics of Concurrent Microfiche Editions of Published Periodicals." *NRCd Bulletin*, vol. 3, no. 1, pp.5-6.

Bishop, Charles. "The Microcard Production of Single Journal Articles." *American Documentation*, vol. 7, 1956, pp.33-35.

"Books and Journals." *Chemical and Engineering News*, April 5, 1976, pp.35-36.

Bovee, Warren G. "Scientific and Technical Journals on Microfiche." *IEEE Transactions on Professional Communication*, vol. PC-16, no. 3, September 1973, pp.113-116 and 178.

Fenaughty, Alfred L. "Demand Printing: A Revolution in Publishing." *Journal of Micrographics*, vol. 8, no. 4, March 1975, pp.201-206.

Gray, Edward. "Our Microform Marketing Strategy." *IEEE Transactions on Professional Communication*, vol. PC-18, no. 3, September 1975, pp.160-163.

Hirschmann, A. "The Primary Journal: Past, Present and Future." *Journal of Chemical Documentation*, vol.10, 1970, p. 57.

International Group of Scientific, Technical and Medical Publishers, Journals Committee. *Results of the Microform Questionnaire*. Amsterdam: STM, 1974.

Kuney, J.H. "New Developments in Primary Journal Publication." *Journal of Chemical Documentation*, vol. 10, 1975, p.42.

Kuney, J.H. "The Role of Microforms in Journal Publication." *Journal of Chemical Documentation*, vol. 12, no. 2, 1972, pp. 78-80.

Lea, P.W. *Trends in Scientific and Technical Primary Journal Publishing in the U.S.A.* Wetherby, England: British Library, 1976.

Leake, Chauncey D. "Primary Journals: Questionable Progress and Present Problems." *Journal of Chemical Documentation*, vol. 10, no. 1, February 1970, pp. 27-29.

Marks, Robert H. "Improving Communications in Science Through Micropublishing." National Micrographics Association, *Proceedings*, vol. 21, 1971, II-154.

McNeill, William H. "Editorial." *Journal of Modern History*, vol. 48, March 1976.

"Microform Survey." *Microform Review*, vol. 4, no. 3, July 1975, pp. 179-182.

"Micropublishing." *NRCd Bulletin*, vol. 10, no. 2, p. 41.

"Micropublishing—The Size of Journals to Come." *Reprographics Quarterly*, vol. 8, 1975, p. 93.

Moore, J.A. "An Inquiry on New Forms of Primary Publications." *Journal of Chemical Documentation*, vol. 12, no. 2, 1972, pp. 75-78.

O'Sullivan, Dermot A. "Synopses Journal Idea Catching on in Europe." *Chemical and Engineering News*, April 14, 1975, pp. 14-15.

Reynolds, Helen L. "Introduction to Symposium on the Primary Journal." *Journal of Chemical Documentation*, vol. 10, no. 1, February 1970, p. 26.

"Scientific Journal in Microfilm—An Experiment in Publishing." *Library Journal*, vol. 84, April 1, 1959, p. 1053.

Somerville, Brendan F. "Abstract Journal Concept Being Examined." *Chemical and Engineering News*, June 12, 1972, pp. 16-17.

Starker, Lee N. "Scientific Papers and Microfiche." [Letter]. *Chemical and Engineering News*, July 16, 1969, p. 7.

"Synopsis Journal Idea." [Letters]. *Chemical and Engineering News*, June 16, 1975, p. 3.

"Which Way Now for Journals?" *Nature*, August 26, 1976, p. 731.

White, Herbert S. and Bernard M. Fry. "Economic Interaction Between Special Libraries and Publishers of Scholarly and Research Journals." *Special Libraries*, March 1977, pp. 109-114.

IMPACT OF MICROFILMS ON JOURNAL COSTS

by **Joseph Kuney**, *Journal and Encyclopedia Department, Wiley-Interscience Division, John Wiley and Sons, Inc., New York*

It has been quite fashionable, the past few years, to forecast the doom of the journal system. But, despite these predictions of disaster, the system is a healthy one and remains the primary instrument of communication among scientists and engineers. Certainly, there are problems which must be solved if the system is to continue to function effectively and efficiently. For, despite the growing seriousness of the problems that face all involved in the journal publishing cycle, the needs fulfilled by journals have neither lessened nor changed. What is happening is the diminishing ability of the traditional journal to render a full spectrum of needs on a cost-effective basis.

One set of solutions has involved the development of alternative services as journal access devices. Abstracts, contents pages, and selective dissemination services are among the alternatives that have developed. But, since all such systems are based on the content of the traditional journal, they have tended to aggravate the problems of the very product on which they are dependent.

To publishers of journals, it is of utmost importance that new alternatives be found and tested. An alternative, which holds much promise for keeping the journal system healthy and useful, is the application of microform technology in the publication and distribution of primary information. Thus, the publisher of journals is now able to reassess the traditional role of the journal in filling a wide spectrum of user needs and to select media options which more precisely fulfill the needs of users and which present a more favorable economic picture in the form of increased revenue and lower costs.

Reprinted from the *IEEE Transactions on Professional Communication*, vol. PC-16, no. 3 (September 1973), pp. 80-81, 175, by permission of the publisher. Copyright © 1973 by The Institute of Electrical and Electronics Engineers, Inc.

I would suggest further that we can learn and understand much about the whole business of the impact of technology on the dissemination and use of information by an examination of the role of microforms in scientific publishing. The practicality of producing and using microimages was shown in the late 1880's. Why then did we have to wait until the middle 1960's for microfilm to take a significant role in the publication and dissemination of scientific and technical information? If we observe closely the factors leading to the successful acceptance of microforms, we will get a quick but basic lesson on what we must look for if we are to solve our current problems and to enjoy the equally successful implementation of computer-based systems of handling, disseminating, and using information.

First, the user's requirement for convenience of handling was met by the introduction of the self-threading 16-mm cassette. This overcame the resistance to the user's unwillingness to fumble with threading a roll of microfilm through a reader. Second, the introduction of the reader-printer fulfilled another requirement of the user, the need to carry away a permanent record of information he perceived as being of interest to him. And, lastly, the literature explosion put a strain on existing library facilities. This strain could be alleviated by microfilm and the saving counted in dollars. Thus it took little calculation on the part of librarians to figure out the amount of space replaced by microfilm publications and the cost of that space in dollars, a cost which doubled or tripled when new library facilities were required. Thus microfilm became a product whose cost could be readily amortized. In short, the product's value could be precisely stated in dollars that did not have to include any valuation on the intangibles of microfilm use.

With this strong base for development, we are seeing the growth of microform usage by both publisher and user. Microfilm readers and reader-printers are improving in ease of use and quality of blowup. In fact, under the stimulus of growing markets, all aspects of the technology are showing rapid improvement, and much of the old resistance to the use of microfilm is fast disappearing.

In the course of this development, publishers have moved to incorporate into their programs the advantages offered by use of microforms. I think we can get a good perspective of the thinking and resultant actions of publishers, particularly the scientific societies, if we take a rather close look at the inception and implementation of the extensive program of the American Chemical Society (ACS). This was really a two-pronged development involving *Chemical Abstracts* as one program and the journals program of the ACS as the other. I will confine my comments to the journals program of the ACS.

It is hardly any secret that, for the past seven or eight years, the financing of journals by societies has become an ever more pressing problem. Possibly it was a more pressing problem for societies than commercial publishers, because the societies were less restrictive in the number of pages published, thus creating upward cost pressures, while at the same time seeking to keep subscription rates to their members at the lowest possible levels.

Another matter of growing concern was the impact of photocopying. While losses to publishers (if any) were and are a difficult matter to measure, it was apparent that the volume of such copying was growing and that, somewhere along the line, the results might become serious in terms of affecting revenue from subscription sales.

An obvious solution to the first matter was to hold the price to members steady while increasing the charges to institutional users. But, as the spread of prices for the same product gets larger and larger, it becomes increasingly difficult to enforce and collect the higher price. Similarly, some method of charging for photocopies would provide the publisher with additional revenues, but again the complexities of assessing and collecting such charges have not, as yet, proved manageable.

But, with user acceptance of microfilm, here was the answer. First, it was a product likely to be purchased only by institutional users and, second, it was obvious that a major use of the film would be for the making of enlarged copies of the film. Thus the ACS decided to make microfilm editions of its journals available on a lease basis, where the fee for the lease included a license to make unlimited photocopies from either the microfilm or the print edition. The price of the package included a subscription to the print edition since this was the means by which the library maintained currency of coverage. The microfilm edition for the current year is not made available until the end of the volume year.

Thus the price for the program was arrived at by adding the cost of the print edition, the cost of the microfilm, and a license fee. The license fee is calculated on the basis of the number of editorial pages published in a given journal. With the original announcement of the availability of the service, the ACS obtained, as an unlooked-for by-product, a definitive market study of price acceptability. The first pricing was based on a license fee of five cents per editorial page published. Thus the license fee, for a journal publishing 2,000 pages per year, would have been $100. This fee was to be paid annually along with the other costs on a renewal basis. The reception to this announcement was rather violent, in the form of letters to the editor of *Chemical and Engineering News* and some rather choice invectives heaped on me personally. Then followed a series of written exchanges between myself and the leaders of the loyal opposition in which we both sought to reach some accord. It is interesting to note that they all wanted microfilm. Only the license charge was at issue. The final result was an agreement on two cents per page for the license fee (still the current rate).

The acceptance of the program by the user community was most gratifying.

The program has continued to grow and currently the ACS has more than 1,400 microfilm subscriptions to its journals. These subscriptions represent some 200 institutions, about half of which take the full package of some 21 journals. Thus the microfilm program has become a significant source of net revenue for the journals program of the ACS.

It has now become apparent that microforms offer further advantages in terms of meeting the publishing objectives of societies. The matter of the cost and pricing of the printed editions remains a serious problem. One avenue of relief, offered by microforms, is the virtually unlimited low-cost capacity provided by the compaction of the microform process. By moving to reduce material in the printed editions and placing it in the microform without the expense of typesetting, significant savings can be effected. The increased use of the microfilm editions would enable the publishers and authors to utilize the more expensive printed journal for a shorter, more concise form of paper, better suited to fill the current awareness needs of most users. There are definite signs that publishers are beginning to move toward such a system of publication. But, for the present, the ACS has taken the first steps to achieve this goal.

Specifically, the ACS now makes available to editors and authors space in the microfilm editions of ACS journals for the publication of material supplementing that published in the printed journal. Thus editors, under heavy economic pressure, may adopt a more stringent attitude on what they will publish in the printed journal since there is now an outlet for whatever additional material might be required in the microfilm edition. Similarly, authors will be encouraged to accept microfilm as an adequate means of dissemination, because more of their work can be included in the permanent record, and for abstracting and indexing, the supplementary material is submitted to *Chemical Abstracts*. The prospect of lesser page-charge billing also provides an incentive to authors. Looking ahead, it seems reasonable to project that, when the economy of the microfilm edition is fully realized, page charges for the printed edition may be eliminated.

Briefly, the system works as follows. After editor and author have reached agreement on what is to be included in the microfilm edition, the entire manuscript, including the supplementary material, is sent to the editorial production office. When the portion of the manuscript to be published in the printed edition has been put into final page form, the supplementary material is sent to the microfilm-processing operation. Added to the article published in the journal is a footnote indicating that additional related content has been put into the microfilm edition with instructions on how to obtain either microfiche or hard copy, including prices. The supplementary material is paginated, with numbers starting with the last page of the journal paper and suffixed with the letter "M." At this stage of the process, a copy of the supplementary material is sent to *Chemical Abstracts* for abstracting and indexing purposes. When the issue is microfilmed, the supplementary material is positioned following the article to which it applies. In the interim between publication of the journal and the issuance of the microfilm edition, users may obtain either microfiche or hard copy of the supplementary material at the ACS office.

Admittedly such a system provides a somewhat less than convenient access problem for the user who has need for the supplementary material. We can anticipate that sometime in the future, we will have developed the electronic capacity to provide immediate access. But, for the moment, the ACS system has moved to improve the access capability by making available with the print issue, at additional cost, microfiche of the supplementary material for that issue. This program was started in 1973 and is being well received as a further indication that the trend is one consistent with user needs.

The expense of adding pages to the microfilm edition is negligible since the reductions are made directly from material supplied by the author, thus avoiding the high cost of typesetting and reproduction of charts and drawings. Only in a few cases has the material supplied by the author been inadequate for microfilm reproduction. The ACS is now developing instructions to authors pointing out the need for original copy for good microfilm reproduction. A third or fourth generation of a computer printout does not make for the best possible result in the final microform. This is certainly an area that needs attention, but improvement can be expected as the usage of the microfilm editions for supplementary material becomes more widespread and authors understand the requirements of the system.

During 1972, the second year of operation, ACS journals placed more than 2,000 pages of supplementary material in the microfilm edition. Most of these pages were charts and tables, graphics of one type or another, and bibliographic references. The remaining pages consisted of text matter. Many of the depositions consisted of a single page, while in at least one case the amount of material associated with a single paper added 51 pages to the microfilm edition. About 20 percent of the single-copy orders, received for the supplementary material, were for microfiche and the rest were photocopies.

For every page not carried in the printed journal, the saving in printing, paper, and distribution costs varies from $60 to $100, depending on the circulation of the journal. From this must be subtracted the loss in page-charge revenue, about 60 percent for the ACS. In the main, the material not being placed in the microfilm edition of the ACS journals would not have been carried in the journal. Thus the saving in cost of production has not been a significant factor during the first two years of operation. But, more important, the material would have been lost to the permanent record. There was one worthy exception. The journal *Inorganic Chemistry* placed structure-factor tables, which previously would have been published in the printed journal, in the microfilm edition. The resultant reduction in production costs was about $7,500, less any lost page-charge revenue. It is likely that the usage of the microfilm for the archiving of supplementary material will double in 1973.

A quick calculation will show that moving pages from the printed issue to the microfilm edition will result in significant cost reductions. Of more long-range significance is the growing evidence that shorter versions of papers will better serve the information-seeking needs of most users, without in any way affecting that author's stake in publication. Thus publishers will not only be able to produce a more useful product at lower cost, but they will be able to price their products in a pattern more consistent with the number of users served and thereby gain revenues needed to maintain the publication and distribution of primary information. It is possible to more sharply reduce the printed pages in a journal by moving toward the digest or short-paper concept. The savings in production costs could affect the whole pattern of pricing and lead to the elimination of page charges and to lower prices for individual users of the short-form digest journal.

The record of acceptance, during the first years of operation of the ACS microform program, and the steady growth in the amount of material placed in the microfilm edition suggests that a useful addition to the journal system has been opened. ACS journals are beginning to receive papers prepared for publication in two versions, a brief one for the printed journal and an expanded version to be carried only in the microfilm edition. As editors and authors see the system grow and prove useful, it is to be expected that they will be more and more encouraged to utilize it to its fullest potential, that is, to move toward more emphasis on current awareness in what is published in the printed journal and toward expanded use of the microfilm to provide as complete an archive of chemical information as possible. The overall result will be a journal system significantly improved in terms of the efficiency of transmitting information from author to user and of lower costs of publication and distribution to the benefit of all concerned.

MICROPUBLISHING POTENTIAL IN PROFESSIONAL JOURNAL PUBLICATIONS

by Marjorie A. Laflin, *American Chemical Society*

Introduction

The American Chemical Society (ACS), with over 110,000 members, is the largest scientific society devoted to a single discipline in the world. The three main organizational divisions are Chemical Abstracts Service, Membership, and Books and Journals. The Books and Journals Division is responsible for the business and administrative management of the Society's 17 technical journals, its books, and two more general interest magazines.

The Books and Journals Division of the American Chemical Society has a unique micropublishing program. This paper will describe principally that system combined with the microfiche current issue program, and then touch on other possibilities in use by various other professional scientific societies. It is entirely appropriate to take the definition of "micropublishing" in its strictest sense. That is, the publishing, in microform, of material which has not been published previously. This is exactly what makes the ACS program different from the many other systems in use.

Although there are 17 journals published virtually simultaneously in microfiche and all of the journals and magazines are done at year's end on roll microfilm, a significant part of the ACS program is the micropublishing of what is termed "supplementary material." This is information which has

Reprinted from the *Journal of Micrographics*, vol. 10, no. 6 (July 1977), pp. 281-285, by permission of the National Micrographics Association. © 1977 by the NMA.

never appeared in the hardcopy and was never *intended* to appear in the hardcopy.

Many other publishers take particular sections of an article, or even the entire article, which they would ordinarily plan to print and put these in microform from author-supplied typescript. The American Chemical Society, on the other hand, prints in hardcopy what it considers to be the *entire* article.

What is placed on the microform is termed supplementary—information which would be of interest only to the specialized researcher—the scientist who has much more than a passing interest in the developments of his or a related field. Examples of this type of information are detailed computer printouts such as crystal structure factor tables or extensive specialized bibliographies and the like. It is, in other words, material relevant to the published paper, but which supplies extreme details and/or data.

Supplementary Material

The supplementary material concept began many years ago with the American Documentation Insitutue (ADI). In fact, the American Chemical Society used the ADI service for many years for documents which it did not wish to include in its printed editions. For a fee, the author was allowed to deposit any material he considered important enough to be on record, but that was not to be included in his printed article. Then, for another fee, any requestor could order those documents of interest from the National Auxiliary Publications Service, a part of ADI, in a process which should work quickly, but did not always do so.

As early as 1970, the American Chemical Society began to feel that using an outside organization for deposition of material directly related to articles published in its own journals was not the way to go. There was some concern that, over the years, the path to obtaining that material might become quite long and complicated, and, in fact, that has indeed been the case.

A letter not too long ago from a very distraught librarian uncovered the following situation. The American Documentation Institute had evolved into the American Society for Information Science, which had contracted the handling of existing depository documents to a firm called Microfiche Publications, which had changed locations within New York City frequently enough to make mail delivery from one address to the next impossible. In addition, some of the documents submitted to the American Documentation Institute had been stored with the Library of Congress, rather than the National Auxiliary Publications Service. The frustration felt by that librarian should be obvious.

It was a case of a perfectly logical system evolving into an impenetrable maze.

Initiating a Program

Foreseeing that eventuality, the American Chemical Society took over publishing its own supplementary material in 1971. It began by putting the documents only on the roll microfilm at the end of the year.

In 1973 the number of documents had grown to the extent that it was apparent that the supplementary material had to be made more widely available than just at the end of the year. It was then that the American Chemical Society's micropublishing on micro*fiche* began. With microfiche came the possibility of supplying the supplementary documents, relatively economically, simultaneously with the printed issues themselves.

The first fiche were rudimentary indeed, not because the industry did not have the capabilities necessary but because the American Chemical Society, a *scientific* society, was pioneering in a completely unfamiliar field.

We began by knowing nothing. We let our microfilm service bureau subcontract the making of the microfiche to a second service bureau. Clearly, a mistake. The fiche started to arrive and they were a hodge-podge of errors. The problem was that the micrographic industry seemed to know as little about publishing as ACS knew about microfiche.

Microfiche arrived labeled "Inorganic Chemistry"—but contained supplementary material from *Environmental Science & Technology*. (Therefore, we had insufficient batch labeling.) Or, all the right authors were on the microfiche, but a few pages were missing. (We discovered we had insufficient individual document labeling.) Or the classic case of the undecipherable row of documents. We looked at the microfiche and all the rows were legible but one. You might be surprised at the amount of concentration it took before we realized the fiche must have been made by putting little narrow rows of film together on a wider piece of film. How else could one row be upside down and backwards? Our problem here was plain ignorance of possible micrographic techniques.

By the beginning of 1974 it was obvious that something needed to be done both to improve the quality of the microfiche and the documents we were receiving. The old rules, held for so long for hardcopy, simply would not do for microfiche.

During that same year, we began another, different program with microfiche: publication on microfiche of the technical journal issues themselves. The decision was made not to include the magazines, which have significant use of color and half tones which might lead to less than acceptable fiche. Bids were taken from major suppliers and the contract was awarded to NCR for standard 24× source document filming. The considerable work of starting up production schedules for 16 journals with varying publication schedules was begun. (Four more have since been added, bringing to 20 the number of titles currently available on microfiche from the Society.)

Production

In 1975 there were two separate but related programs going—both supplementary material and current issues. Organization was essential.

First we color coded the headers: white for current issue; brown for supplementary material. We added a logo to let the users know it was an American Chemical Society microfiche; full bibliographic reference—the journal name, volume number, issue number and date, and copyright line. Numbers for the sequence of the microfiche in one set were added along with the reduction.

For supplementary material preparation, we devised NMA standard type layout sheets. They reflect the double page format and the basic information common to all microfiche headers.

In the body of the supplementary material fiche, we filmed what we call our transmittal sheet listing all sets of documents for that issue. A microfilmer would call it a batch sheet and a librarian would call it a table of contents. Next came the eye readable name and page sheets identifying individual articles, with the author's name and the page numbers of his article. These eye legible sheets reassure the anxious reader that the author he is looking for is indeed on that microfiche. Page numbers are necessary because authors commonly have two or three related articles in succession in one journal issue.

For internal organization, sets of supplementary material were also identified by a depository sheet. This is not filmed and gives much more information than the author name and page sheet. It is actually completed in the editor's office, long before the filming process begins.

In order to identify individual sheets within a set, both for the microfilmer and for the careful reader, we devised a unique numbering system. It consists of the journal code, the last page number of the article in the hardcopy issue to which the supplementary material pertains, and the microfilm page number.

The current issue microfiche presented even more problems. How could we make the individual chemist feel at home with microfiche instead of his lovingly mutilated paper issues? First, we knew that page numbers were of the utmost importance. After all, a bibliographic reference is not bibliographic reference without page numbers. So, the first frame had to be an eye legible page number frame. The page numbers are of the entire issue, not just those on the first microfiche. This information corresponds to what is on the spine of the printed issue. Then we provided another crutch, eye legible page numbers on the left hand side of each row. They give the number of the first page in that row. This aids the chemist in look-up time. He knows just about where the page is he's looking for, either from spotting the approximate location immediately or scanning down the column after the microfiche is in the viewer. In either case, it is the original psychological reassurance that is most helpful.

The first year, we filmed the covers of all our current issue journals in the second frame after the inclusive page numbers. This proved to be somewhat less than successful, so we substituted a stylized cover. It was eye legible, and even had the volume number and our phoenix logo.

Those were some of the technical problems we faced in setting up our systems. Situations of far more widespread consequence were ones connected with the American Chemical Society as a scientific, professional society. It is usually quite a shock to micrographic industry personnel to hear that we consider the cost of postage to mail microfiche astronomically high. The current issue microfiche are mailed first class, by individual issues. Currently, that is at least 13¢ each domestically. Compare that with a little under 4½ cents for the same issue in hardcopy at the second class nonprofit rate. [c. 1976]

Why is microfiche mailed first class? Because to use any other method would slow it down considerably and drastically increase the chances of loss. To a scientist, the most important thing is to have his research in front of him *immediately*. It simply would not do to have a microfiche issue arrive very much later than the corresponding hardcopy. So we mail first class to make up some of the time lost in producing the microfiche.

Another unique problem for current issue microfiche is bingo cards, those small, reader service cards. It seems that chemists love them, or at least many say they can't live without them. Our solution: manually stuff the cards into the envelopes with the microfiche before mailing so the chemist will be able to request information.

Supplementary material microfiche created special problems for us in re-educating authors and editors. Old habits die hard, particularly the ingrained habit of authors to supply glossy photos of figures. Another disaster is the photoreduced computer table, or a table that has 15 sections and 15 section headings on 15 *extra* pieces of paper.

We had to educate editors not to accept those things. By the time documents reached the microfilming stage they could not be returned for revision. The hardcopy was already in page proof and there could be no holding up an article while a deficient supplementary chart or table was corrected.

Supplementary material also creates extra work in the peer review process and it must be considered as part of the whole article when it is being abstracted in *Chemical Abstracts*.

Philosophical Aspects

So why do we have supplementary material? Advantages are that the author is allowed to contribute more to the permanent scientific record. This enhances his reputation. It also helps other scientists by making information permanently available. And, in the American Chemical Society system, he does not have to pay for this privilege, as with NAPS or the new American Institute of Physics program. Not only that, material not typeset is not subject to page charges (the per page fee which helps to defray the compostition cost of the article).

Also, supplementary material saves space in the printed journal. How much space depends upon many things, from the ability of the individual journal editor to hold down the length of contributions to his journal to the willingness of the author to accept microfiche as a valid way of preserving information.

Besides the economic advantages to the author, there are other pluses. From the American Chemical Society's point of view, the printed journal looks better and serves its reader better. One of the basic tenets of information science is the information explosion. By putting specialized information on microfiche, the average reader is better served by not having to look through overly long articles. This helps cut down on the "I've got too much to read" syndrome.

The main *dis*advantage is the problem of reeducating the authors, editors *and* subscribers. We must get authors to generate acceptable original documents. We must train editors not to accept reams of meaningless paper, simply because it will not be typeset. And we must tell everyone that microfiche are not free. Quite the contrary. Professional societies do not save money by microrepublishing their journals. A highlight of the annual American Library Association meeting in July 1976 was hearing Francis Spreitzer of the University of Southern California tell the librarians that microfiche cost money. To the American Chemical Society, a major disadvantage of microfiche is the cost of producing it, due to the extreme labor intensity of such a specialized product on such a small scale.

But the program is growing. There is no doubt of that. And as it does, we are prepared because we have already taken our lumps. We met the enemy, it was us, and we won. Everyone from the American Institute of Physics to Pergamon Press has followed our lead—with promotion ideas, mailing philosophy, and especially those left hand side page numbers—and we are naturally proud of it.

New Approaches

The American Chemical Society began micropublishing its supplementary material in 1973 and began microrepublishing its current issues in '75. Obviously something is needed for '77. It is the American Chemical Society

Customized Article Service. This is a form of selective dissemination of information (SDI). The subscriber will receive a hardcopy subscription to the single journal most closely related to his area of interest. In addition, he will also receive other journal articles matching his interest profile. But these additional articles will be taken from *any* American Chemical Society journal and placed on microfiche—making, in effect, a customized, microfiche journal.

1977 will also see the first issue of the *Journal of Chemical Research*. This is a joint publication of The Chemical Society (London), the French Société Chimique de France and the German Gesellschaft der deutscher Chemiker. The typset printed edition of the *Journal of Chemical Research* will feature only short summaries of articles—one or two pages. All the rest of the information will be in an "M" edition. The M stands for microfiche or it can stand for miniprint, for those who have not yet seen the light. This will be an entirely new journal, not a new form of an old title, so cost comparisons may be difficult to make. However, our foreign professional society colleagues obviously believe this will be a more economical way to handle the scientific literature.

Clearly, microforms are being accepted by scientific and professional societies. But in the halls of scholarly publishing, the old ways die hard. There is little room for compromise, but when micrographics shows it can build us a better mousetrap, we will welcome it with open arms.

THE SHAPE OF LITERATURE TO COME

by **L.C. Cross,** *Director of Publications, The Chemical Society,* *and* **I.A. Williams***, Publications Services Manager, The Chemical Society*

The primary research journal has long been seen as inefficient in both its main functions—archival and current-awareness. Numerous theoretical proposals have been made to rationalize the situation by separating these two prime roles and the arguments for such a course have been frequently stated, but until recently these were, for the most part, based upon theoretical considerations of information-flow, with the economic benefits seldom evaluated and no practical studies attempted.

Cost

Within the past five years, however, alarming increases in the cost of printing, paper and postage have been accompanied by decreases in circulation. While the rapid increase in the numbers of papers submitted for publication, a phenomenon of the period 1955-70 in particular, may be easing off, the evidence is at present slender. During that period the circulations of journals tended to increase, at least as far as full-price sales to institutions were concerned, and the demand showed little sign of being influenced by the price increases inevitably associated with increasing size.

However, from about 1970, there has been a steady decline in demand for journals. A number of factors may be involved: institutions are pruning

Reprinted from the Chemical Society, *Chemistry in Britain*, vol. 11, no. 6 (1975), pp. 224-6, with permission.

multiple subscriptions; some industrial organizations have closed down; the use of photocopying (legal or otherwise) has had its effect. But the plain fact is that the publisher has to recover his increasing costs from an ever-smaller number of sales.

The cost of producing a journal is made up of several elements:
(*i*) There are those which, for a journal of a given length, are independent of the number of copies produced, *i.e.* 'fixed costs'. These include general overheads such as staff salaries, rent, rates, electricity, postage on correspondence with authors and referees, and largest by far, the cost of preparing the 'master' from which the journal is printed.
(*ii*) There are elements which vary (not necessarily linearly) with the number of copies produced: these include the cost of actually putting the ink on the paper (machining), the cost of the paper itself, and, of course, the postage bill.

The production of a specialized journal, to a standard that users have a right to expect, is a complex and expensive business. These is little room for economy, and attempts to cut costs by altering one part of the total system usually involve additional costs at another part. The possible savings could be discussed at length, but suffice it to say that no combination of currently available printing techniques will produce an acceptable journal of the complexity of *Journal of the Chemical Society*—and with a comparable print run—at significantly lower cost than is at present being achieved. If the present rate of fall-off in subscriptions continues, then a journal corresponding in size and complexity to *JCS Perkin 1* will, by 1982, cost a subscriber at least 60 percent more in real terms than it does at present. We believe that the Chemical Society will be failing its role as a communicator unless it provides the reader with the information he needs, at a price he can afford. Sales of the Chemical Society journals to individuals—even at the greatly reduced prices that are available to members—account for only 7 percent of the income received, so already the reader is, in general, dependent upon the availability of journals in a library. For economic reasons, many librarians are looking critically at their periodical holdings and relying on methods other than direct availability of the journals to satisfy the demands of their users.

The present research-information flow system is highly inflexible. A subscriber to a journal—even a fairly specialized journal—has to take, and pay for, a large amount of information that he will not need. In the context of a conventional printed journal there is no way around this which makes economic sense. However the papers which make up a journal may be repackaged, the publisher still has to produce a 'master' of some kind (usually made of metal type) from which the journal is printed, and this represents a fixed cost independent of how many (or how few) copies are printed from it. This fixed cost, together with the others already mentioned, has to be recovered by spreading it over the number of copies sold. If circulation falls, the total cost of produciton does not fall in proportion, so the unit cost increases. To sub-divide the existing journal packages still further would result in a larger number of journals, all with lower circulations than the present ones.

A New Approach

The Chemical Society has already taken steps to reduce the fixed costs of some of its journals by taking part in the supplementary publications scheme, whereby material associated with a published paper, which needs to be available but not necessarily printed and bound and available on the library shelf, is deposited and made available only to those who request it, either as microfiche or as hard copy. In the few years that we have been doing this, we must have saved the Society at least £20,000, with no evidence that anyone has been seriously inconvenienced.

In the U.S.S.R., this approach hás been taken a step further, by the voluntary or compulsory deposition of manuscripts with VINITI (the all-union institute for scientific and technical information) or with one of about 30 other deposition centres throughout the Soviet Union. If the paper has been submitted *via* a primary journal, then an abstract or, often, just a title and a reference number, may be published in the journal concerned. An abstract appears in *Referativnyi Zhurnal*, and the title is listed in VINITI's catalogue of deposited manuscripts.

While this approach clearly has the advantage of cutting down the publishing costs, it could be argued that it adds a serious obstacle between the would-be user and the results he may wish to study. We feel that the full texts of scientific papers should continue to be made widely available, as quickly and as cheaply as possible.

Our U.S. colleagues have been experimenting with the use of 'mini-print' in an attempt to curb the increases in production costs. This system involves the printing of the 'discussion' sections of papers in the conventional way, with the 'experimental' sections being reproduced directly from the authors' type-scripts at one-third (linear) original size. We could save money by adopting this method of production but the savings are not of the order of magnitude we consider necessary to ensure the long-term financial balance of the Society's primary publications. That is not to say that the American Chemical Society is wrong to use such a system: the basic differences between the U.K. and U.S. situations are that the print-runs of American Chemical Society journals tend to be much longer than ours (up to three times) and that they are able to recover a substantial proportion of their composition costs by means of the page-charge. The page-charge is, in effect, a subsidy by the federal government of journals whose circulation is primarily domestic. In the case of *Journal of the Chemical Society*, about 60 percent of the papers published originate in the U.K., but only about 7 percent of the sales are domestic. In our case, the levying of a page-charge would constitute a subsidy by the U.K. either privately or by H.M. Government) of a product destined for export, to the extent of 40 percent to the U.S. The Society—and presumably any British Government—would not regard such subsidy as desirable. The longer print-runs of American Chemical Society journals mean that their savings in paper and machining by the use of miniprint would constitute a far higher proportion of their production costs than such savings would be in our case.

Experimental Journal

Following detailed consideration by the Publication Board of the problems of the primary journal literature, involvement in the development of a new design of research journal has been authorized, and an experimental issue of a synposis/microfiche journal has been prepared. Basically, the concept is that the general current-awareness needs of the reader will be catered for by means of a conventionally-printed mini-journal which will contain very brief, carefully designed accounts of the researches being reported, while the full texts of the papers (as authors' typescripts) will be available on microfiche.

The CS experimental synopsis/microfiche journal has already been circulated fairly widely to authors, librarians, and sister societies at home and overseas for comment. Copies are available on request. It must be emphasized that it is by no means the last word in presentation and content, and when the synopsis/microfiche journal proper appears in 1977, its form will take account of the many constructive and helpful criticisms that we have received already, and doubtless more that we shall receive in the near future. [This has already appeared, 1978. Ed.]

The experimental synopsis journal (Mark 1) was based on *JCS Perkin 1* and consists of synopses of papers already published there. Some of the synopses were prepared by the authors of the original papers, some were produced entirely in the editorial office, and some are the results of collaborative efforts. They represent a number of different approaches to synopsis construction, and it is hoped that they will be used to indicate what readers would (and would not) like to see in a synopis journal. Already, from the feedback we have received, it is apparent that we should have included at least the leading literature references in the synopsis as well as in the full-text version. The use, originally based on studies of ease and speed of scanning, of a very high proportion of reaction schemes and structural formulae to indicate the results has proved extremely popular, but it is clear that readers would prefer to have a maximum of information in the shape of experimental conditions, and so forth 'on the arrows'.

We are extending study of synopsis construction to papers from the fields of inorganic, physical, and physical organic chemistry. We hope to receive from authors their own ideas on how their own papers could have been rendered in synopsis form. We should be equally interested to hear about specific papers (or types of papers) that would present particular problems when attempts are made to render them into synopsis form.

Turning now to the microform full-text version, we recognize the common misgivings about the use of this medium. This is perfectly natural, but we are confident that once readers become accustomed to its use and realize how infrequently in fact they refer to the full paper, they will appreciate the very real advantages of the system—not least its economic advantages and the benefits that flow from its decreased bulk *vis-à-vis* the traditional journal.

Microfiche

The microfiche that will form part of Mark II of our experimental synopsis/ microfiche journal will also be experimental in character, containing various layouts of typescripts. This will enable the optimum layout to be defined in future instructions to authors.

Microfiche may not be the ideal microform for long-term archival retention in libraries, so we shall make arrangements for libraries to be able to obtain microfilm versions of the full texts at the end of the year—just as they can now obtain microfilm versions of the conventional journal. If possible the choice of positive or negative microfiches will be offered, since negative fiches are considered by many people to give better results in reader-printers when hardcopy full-size prints are required.

Individuals may wish to subscribe, in the main, just to the synopsis journal, but libraries will probably wish to have the whole package, *i.e.*, the synopsis journal plus the whole set of microfiches. However, one-off copies of individual microfiches will be made available quickly and at a reasonable price, to pass on to the customer the benefits of the flexibility of production that we shall obtain.

The new system will offer the individual subscriber better value for money and it is hoped that, since the synopses are designed for cheap and effective current awareness, more chemists will become involved with the literature of their science by once again reading their personal copy.

Since most of the effort required to prepare the printing master of the conventionally printed journal will have been removed, it should be possible to offer the author a much better 'time to publication' as well as a much wider general interest readership than his paper at present achieves.

The advantages of microfiche to the publisher (and therefore to the subscriber) are many; specifically, the very low fixed cost of producing the master fiches, and the ease with which small numbers of copies can be produced, mean (*i*) that a decline in circulation of a microform publication has much less effect on the unit cost than a corresponding decline in circulation of a conventional journal; (*ii*) that the stock that needs to be kept in order to satisfy demand for back-numbers is nil, with useful implications so far as warehousing space and locking-up of capital are concerned.

There is already one synopsis/microfiche journal. The German technical journal *Chemie-Ingenieur-Technik* has included synopses since the beginning of 1974, and to judge from the numbers of synopses appearing it seems to be very popular with authors. Dr. Helmut Grünewald, the publications director of the Gesellschaft der deutscher Chemiker, has long been an advocate of this approach to publication of scientific papers, and it is a pleasure to record our gratitude for many stimulating discussions. We are also grateful to the many chemists who have already offered comments and criticisms, and will continue to stimulate discussion of these developments wherever we can.

At the Society's Autumn Meeting, to be held at the University of Reading in September, we are arranging in association with a number of suppliers of microform equipment an exhibition-demonstration of the relevant equipment that is currently available, as an addendum to a presentation on the synopsis/ microfiche journal. Contrary to widespread belief, microfiche readers are not unduly expensive, they do not have to be confined to libraries, and indeed many people possess their own microfiche readers. The quality of the equipment available is improving all the time, and prices are tending to fall as more and more people begin to use microform.

And what of the future? The Chemical Society synopsis/microfiche journal goes only part of the way to cure the information-flow problems of research journals—the twin blights of dilution (too many papers of no interest to the subscriber) and dispersion (papers of interest spread through too many journals). Fortunately, several foreign publishing learned societies are also interested in the synopsis/microfiche journal concept and a level of collaboration on publications, far greater than any to date, now seems possible. If this can be achieved in a rational way and the total of papers produced in such countries can be pooled, the possibility of multiple repackaging into a sensible number of specialized parts becomes economically possible. One may yet see the day when the individual can receive most, if not all, of his requirements in one package.

SUBSCRIPTIONS ON MICROFICHE: AN IRREVERSIBLE TREND

by **Dr. Edward Gray,** *President, Microforms International Marketing Corporation*

Obviously, there aren't many approaches to the conversion of conventional serials publications to microforms. The rivalry is actually between microfilm and microfiche.

The conversion to microfilm has been aided by a rapid improvement in technology which has brought about reliable cartridges, better readers, electronic finders, and the extensive use of reader-printers. As a result, the microfilm is generally considered to be the more adequate medium to which larger collections of journals and serials should be converted. On the other hand, with some exceptions, microfiche has appeared to be the ideal medium for monographs, reports, printouts, and text confined to a few hundred frames. This, in general, was the outlook that explained, for instance, why University Microfilm has progressed far more rapidly than Microcard Editions which had emphasized microfiche, but directed its search for the same type of material.

In the last couple of years, however, a new technological development has taken place, almost without our noticing it: the microfiche copying machine. As a matter of fact, may I suggest that we are at the beginning of a new era in the technology of copying, and that there is already more than ample evidence to indicate that this trend is irreversible.

The arithmetic is simple. It begins with the high cost of copying by Xerox or any other machine. For many years, librarians have used the copying machine on a large scale and with obvious results in cutting a reference library's multiple subscriptions to each publication. A considerable number of libraries

Reprinted from *The Journal of Micrographics*, vol. 8, no. 5 (May 1975), pp. 241-244, by permission of the National Micrographics Association. ©1975 by the NMA.

around the world are presently receiving only one basic copy of a given journal, but are "Xeroxing" specific articles, some of them for quite a number of patrons. Suppose, for example, an issue of 100 pages includes 10 articles averaging 10 pages each. A researcher might get copies of articles at a cost of approximately $1.00 for 20 pages.

Now, however, if the issue is available in microfiche, a diazo copy—which can now be obtained as easily as a Xerox copy—will probably cost 5 cents, or even less. The difference is that the microfiche covers not only one but fully 98 pages. Considering, however, that only 20 pages from this NMA Standard microfiche are of interest to individual researchers, the difference in cost is equally convincing, i.e., 5 cents for the microfiche against $1.00 for the 20 pages in Xerox copy; respectively, 1/20 the cost!

This arithmetic is so convincing that some industrial libraries, while waiting for publishers to release their current subscriptions in microfiche, are making the microfiche of basic journals themselves.

The library of the chemical complex Ugine Kuhlmann in Paris is one of them. The issues, as received, are cut and prepared for shooting in the library. Bell and Howell—France will then shoot the microfiche and deliver a silver master. Another Bell and Howell diazo duplicator then reproduces the fiche for scores of researchers interested in pre-established journals or in specific subject articles.

Even considering the expenses for preparing and obtaining a custom master, the librarian has calculated important savings against paper copying. If a fiche were to come directly from the publisher, not only would the saving be increased but the use of this procedure should spread rapidly, especially among research libraries.

How many others have followed Ugine Kuhlmann's example? We do not have a general picture at this time. It is well known, for instance, that the Centre National de la Recherche Scientifique (CNRS) is doing a similar job—on a subscription basis—on a national and even international scale.

According to a survey by the American Library Association (ALA), there are 37 academic and public libraries in the U.S.A. that are performing reprographic services in microfiche. We know very little regarding industrial libraries for which this approach would seem essential.

There are already some publishers who are announcing the release of such simultaneous microfiche editions. Even they, however, are not encouraging it; they are, rather, announcing it only to show that they are keeping up with the times.

Nevertheless, there are two experiments in progress, which indicate a change of climate. One of them is being conducted by Pergamon Press and its micropublisher, Microforms International Marketing Corporation (MIMC). The second is the American Chemical Society (ACS) experiment.

As early as 1972, MIMC attempted to make available—in addition to microfilm—a simultaneous microfiche edition of more than a hundred journals. The initial attempt has shown that many libraries have entered standing orders for microfilm to be supplied at the end of each subscription year, but only a few have shown an interest in subscribing to a microfiche released simultaneously with the paper issue, and paying additionally for it. (One of these few is the Proctor & Gamble library.)

The program for a simultaneous microfiche release was, therefore, halted—actually postponed, pending further technological developments.

This year this program has been revived, on an experimental basis, with consideration being given to the possible detachment of the microfiche from the paper edition. Chosen for the experiment was *Tetrahedron Letters,* a weekly medium for the rapid dissemination of preliminary communications in organic chemistry, which a large number of chemists look forward to as eagerly as the general public awaits the Sunday edition of the *New York Times.*

To acquaint researchers with the microfiche edition, it was decided to supply eight consecutive issues free to 500 selected institutional subscribers—including 100 who were aware of this project and made sure they would be among those selected.

Unless otherwise requested, negative microfiche have been mailed to U.S. and Canadian libraries, and positive microfiche to the others, as it was considered that copying machines for microfiche and reader-printers are more prevalent in the Western Hemisphere. Apparently this was an erroneous assumption, as there has been a number of requests from Europe asking to change the positive microfiche to negative.

A questionnaire has been sent to each recipient in order to ascertain the receipt of the polarity requested, to establish if the microfiche is arriving sooner than the airmailed paper copy, and to invite comments regarding the intensity and resolution, with a view toward further improvements.

We have undertaken this experiment with the intitial idea of continuing to produce a commercial microfiche edition at the end of the test period. However, during the experiment, a number of libraries (many more than anticipated) have indicated their intention to renounce the existing hardcopy immediately in favor of the microfiche. Hence, we have been faced with problems regarding the printout commitment of the publisher as established at the beginning of the subscription year.

On the other hand, some users have asked if we are not handling this matter too abruptly. They have suggested that the increasing availability of simultaneous microfiche editions may have too many important implications for its potential users to make an immediate decision. Libraries that wish to implement it may not be prepared to do so at this time, especially in regard to hardware and to organizational problems.

For these reasons, we have decided to mark time for the remainder of the current year to allow subscribers ample time to give full consideration to the desirability of a microfiche simultaneous edition.

In 1976 when this project is resumed, *Tetrahedron Letters* on microfiche will be produced on a commercial basis; when renewing the subscription for 1976 subscribers will have the opportunity to decide:

a. If a microfiche subscription is advisable in addition to the paper edition; or
b. If a microfiche subscription is advisable in lieu of the hardcopy.

As a result of the 1975 experiment, a simultaneous microfiche edition on a commercial basis will be prepared by MIMC for a number of Pergamon Press journals in 1976. Actually the specific journals to be offered in microfiche in 1976 (probably mostly in chemistry) as well as the rating policy are the object of present research on the basis of the 1975 tests.

Another experiment, which also has it in view to acquaint researchers with a free microfiche release, is being made by the American Chemical Society. In fact, it involves all their journals except *Chemical Abstracts*. ACS is supplying the microfiche of current issues free to their microfilm standing-order customers. However, anyone can enter a microfiche subscription for 1975 at the same price as the paper edition. Actually, for eight ACS journals, there is also available a ''supplementary'' microfiche edition covering texts not published at all in the paper edition.

These experiments probably will not be the last, but chances are they shall have an impact on the entire publishing field. A very important step forward has already been taken in recent years, as publishers have begun to consider microfiche an important medium for subscriptions in an era of paper shortages and to encourage its release. The microfiche subscription appears to be no longer necessarily connected with a subscription to the corresponding paper edition, and it is obvious that its cost will gradually decrease as the demand brings savings on the print-run of the paper edition, which is becoming increasingly exorbitant.

No matter what present experiments show, it is obvious that we are indeed witnessing an irreversible trend.

MICROFORM PUBLISHING: SALVATION FOR SHORT-RUN PERIODICALS?

by **Warren G. Bovee,** *College of Journalism, Marquette University*

When *Life* magazine died, the obituary received front-page space in the newspapers, but when *Better Health* or *Charisma Digest* or *Gas Age* (and at least 1,300 other small-circulation periodicals) passed away, the death notice was only a few lines in the "Cessations" section of the 1971-72 *Ulrich's International Periodicals Directory.*

No doubt, it has always been thus: when battle casualties are announced, generals get more attention than privates do. But there are more privates than generals; there are more small-circulation, specialized publications than mass-circulation, consumer magazines. And for those who are interested in the total area of magazine journalism, the plight of the numerous small publications is at least as important as that of the few giants.

Magazines go out of existence for a great variety of reasons: competition from other media, changes in public interests and tastes, death or retirement of strong editors, and so on. But certainly one of the principal causes is economic—the inability of income to keep up with soaring expenses. Except for the few publications which can meet deficits with subsidies (*Commonweal*, for example) or tax write-offs (as is true of *The New Republic*), those which face a large or extended excess of expense over income must either merge or die.

One of the popular notions today is that this economic crunch is hitting hardest at the general consumer publications. No doubt, many of the big slicks have died and others are hurting; whereas, in contrast, many special interest periodicals seem to be doing very well. But some of the highly specialized

Reprinted from ERIC Document 084 557 (August 22, 1973)

publications—especially those with circulations under 50,000 and with little advertising income—are in an exceedingly precarious position.[1] The few such small circulation publications which do contain paid advertising have little hope of significantly increasing income by raising advertising rates. Because circulation is low and advertising sales and production costs are high, many of them already have exceedingly costly page-per-thousand rates. As a result, present and potential advertisers are finding it more economical to employ alternative means—especially direct mail—for reaching their customers. Additional advertising rate increases, therefore, would only further price these publications out of the market. Thus for most small-circulation periodicals, the last hope for increasing income seems to be to raise subscription prices. But here, too, one questions how much higher these prices can go. Just as an example, Table 1 shows some of the increases that have taken place during the last half-dozen years.

Table 1
COMPARATIVE SUBSCRIPTION PRICES
1967 - 1972-73

Publication (frequency)	1967 Price	1972-73 Price	Percentage Increase
Chemical Reviews (BM)	$20.00	$ 39.00	95%
Child Development (Q)	15.00	25.00	66%
Christian Century (W)	7.50	12.00	60%
Humanist (BM)	3.00	7.00	133%
Insulation/Circuits (M)	15.00	25.00	66%
Journal of Chemical Physics (SM)	35.00	110.00	214%
Philosophy of Science (Q)	10.00	15.00	50%
Physics of Fluids (M)	20.00	47.00	135%
Railway Age (W)	6.00	15.00	150%
Telecommunications & Radio Engineering (M)	75.00	135.00	80%
Textile Technology Digest (M)	25.00	100.00	300%

Not all small publications have had to make such enormous jumps in their subscription costs, of course. But any subscription price increase normally results in some loss in circulation. Furthermore, as circulation decreases, the printing cost per copy increases. Thus it is easy to see how even a series of small "upward adjustments" in subscription prices can easily direct a publication into a downward spiral toward oblivion. If there are only slim chances of achieving salvation by going through the door marked "Increase income," then the only hope seems to lie in trying the door labeled "Cut costs." That door, obviously, is not easy to locate. In fact, it is because costs in such major items as paper, printing, and postage are going up that short-run magazines are in a bind in the first place. If there were a way of avoiding some of these factors which are contributing to escalating costs, there might be hope. Fortunately, the new technology has provided magazines—and especially the small-circulation magazines—with such an option. I am referring to what is called micropublishing.

Micropublishing can be achieved in a variety of ways, but the process which seems most serviceable for short-run periodicals is that which involves the use of *microfiche*.[2] As anyone who has done extensive library research knows, a standard microfiche is a piece of film, about the size of a picture postcard, on which can be produced in miniature up to 98 pages of any written or pictorial materials—including magazine pages. By inserting a fiche into a suitable viewer, one can enlarge each frame to the original page size for easy reading. Microfiche has a great number of advantages, but one of the greatest is its economy compared to the cost of printing. Once a publication is ready to be sent to a printer—in other words, once the composition, layout, and pasteup or form make-ready processes have been completed—it is possible to produce duplicate copies in fiche at a fraction of the cost required to print these copies on paper.

Perhaps some specific examples will make this clear. Let's say we have a rather typical publication: 96 pages, 8½″ × 11″ trim size, printed offset on 70 pound stock, and containing 10 moderate-size half-tones. And let us compare, at various circulation levels, these printing costs (including the costs for plates, paper, ink, press time, and binding) with the costs for producing these copies in microfiche. The results would be approximately as indicated in Table 2.

Table 2
MICROFICHE COMPARED TO PRINT
(96 pages - 8½″ × 11″ - Black on white)
Ten Halftones

Number of Copies	Cost of Microfiche	Cost of Print	Savings Using Fiche*
1,000	$175	$1,105	$930
5,000	$700	$2,225	$1,525
10,000	$1,330	$3,625	$2,295
50,000	$6,490	$7,225	$735
75,000	$9,675	$10,115	$440

*Excluding circulation costs.

Two important cautions should be noted in these and in other cost comparisons. First of all, the printing costs given here are those charged in the midwest by experienced and highly reliable printers who provide good quality service.[3] Other printers in other areas of the country might charge anywhere from ten percent more to ten percent less than the figures listed on these tables. Even if one reduced these printing costs by ten percent, however, fiche would still have an economic advantage for press runs up to approximately 50,000. Secondly, the cost of mailing the finished product to subscribers has been omitted from these comparisons. In spite of the fact that a fiche is only four by six inches in size and weighs only one-sixth of an ounce, it costs more to mail microfiche than it does to mail a printed publication. [1973, Ed.] This is due to one of the anachronisms of present postal regulations, which insist that only periodicals composed of "printed sheets" can qualify for second-class mailing privileges. Fiche must be mailed either third class (at an increased cost, compared to second class, of about one-half cent to three cents per piece) or first class (at an increased cost of about four to nearly seven cents per piece.) Thus, even though microfiche has, according to Table 2, a small cost advantage even beyond the 50,000 circulation category, beyond that point the savings would probably be offset by the greater postal costs.

The circulation figure up to which microfiche publishing is less expensive than print publishing is of major importance. To the best of my knowledge, no one knows the circulation of all the some 30,000 periodicals published in the United States. But in conjunction with a research project unconnected with this one, a check was made of all the periodicals subscribed to by the major libraries at Marquette University. Even omitting all periodicals which have ceased publication, which are published outside the United States, which are published less frequently than quarterly, which are published by any unit of the government, and which have circulations greater than 35,000, we discovered that this one library complex contained 1,666 short-run periodicals. Every one of these publications—and undoubtedly many more—could probably save a considerable amount of money by switching from printing to microfiching.

Since the figures given in Table 2 apply to only a single issue of a magazine, one has to multiply these figures by the number of issues published per year in order to appreciate the annual savings which are possible by switching to microfiche. A monthly magazine with a circulation of 10,000, for example, could save $25,000 a year if microfiching were substituted for printing.

Comparable savings are possible for publications of different quality or format. For example, four-color reproduction is economically feasible for most printed publications only if they have enormous circulations, high subscription costs or heavy subsidies. But when microfiche is used, full-color reproduction is feasible for the publications with a small print order. Table 3 indicates some of the comparative costs. It should be noted, furthermore, that

Table 3
MICROFICHE COMPARED TO PRINT
(Four-color Reproduction on One Signature)
Ten Color Separations

Number of Copies	Cost of Microfiche	Cost of Print	Savings (or Loss) Using Fiche*
1,000	$500	$2,955	$2,455
5,000	$2,500	$4,075	$1,575
10,000	$5,000	$5,475	$475
50,000	$25,000	$11,400	($13,600)
75,000	$37,500	$13,550	($23,950)

*Excluding circulation costs.

the print costs are based on the assumption that only ten color separations would be used, and that all of the color would be printed on a single signature. Greater use of color would, of course, greatly increase the printing costs. But the same is not true for the microfiche version. Since the fiche is, in effect, a single piece of film, every miniature page on that fiche could be in full color without any addition to the cost.

As a final example, let us consider journals of the size of the *Journalism Quarterly*—in other words, publications with the smaller, 6″ × 9″ trim size but with nearly two hundred pages of editorial material. If, instead of being printed, these journals were produced on standard microfiche, two fiche would have to be used. (It would be possible to use a single ultrafiche—some of which have a capacity of up to 3,280 pages—for these publications, but the viewers needed to read ultrafiche are not widely available.) In spite of a nearly two-fold increase in the microfiching costs, the fiche version is still considerably less expensive than the printed version for short-run periodicals.

But if microfiching is really the water of salvation for small circulation publishers, why is it that so few of those publishers are lining up at the baptismal font? Part of the answer can be found in the history of other technological innovations in the field of communications. Consider, for example, long-playing records, FM broadcasting, ultra high frequency and then color telecasting—in all of these instances there was a period during which the companies were claiming there was no point in investing in the equipment because there were so few products available. Whey televise in color if most people do not have color tv sets? Why buy a color tv set if most programs are being televised in black and white?

In all of these other instances, of course, the dilemma was eventually resolved. It took an act of Congress to convince television set manufacturers to produce sets capable of receiving UHF as well as VHF channels, but otherwise the communications companies and industries themselves took the initiative once they were convinced that the innovations would have market acceptability.

But it is precisely in reference to this point—market acceptability—that the publishers of small-circulation magazines are digging in their heels. The publishers strongly doubt that their readers will accept a microfiche in place of a printed publication. Their doubts seem well founded. A fiche magazine cannot be read until the fiche is inserted into a suitable viewer, and it cannot be read at all unless the subscriber purchases or has access to such a viewer; a printed magazine, on the other hand, can be read as soon as it arrives in the mail. All this appears to indicate that the subscriber would resist rather than accept a microfiche publication. In other words, microfiche publishing may be a great idea, but it won't sell.

At this point, however, it is important to recognize that most small circulation publications have two types of subscribers: the individual who, either directly or through his membership in some organization, acquires his copies primarily for his own personal use; and the institution—primarily the scholarly, scientific, industrial, or research library—which acquires copies for the convenience of all who are patrons of that institution. For most of the individual subscribers, it is true, there is little incentive to request fiche rather than a printed publication. Although microfiche viewers cost less than half the price of a standard office typewriter, not many individual subscribers have, as yet, purchased their own personal viewers. And reading a fiche on a viewer is less convenient than reading a printed publication. Individual subscribers, therefore, could probably be moved to accept fiche only if it were to their economic advantage to do so. Since microfiching is less expensive than printing, it would seem reasonable for publishers to offer fiche subscriptions at a cost lower than that for printed publications, or at least to maintain fiche subscriptions at the present level when the subscription price for the printed version has to be increased. Such cost differentials would encourage a gradual movement to microfiche publishing, to the benefit of both the magazine publishers and the magazine readers.

But for the institutional subscriber there already exists a strong incentive for preferring microfiche to print. The librarian's interest in a periodical does not end after the magazine has been received, catalogued and placed on the shelf. At some later time, the librarian must remove the individual copies from the shelf, have them bound as an annual volume, and then find shelf space again for the bound volume. These additional activities involve expenses which could be eliminated or significantly reduced if the periodical were in the form of fiche instead of print.

For example, according to a study made by the Center for Research Libraries, binding costs alone now range from $7.00 to $11.00 per periodical.[4] The same report also indicated that "large university research libraries typically receive 10,000 to 20,000 or more current serials."[5] In other words, since microfiche does not need to be bound, librarians can foresee the saving of thousands—even of hundreds of thousands—of dollars each year in binding costs if the libraries could obtain fiche rather than print versions of periodicals.

And this is only the tip of the iceberg, for also of major importance is the savings in space which is made possible through microfiche publishing. A journal in the form of fiche occupies approximately five percent of the space required for its printed equivalent. In other words, the publications that occupy twenty running feet of shelf space when produced in printed form can be fitted into a shoe box when produced in microfiche.

Fiche also eliminates other problems, such as the unavailability of printed copies during the time when they are "out for binding" and the enormous difficulties in replacing bound volumes if they are mutilated. Moreover, most libraries today are completely equipped with microfiche viewers and even with reader-printers, from which a patron can obtain a hard-copy enlargement of a microfiche frame for only ten cents.

The present situation for the subscribers to short-run periodicals, therefore, seems to be this:

Most individual subscribers would probably be opposed to microfiche magazines, and will continue to be opposed until such magazines are more widely available and less expensive than printed periodicals.

Most institutional subscribers—particularly libraries—strongly favor microfiche magazines, especially if they can be obtained at the same time that the printed equivalent is available.[6] This situation suggests that the best course of action for the near future would be to publish short-run publications in two forms: in microfiche for libraries and for the few individual subscribers who own and are accustomed to using microfiche viewers; and in print for all of the other subscribers.

A publisher might be tempted to reject such a suggestion, for it seems to wipe out the major advantage—economy—possessed by microfiche. It is obvious, of course, that, if the circulation of a publication stays the same, for every copy produced in fiche there would be one less copy produced in print. And since the per-copy printing cost increases as the number of copies printed decreases, a publisher might think that partial conversion to fiche might raise, instead of lower, his total costs.

But a reexamination of Table 2 reveals that this is not necessarily true. For example, according to that Table, costs for a periodical with a circulation of 10,000 would be approximately $3,625 if all of the copies were printed. If only half of the copies were produced in print and the other half were produced in fiche, the *combined* cost for the two forms would be only $2,925—a savings of approximately $700 per issue. In other words, the economic advantages of fiche are so great when small quantities are involved that even a partial conversion can provide some savings.

In general, therefore, the transition to microfiche on the part of small-circulation magazines can be described as a push-pull movement. The push is coming from the libraries which subscribe to these magazines—and for short-run, specialized publications, library subscriptions constitute a relatively high percentage of the total subscription list—as these institutional subscribers demand microfiche in order to reduce their own soaring costs. At the moment, however, the energy behind the pull is much stronger than that which is behind the push.[7] If this tendency continues, the conversion to microfiche may take place in spite of the reluctance of some magazines to be converted. But perhaps in the magazine world, even forced salvation is better than eternal damnation.

References

1. "Small Magazines Face Gravest Crisis," *The Milwaukee Journal*, May 28, 1973.

2. Mary L. Fischer, "The Use of COM at Los Angeles Public Library," *The Journal of Micrographics*, vol. 6, no. 5 (May/June 1973), pp. 205-210. Periodicals are also frequently produced on microfilm, but Miss Fischer identifies (p. 209) five advantages which microfiche has over microfilm: lower cost for the film, less space needed, faster access to data, less expensive viewers, and less time for production.

3. The basic printing figures were provided by Kalmbach Press, Milwaukee, Wisconsin, which does both commercial and magazine printing. The figures were reviewed for general accuracy by Modular Publications, Inc., Senatobia, Miss., a new plant specializing in short-run periodicals. Microfiche costs were obtained from the Eastman Kodak Company.

4. Center for Research Libraries, "Background and Proposal for a National Lending Library for Journals," a report prepared for the January 5, 1973 meeting of the Council for the Center for Research Libraries, Chicago, Illinois, p. 30.

5. *Ibid.*, p. 33.

6. Several micropublishng companies—for example, Bell & Howell and Xerox University Microfilms—sell microfiche versions of current periodicals. A provision in the contracts which these companies have with magazine publishers, however, prohibits the micropublishing companies from making the microfiche versions available concurrently with the printed versions. Thus, at the present time, concurrent publication of microfiche and printed versions of periodicals is possible only if the magazine publishers themselves initiate and control the microfiche operation.

7.   See the Center for Research Libraries report cited above. Because of economic pressures, libraries belonging to the Center have already cancelled an average of 300 periodical subscriptions (with some libraries cancelling as many as 2,000 subscriptions); in addition, they are cooperating in the establishment of national and international lending libraries for periodicals. Such lending libraries will enable the individual libraries to further reduce their own periodical holdings while continuing to serve their patrons by borrowing copies or photo reproductions of periodical articles from the central lending libraries.

ACCESS TO JOURNAL LITERATURE: SHORT-TERM AND LONG-TERM PROSPECTS

by **David Barr**, *Bibliographic Services Manager, University Microfilms Ltd. [Presently Sub-Librarian (Social Sciences), Hatfield Polytechnic]*

Introduction

The Royal Society stated before the enactment of the 1956 Copyright Act that "science rests upon its published record, and ready access to public scientific and technical information is a fundamental need of scientists everywhere. All bars which prevent access to scientific and technical publications hinder the progress of science and should be removed." This statement related to the making of extracts from books and periodicals, but it now seems possible that these carriers of information themselves are imposing limitations on access to information.

The very rapid rate of inflation currently being experienced in the cost of periodical subscriptions is provoking anguished comment from both publishers and librarians. In the short-term, this is naturally leading to adaptation of existing systems—mostly to their contraction—but it does bring to the fore the need for a longer-term and more fundamental reappraisal of the "vehicles" used for the dissemination of information, and there is clearly a requirement for both librarians and publishers to be involved in this process.

[The opinions expressed in this article are those of the author and not necessarily those of University Microfilms Ltd.]

Reprinted from *Aslib Proceedings*, vol. 28, no. 3 (March 1976), pp. 116-119, by permission of the publisher.

The Oxford booksellers, B.H. Blackwell Ltd., recently held a conference of serials librarians and publishers, which served the useful purpose of bringing together the parties affected by current economic problems in that field. By far the most striking outcome of this event was an appreciation that publishers and librarians are suffering from different aspects of these same basic problems. The pressures on publishers are steep rises in the cost of paper and printing, dangerously low profit margins in many cases, but a continuous flow of papers worthy of publication, many of which must be rejected; indeed, top-quality journals reject the majority of items received. The pressures on librarians are subscription increases coupled with financial stringency and a consequent need to cancel some subscriptions; equally, however, they are still required to meet a demand for information in published journals.

Many scholarly journals which were born in the last ten years came into being through a union of entrepreneurial opportunity and expanding consumer finances. The very specialist nature of some of these ventures and their low-circulation figures are now the main threat to their continued existence. But it does not follow that the readers of these journals will cease to want access to the information contained in them.

Short-term Solutions

In practical day-to-day terms, this situation involves librarians in taking a closer look at identifying the materials in their libraries which are known to be used and in seeking ways of providing access to more copies of material in heavy demand while cutting back on holdings of material with minimal or no demand. In management terms, this process is probably no bad thing in itself, although one American librarian who had actually implemented such a study which resulted in cancelling 500 subscriptions, described the reaction of fellow-librarians as one of "dynamic outrage."[1] However, the severity of current difficulties is illustrated by reference to two suggestions which have been made in recent years, one to expand access to heavily-used items, and the other to eliminate wastage by reducing acquisitions.

The first of these examples appears in a Bath University publication by Line, Sandison, and MacGregor,[2] where it is suggested that journal publishers should consider identifying the core collection of high-quality articles within their backfiles and reproducing them in bound volumes. The argument is as follows:

A particularly attractive feature of this idea is that, unlike many ideas suggested and favoured by librarians for reducing their costs, it would benefit publishers as well as librarians. The number of backsets a publisher has available after a number of years is very small indeed, or non-existent; he aims to make a profit or keep going on the sale of current issues, not of back volumes. If he could produce selections of articles on the lines suggested, these would be a saleable commodity and provide an added source of profit. He could reprint (e.g. by offset litho) at fairly low cost. The benefits to librarians are obvious; apart from the savings in cost in their not having to buy complete back-runs of serials or rely heavily on inter-library borrowing, a great deal of space would be saved. An alternative would be the provision of xerox copies of individual articles, but these are hard to store and make available through catalogues; a bound volume covering a few years represents a better solution.

Since that was written in 1972, reprint publishing has become almost wholly uneconomical, and the only survivors in that intermediate role are micropublishers. The reason is that micropublishers pay royalties on microform sales, and journal publishers get at least as much of a financial return as they would from an activity such as that described above. In addition, the librarian gets full-text storage in microform, absorbing very little space. The full-text aspect is vitally important, since core collections inevitably engender occasions when certain articles are not available to readers. In addition where only a limited number of articles is available, some effort would have to be expended on recording which of those articles were held in the library. This is time-consuming and costly and would probably be rejected, since librarians do not usually catalogue the contents of books of readings.

The second of the suggestions tackled directly the problem of reducing holdings of material which could not be justified by their usage levels. This appeared in *Aslib Proceedings* in June 1974.[3] Houghton and Prosser were developing a procedural model intended as a code of good practice to enable special librarians to effect economies in their journal holdings by systematically planned use of the BLLD holdings. The Dainton report[4] recommended that "the relative costs and the advantages to both the user and the supplying library of supplying a request by loan or by photocopy should be investigated." Houghton and Prosser argued that "the acquisition, lending, photocopying, and storage policies all too often evolve in isolation from the BLL's central resources." They spent as much time criticizing the model of Brookes as in constructing their own, but it is significant that in neither case did they take into account the possibility of studying the economics of serials in microform as an intermediate stage between full-text storage on paper on the one hand and borrowing or acquiring photocopies from the BLLD on the other.

Their own model appears to be still in the early stages of development, so it would be wrong to pre-judge it. However, their rejection of Brookes' model is not altogether valid because it entirely overlooks the cost-saving potential of microform, and because without some such consideration, any model which places cost against use as the fundamental criteria for rationalization must be regarded as incomplete. Applying Brookes' criteria, they found a situation in a large industrial research library where only 41 of the 316 titles were economical to retain, and from specific subject fields within that collection only 29 of the 57 journals would be retained since they produced 89 percent of total usages. Their conclusion that the results prove to be un-realistic in terms of immediate library provision is invalid, because, if 50 percent of the holdings represent only 11 percent of usages, but for some reason it is deemed undesirable to be without these 50 percent, then the logical argument must be to retain as many of them as possible in the cheapest available medium permitting access to full-text information, i.e. microform.

Long-term Solutions

Financial pressures on both publishers and librarians are inevitably going to lead to changes in the formal publication system. The use of microform as outlined above will serve only as a short-term solution to the storage of existing published materials. The great danger is that microform will be used as an implement for instigating the dissemination of large amounts of unpublished or "semi-published" material. The large microform-based clearing-house systems which are becoming more prevalent in the United States contain vast amounts of duplicated or ephemeral items which have been subjected to little or no editorial control, such systems being fed and supported by the need of academics and pseudo-academics to be seen to be producing papers. This leads ultimately to a mere proliferation of documentation rather than to a genuine expansion of the information system, and such systems represent an abuse of both computer and microform technology in relation to the provision of information.

Clearing-house systems can be seen as an alternative to the formal publication system, but they have a number of undesirable side-effects. What is urgently needed is a fundamental review of methods of disseminating the kind of information which has been traditionally included in journals. This does not mean complete abolition of existing systems, or substitution by alternatives like clearing-houses, but rather a systematic development of what is best in both. The two prime requirements for any new development are clearly proper editorial and bibliographic control. The former, although sometimes a subjective and arbitrary process, is best conducted by persons knowledgeable in the subject matter concerned and skilled in editorial techniques. The latter is best handled by a centralized system of control managed by librarians who understand the requirements for bibliographic description of, and access to, scholarly materials.

The need for the co-operation of both publishers and librarians is self-evident. There is a genuine demand for access to the results of research and other scholarly papers; on the other hand, the present system can neither cope with nor afford the scale on which this is necessary. Consequently much that is published is referred to infrequently if at all, and much that is rejected could have been of some use even to a very small number of readers.

Scholarly journals of high quality will continue to be published and rightly so, but it may be worth considering the creation of a central depository for the 'overflow', *i.e.* items which would be subjected to editorial scrutiny, but which it would be more rational to publish on microfiche held in a limited number of locations, and from which librarians could plan their acquisitions much more selectively than at present.

The onus is on librarians to influence future publication patterns rather than to allow themselves to be wholly governed by them. The creation of the National Lending Library was the single outstanding example of self-help by librarians in this field. Publishers may complain on occasions about its effect on their vested interests, but it is a real sign of the powerful influence which the library profession can bring to bear in an area in which it has considerable knowledge and experience to contribute. Libraries are still the largest segment of the market for scholarly documentation, and librarians ought to be actively involved in future developments for their own sake, and, above all, on behalf of the communities they serve.

References

1.   Gore, Daniel, Sawing Off the Horns of a Dilemma, or, How to Cut Subscription Lists and Expand Access to Journal Literature, *in* P. Spyers-Duran and D. Gore, eds. *Management Problems in Serials Work: Proceedings of a Conference Held at Florida Atlantic University, Boca Raton, Florida, March 26-27, 1973.* Greenwood Press, 1974.

2.   Line, M.B., Sandison, A. and MacGregor, J. *Patterns of Citations to Articles Within Journals: A Preliminary Test of Scatter, Concentration, and Obsolescence.* Bath University Library, BATH/LIB/2 October 1972.

3.   Houghton, B., and Prosser, C. Rationalization of Serial Holdings in Special Libraries, *Aslib Proceedings,* 26 (6), June 1974, p. 226-35.

4.   *Report of the National Libraries Committee.* London, HMSO, 1969 (Cmnd 4028).

V ■ EXTENDED APPLICATIONS OF MICROFORMS FOR SERIALS

INTRODUCTION

Once microform acceptance has been accomplished, extensions and refinements can be considered. COM (Computer Output Microfilm) serials lists and microform dissemination of journal copies for users are only two applications that can be utilized by the adoption of microforms for serials. Serials management can be greatly facilitated by continually updated COM serials listings, with only one place to look, in an intergrated file, rather than consulting one main book listing and numerous supplements. This COM serials listing would be designed to service both staff and patrons. Further use of computers can provide access to microfiche material and provide almost instantaneous copies. By means of console displays controlled by the user, he can have direct access to a properly indexed serials collection. Copies, in either hard copy or microform, can be disseminated to the interested users by means of reader/printers, thus reducing destruction to the material in comparison to the risk of losing by theft or mutilation the only pages in hard copy. By means of a computer-microform system several readers can view the same material simultaneously, by means of fiche copies. And the material can remain intact (relative to heavy hard copy usage).

Once microforms have been integrated into essentially hard copy periodical collections, there might be further evidenced a movement toward a fully operative microform-computer serials system. The time is now; the future is upon us.

Additional Readings

Avedon, Don M. *Computer Output Microfilm.* 2nd ed. Silver Spring, MD: National Microfilm Association, 1971.

Avedon, Don M., ed. *Fundamentals of Computer Output Microfilm.* [Pamphlet]. Silver Spring, MD: National Micrographics Association, 1974.

G.G. Baker and Associates. *A Guide to Computer Output Microfilm.* 4th ed. Guildford, England: G.G. Baker and Associates, 1975.

Belch, David E. "The Computer Controlled Periodical System at the San Francisco Public Library." *Library Resources and Technical Services*, vol. 13, no. 4, Fall 1969, pp. 531-532.

COM Is... [Flyer]. San Diego: Datagraphix, n.d.

Friedman, Elaine S. "Library Applications of Computer Output Microfilm: An Annotated Bibliography." *Special Libraries*, December 1977, pp. 447-454.

Gwinn, Nancy E. "A National Periodicals Center: Articulating the Dream." *Library Journal*, November 1, 1978, pp. 2166-2169.

"Input." [Letters]. *Journal of Library Automation*, vol. 8, no. 1, March 1975, pp. 79-80.

National Micrographics Association. *COM and Its Applications.* Silver Spring, MD: National Micrographics Association, 1976.

National Micrographics Association. *Proceeedings.* Silver Spring, MD: National Micrographics Association, 1976.

North, John. "Card Catalog to COM." *Library Journal*, October 15, 1977, pp. 2132-2134.

Pitkin, Gary M. *Serials Automation in the U.S.: A Bibliographic History.* Metuchen, NJ: Scarecrow Press, 1976.

ROM Newsletter, vol. 1, 1977—. Menlo Park, CA: Information Design, Inc.

Roth, Dana L. "Scientific Serial Lists." *Journal of Library Automation*, vol. 5, no. 1, March 1972, pp. 51-57.

Smith, Robert B. "Breaking New Ground in Library Work." *Network: International Communications in Library Automation*, vol. 3, 1976, pp. 26-27, 28.

West, Martha W. and Brett B. Butler. "Microreadings: Easing Obstacles to Library Distribution of Information." *Journal of Micrographics*, vol. 8, no. 1, September 1974, pp. 17-22.

HARD COPY PRINT-OUT IN LIBRARIES

by **Mark Levine,** *Readex Microprint Corporation, New York, N.Y.*

Micropublishing, in its true sense, is a mildly mixed blessing for libraries. Like so many things in life, it seems to be both indispensable and impossible to live with to many librarians. The core of the difficulty lies in the difference between microreproduction as it is applied in industrial systems and micropublishing. When a user decides that micro-reproduction is needed in a particular application, he properly follows steps of examination and analysis of his data handling problems and, usually with the help of consultants and vendors, establishes a system to meet his needs. If he is working on an engineering drawing problem, he will usually use the aperture card as the basic form and will acquire the necessary equipment, cameras, viewers, duplicators, print-out devices and retrieval machinery to make his system function in accordance with the requirements which he has established. In other words, within the spectrum of what the micrographic industry makes available to him, the user is the determiner of what microform he will use and he is in a position to select, adapt and modify available microforms and equipment to meet the needs of his system.

On the other hand, the acquisitions librarian finds himself in an entirely different position. He seldom has any choices at all in the form in which his library materials will come to him. *Portnoy's Complaint* will arrive at the library with a yellow dust jacket wrapped about a conventionally bound book—and that's it. Later in the year, perhaps, there will be the choice of hardbound versus paperback. This lack of choice in such materials is not, of course, a problem, except for the small percentage of books whose dimensions

Reprinted from National Micrographics Association, *Proceedings,* vol. 18 (1969), pp. 270-275, by permission of the publisher. © 1969 by NMA.

are so large as to preclude conventional shelving or for the dictionary which is large and heavy enough to require a bookstand.

Librarians have been coping with such problems for so long that they no longer are problems. Now, however, micro-publishing is a major factor in the library and the lack of choices is almost complete. *The New York Times,* a major micrographic publication, is available only in 35mm roll film. If the library needs the *Times,* 35mm film it will be. ERIC materials may be purchased conventionally printed or on microfiche. Assuming the microform is purchased, and it usually is, it will be fiche, and it will conform to the formats which ERIC chooses—not the format the librarian might choose. The Nineteenth Century British Sessional Papers are available only in a Microprint edition; if the library needs the Sessional Papers, Microprint sides it must be. As you know, Microprint is the trademark of Readex Microprint Corporation for ink-on-paper micrographic materials.

Is there really any wonder that the librarian feels locked in and frustrated? Should we be surprised that we keep hearing the request, plaintive at times, from Librarians, for standardization among the micro-publishers? Of course not, but standardization is really not likely to come, any more than it has come in conventionally printed materials. Aside from the economies of the situation, new developments in both the microform and in retrieval requirements and methods will keep the pot boiling for a long time.

The librarian's problem is simply that he must be able to provide always a means of viewing and often a means of producing hard copy from the microforms in the library's holdings. Any substantial library must today have a multiplicity of viewers and reader-printers. And perhaps more difficult, the equipment often will be operated by the untrained library user. There is ample basis for librarians thinking that this is no way to run a library.

Yet, run it they must and, as it affects each of us, it is necessary to understand fully the problems which face those in the library world who must come to grips with micrographics.

The problems vary—there is really no typical library—and the methods of handling the problems also vary. In order to understand something of the situation today I would like first to describe to you the operation of three libraries as they deal with hard copy print-out from their microform collections. Recognize that these three libraries are deeply committed to micro-publishing. I said that there is no typical library, and surely these are not, but they do represent a segment of the library world which is leading the movement toward greater use of microforms.

The Information Retrieval and Dissemination Center of Levittown is an unconventional library—its patrons never visit the library at all. Established this year under a Title III federal grant, the Center serves the Levittown, Long Island Public School System. It operates from the premises of the Levittown

Public Library which is a participant in the Nassau County Library System along with 51 other libraries. The mission of this establishment is to supply source materials for study to the secondary schools of Levittown on request. The direct holdings of the Center are all microforms, mostly of periodicals. Most of the materials are in 35mm roll film with some microfiche. A substantial collection of Microprint sides is available through the Nassau Library System and additional film from the public library and the Nassau System is available. In all, approximately 5,000 reels of microfilm, some microfiche, and 140,000 Microprint sides are readily available.

Any of the 475 teachers in the secondary schools may request materials for their 9,000 students. In addition, 2,500 10th and 12th grade students may make direct requests. The Center staff of five will research the topic, print-out appropriate materials, and usually within two to three days, supply the documents to the requestor. Single copies are supplied unless a teacher has requested multiple copies for class use. No charges are assessed.

The Center works with Microprint sides, positive and negative film and microfiche. Equipment includes a Dennison-Readex Enlarger-Printer, 2 Filmac 400B Reader-Printers, a Xerox print-out device and two Copia II photocopiers. The Filmac units are basically used for negative film and fiche in order to assure that the hard copy print-out will be positive. The Dennison-Readex machine is used for Microprint sides and positive fiche and the Xerox for positive film. The Copia units are used to produce multiple copy from the print-out when required and are also used for one-to-one copying of eye-legible materials.

Approximately 30,000 documents have been disseminated in the first six months of the program. What is probably most significant about the operation is that as far as Raymond Turgeon, the Director of the Center knows, the program is unique. Whether future centers will operate in the same manner and with the same equipment requirements is speculative, but more operations of this kind will be along and their problems will be similar.

Syracuse University Libraries serve a student body of 20,000 and faculty and staff of over 5,000. A major facility, the libraries house more than 1,300,000 books, periodicals and pamphlets. Holdings, including microforms, manuscripts, recordings and similar non-book materials, total about 15,000,000 items. The microform holdings include 17,000 reels of film, 111,000 microfiche, nearly 800,000 Microprint sides and a relatively small amount of Microcards. The material is located in appropriate sections of the Library: Documents, Periodicals, etc. Viewers are grouped in one room to which the patrons carry the microform. Because the main library building utilizes carefully monitored check points at each exit, no restrictions on movement of library materials within the building are imposed. Should a patron require hard copy from the microform, he carries it to the Copy Service desk and, while he waits, an operator produces the hard copy. If necessary, the patron moves into the equipment area to aid the operator in locating the precise pages required. The charge is 10 cents per copy. The Library also handles requests for hard copy print-out from industry in the Syracuse area as well as requests through an interlibrary loan system.

At present, the Copy Service group operates with a Dennison-Readex Enlarger-Printer and a Xerox for all hard copy print-out. The Group also provides one-to-one copies of conventionally printed materials using Xerox equipment. It should be noted that the present building was occupied in 1907 and that a new library structure is under construction. When opened in 1971, it is likely that the operation of the Copy Service group will change markedly.

East Stroudsburg State College, located in Pennsylvania's Pocono Mountains, is perhaps typical of the rapidly growing colleges in the nation. An undergraduate student body of 2,300 is projected to reach 7,500 in the next decade. In the past nine years, the library's book budget has increased from $8,000 to $275,000. And while in a relatively new facility, money has been appropriated for a new library building and planning is well along toward construction. Perhaps atypical, however, is the approach of Library Director Russell Emele to microforms. Approximately 20 percent of the library's book budget is allotted to microform materials. With holdings of 150,000 volumes of conventional books, the library has 150,000 unitized microforms, mostly microfiche and Microprint sides, and 18,000 reels of microfilm.

Microforms are stored in the open stack area, both in conventional cabinets as well as in special boxes which are shelved with the books and periodicals. If for example, the library holds the first ten volumes of a periodical in microfilm and the remaining issues in conventional form, the film is boxed and shelved with the later bound volumes. All microforms are accessible to the patrons. Approximately twelve viewers are located along two walls of the stack area along with print-out equipment. At present the library owns a coin-operated Dennison-Readex Enlarger-Printer, a Filmac 100 and a Filmac 200. This equipment is used by the patron who receives instruction from the staff upon request. A ten cent charge is made per copy. Future equipment will all be coin-operated.

Requests from other libraries for hard copy are handled by the staff. Such requests come from both other elements of the State University System and from private college libraries. Substantial print-requirements from the 197-member faculty are also handled by the library. Much of this material is required for personal research. At times these requirements have become burdensome because of the tendency of some faculty members to by-pass the use of viewers completely and to request hard copy of a complete book or periodical. The library tries to discourage this tendency.

The design of a micrographic system for library use is a complex problem.

As with many information systems, much of the storage is seldom used. Location of the desired material is particularly difficult in many instances because much of the effort is involved in breaking new ground. For example, nineteenth century periodicals, for the most part, are not indexed. The micrographic system for such materials must make it as easy as possible to scan the publication for the item of interest. Once located, the viewing equipment should be of such quality as to discourage the indiscriminate production of hard copy. But the hard copy must readily be available when needed.

Many other elements of the library system need to be considered. Library security, for example, has always been a problem with hard-bound books, but few thefts of micropublications have been reported. With the more general availability of viewers, some librarians have started to be concerned. After all, there is hardly anything easier to slip into a pocket than a 4'' x 6'' microfiche. Indeed, one librarian, not at all in jest, viewed with considerable alarm the prospect of an inexpensive viewer simply because he felt that thefts of micrographic materials would increase. Keeping equipment prices high is surely not a real answer to the security problem, but we must find out what the answers are; and the answers will be different in different situations.

The subject today is hard copy. However, it is impossible to talk about hard copy in libraries without considering that we are really talking about a group of micrographic systems which are imposed on a more traditional library system. With regard to the hard copy equipment itself then, there is a constant requirement; the ability to generate hard copy from an increasingly broad spectrum of microforms using equipment which is designed with the total library environment and operational requirements in mind. We must also remember that simplicity of operation and minimal maintenance requirements are, perhaps, even more critical in the library than in many other applications.

There are more than 27,000 libraries in the United States and Canada. By no means all of these are potential users of hard copy print-out equipment; indeed many do not, and probably will not in the near future, have any microforms in their collections. But, there are more than 3,000 university, college and junior college libraries and there are nearly 5,000 public libraries with book budgets above $25,000 per year. In addition, there are in the United States more than 17,000 public school libraries at all levels having full-time librarians.

The potential for microforms in the library world is obviously large. Yet many librarians are frustrated by the problems which seem to sprout endlessly as they attempt to find a way to use these materials effectively. Many experiment and innovate while working with the micropublishers and equipment suppliers. Many others, probably a majority, hold back to the extent to which they can, awaiting the millenium of standardization of form and equipment perfection. The size of the second group will shrink only at a rate proportional to the effort which we in the micrographic industry expend in understanding the problems of the library world and in dealing creatively with these problems.

I will not attempt, because I must fail, to tell you in what manner micrographics ultimately will take their place in the library. Hard copy print-out will be vitally important—we know that already. But from this period of experimentation and innovation many different answers will emerge. We really have no choice; if effective microform systems are to emerge they will do so only if we in the micrographics industry supply the leadership.

REDUCTION WITHOUT TEARS:A PRIMER ON COM (COMPUTER OUTPUT MICROFILM), AN ALTERNATIVE TO COMPUTER PRINTOUT

by Carl M. Spaulding, *Council on Library Resources, Inc.*

The Line Printers

The earliest electronic computers were designed to deal with mathematical problems which required rather small amounts of data input and generated relatively little output. Consequently the heavy-duty typewriters used for input/output functions on those computers served satisfactorily. However, as business and industry began to use computers for what quickly became known as data processing, much faster printers were developed to handle large volume output of lists, reports, invoices, statements, and checks. These high speed printers are usually called line printers, because they print a line at a time, or impact printers, because they print by means of many small hammers which drive paper and ribbon against embossed alphanumeric characters.

Line printers have not evolved much since their development in the 1950s and early '60s, particularly with regard to speed. Although the sight of a line printer churning out copy at the rate of a thousand lines a minute gives the layman an impression of furious speed, line printers are often bottlenecks in computer systems. Their rates of operation—typically 1,000 to 3,000 characters a second—are entirely inadequate for dealing efficiently with information streams from the computer at a rate of 100,000 or more characters a second.

Reprinted from *American Libraries,* vol. 7, no. 7 (July-August 1976), pp. 468-9, by permission of the author.

COM Comes In

One answer to the need for higher-speed computer printout was provided by Stromberg Carlson in 1956, when that company unveiled its Model 100 computer output microfilmer, a device which converted electronic signals to characters on microfilm. This was the first of what we now call COM (Computer Ouput Microfilm) recorders. Acceptance of COM grew slowly until the early '70s, when sales and the number of applications began to increase rapidly. In 1969 there were approximately 500 COM recorders in the U.S.; now one COM equipment manufacturer has more than 1,000 machines in the field.

How COM Works

In brief, a COM recorder consists of an automatic microfilm camera which rapidly films an electronic display of alphanumeric characters. The electronic signals which control the camera and define the characters on the display may come directly from an electronic computer (this type of operaton is called "on-line"), but more often the COM recorder is "driven" by signals read from a magnetic tape. The tape is written by a computer and then physically transported from the computer site to the location of the COM recorder (called "off-line").

There are several kinds of electronic displays used with the various proprietary COM recorders. The most common is similar to a television receiver picture tube, but textual information rather than animated scenes is projected on the COM screen. Because there is so little mechanical motion in these essentially electro-optical machines, they operate at relatively high speeds. Generally, the higher the price of the recorder, the greater the speed. New COM recorders, running almost silently, record from 10,000 to 50,000 lines of text a minute—in sharp contrast with the noise and fury of impact printers thrashing out text at 500 to 1,500 lines a minute.

Among the other electronic mechanisms for imaging characters on COM film are: 1) arrays of light-emitting diodes similar to those used on electronic wrist watches and pocket calculators; and 2) sharply focused electron or laser beams which "write" directly on the film.

COM recorders exist for making 35mm film but most COM output is 16mm film or 105mm by 148mm (4 × 6 inch) microfiche. A number of reduction ratios are available: 24x and 48x (the two most common), 42x, and even 72x.*

*It is not technically correct to denote reduction ratios by the symbol "x". However, popular usage of x for denoting both magnification and reduction ratios has brought about its acceptance for all but the most precise usage.

The difference between the information capacity of a 24x microform and one of higher reduction ratio is quite significant. For example, a 24x microfiche has about one fourth as many images as a 48x microfiche. This means that up to 420 pages are recorded on a 48x microfiche.

Advantages of COM

In addition to its high operating speed COM has these desirable characteristics:

1.   The enormous reduction in cost, weight, and bulk of a COM publication as compared with a paper one is a vital factor in many applications as when a large number of copies of a lengthy document must be disseminated by mail.

2.   COM recorders can incorporate "forms-overlay" slides or superimpose the image of a preprinted form on textual information being recorded on film. These overlay slides can be quicky changed between jobs. Because line printers do not have an equivalent feature, a supply of many different forms must be kept on hand. Coupled with the need to stock multiple-copy forms of several types, this can be a sizable logistics problem for a computer center.

3.   Rerunning a job because of operational errors or equipment malfunction is expensive and time-consuming with an impact printer, but is inexpensive and can be quicky done with a COM recorder.

4.   Line printers can print a maximum of only six to eight copies at a time; and, as the number of copies increases, the quality of the bottom copies deteriorates. On the other hand, any number of high-quality copies of COM film or fiche can be made immediately after production of the original or at a later time. The cost of copies is very low. For example, duplicate fiche typically cost from 10 to 20 cents each depending upon quantity and type of film stock.

5.   Since the COM media are physically small, it is practical to store large numbers of master films or fiche for reference or on-demand duplication at a later date.

6.   The number of different characters which can be printed by a line printer is strictly limited by its essentially mechanical nature; the larger the number of characters in a set, the slower the speed. Because COM images are derived from electronic displays, it has been possible to build COM recorders capable of projecting virtually any set of characters, regardless of their number or the complexity of their shapes. While such recorders are in the minority, they do exist in several places around the country.

COM's Limitations

It should not be inferred from this list of virtues that COM film is suitable as a replacement for computer printout in all instances. For example, COM obviously cannot be used for printing checks, address labels, or other items which must be read by the unaided eye. In general, COM microfilms, like conventionally produced film and fiche, are unsuitable when the cost of the necessary reading machines cannot be justified or when physical circumstances preclude their efficient use. Furthermore, COM microforms cannot be annotated, nor in most cases can a user refer back and forth between two or more microforms as he can with print materials.

COM and the Library

A sizable number of libraries have converted their catalogs from card and book format to COM format. The growing acceptance of COM catalogs is demonstrated by the fact that two companies with considerable experience in marketing bibliographic products are now selling sophisticated, motorized reading machines designed specifically for COM catalogs on 16mm film. Conversion to microform can be particularly attractive to libraries with computer-generated book catalogs requiring frequent cumulation and reissuing. The list of institutions that have developed or are developing COM catalogs is growing rapidly, and includes the Baltimore County Public Library and the libraries at Northern Virginia Community College, the Georgia Institute of Technology, the University of British Columbia, and the University of Toronto.

COM is also being used to turn out products such as union lists of holdings, authority files, patron files and on-order lists.

Micropublishing With COM

A few months ago, the Library of Congress and a group of cooperating libraries completed a successful test of the utility and acceptability of several microform versions of the eighth edition of the *Library of Congress Subject Headings*. By publishing on microforms (some of which were COM-generated and some of which were produced by filming computer printout sheets, thus simulating COM), LC was able to distribute the *Subject Headings* text months before the printed version was available. Building on this success, LC plans, with approval of the GPO, to publish soon a cumulated COM edition of the

Register of Additional Locations. It is important to realize that both of these innovative micropublication projects are possible because of the existence of large machine-readable data bases created by the MARC Development Office.

We can expect that other important micropublications will be extracted from LC's machine-readable data bases, particularly the MARC records, and be made available to libraries in general. Furthermore, there are several other large-scale library automation programs (such as OCLC) with associated files of machine-readable records. These files total millions of bibliographic records from which it seems quite likely that a variety of catalogs, bibliographies, and related listings will be micropublished.

A COMPUTER OUTPUT MICROFILM SERIALS LIST FOR PATRON USE

by **William Saffady,** *Wayne State University, Detroit, Michigan*
[Presently at SUNY, School of Library Science, Albany, N.Y.]

As a marriage of dynamic information-handling technologies, Computer Output Microfilm (COM) is a systems tool of potentially great significance to librarians. Several libraries have reported successful COM applications initiated within the last few years. The two most recent—Fischer's description of four COM-generated reports used by the Los Angeles Public Libraries and Bolef's account of a COM book catalog at the Washington University School of Medicine Library—stress the time, space, and cost savings so frequently reported in analyses of the advantages of COM[1, 2]. This article describes the substitution of microfilm for paper as the computer output medium in one of the most common library automation applications, a serials holdings list intended for use by library patrons. It is interesting that, at a time when librarians are insisting on the importance of patron acceptance of technological innovation, the recent literature reports COM applications intended solely for staff use. Bolef, in fact, lists staff rather than patron use among the characteristics of potentially successful library COM applications. The report that follows suggests, however, that careful attention to the selection of an appropriate microformat and viewing equipment can successfully extend the effectiveness of COM to include patron-use library automation applications.

Reprinted from *Journal of Library Automation*, vol. 7, no. 4 (December, 1974), pp. 263-266, by permission of the author.

The Application

The *Union List of Serials in the Wayne State University Libraries* is a computer-generated alphabetical listing, by title, of serials held by the Wayne State University library system and some biomedical libraries in the Detroit metropolitan area. Sullivan describes it as "informative in purpose and conventional in method."[3] As with many similar applications, serials holdings were automated in order to unify and disseminate hitherto separate, local records. The list is primarily a location device, giving for each title the location within the library system and information on the holdings at each location. It is updated monthly, the July 1974 issue totalling 1,431 pages. In paper form, twenty copies produced on an IBM 1403 line printer using four-ply carbon-interleaved forms were distributed for use throughout the library system.

The list shares some of the characteristics that have marked other successful COM applications.[4] It consists of many pages and has a sizeable distribution. Quick retrieval of information is essential. Use is for reference rather than reading. There is no need to annotate the list and no need for the paper copies, although the latter requirement would not rule out the use of COM for this particular application. Patrons simply consult the list to determine whether the library's holdings include a particular serial and then proceed to the indicated location. It is interesting that serials holdings lists, long recognized as an excellent introductory library automation application, should also prove an excellent first application for COM.

Complexities of format and viewing equipment selection aside, the conversion of output from paper to microfilm presented no problems. Since the Wayne State University Computing and Data Processing Center does not have COM capability, the University Libraries, after careful consideration of several vendors, contracted with the Mark Larwood Company, a microfilm service bureau equipped with a Gould Beta COM 700L recorder. The Beta COM is a CRT-type COM recorder with an uppercase and lowercase character set, forms-overlay capability, proportional spacing, underlining, superscripts, subscripts, italics, and a universal camera capable of producing 16, 35, 70, and 105mm microformats at several reduction ratios. A decisive factor in the selection of this particular vendor was the Beta COM's dedicated PDP-8/L minicomputer that enables the COM recorder to accept an IBM 1403 print tape, thereby greatly simplifying conversion and eliminating the expense of reprogramming.

Microformat Selection

As Ballou notes, discussions of COM have tended to concentrate more on the computer than on micrographics, but for a patron-use COM application the selection of an appropriate microformat is of the greatest importance.[5] However, there has been an unfortunate emphasis placed, both in the literature of micrographics and by vendors, on microfiche, the format now dominating the industry, especially in COM applications. Such emphasis ignores the fundamental rule of systems design, that form follows function. Each of the microformats has strengths and weaknesses that must be analyzed with reference to the application at hand. For a patron-use, COM-generated serials holdings list, ease of use with a minimum of patron film handling is a paramount consideration. Microfiche is clearly unsuitable for a list of over 1,400 pages. Even at 42× reduction, the patron would be forced to choose from among seven fiches, each containing 208 pages. The difficulties of handling and loading, combined with library staff involvement in a program of user instruction, make fiche an unattractive choice.

Instead the relatively large size of the holdings list suggests that one of the 16mm roll formats offers the best prospects of containing present size and future growth within a single microform. The disadvantages of the conventional 16mm open spool—the necessity of threading film onto a take-up reel before viewing—can be minimized by using a magazine-type film housing. The popular cartridge format eliminates much handling, but cartridge readers are very expensive, necessitating a considerable investment where many readers are required. Even with the cartridge, it is still possible for a patron to unwind the film from the take-up reel, necessitating rethreading before viewing. Fortunately, microfilm cassettes overcome this difficulty. Unlike the cartridge format, 16mm cassettes feature self-contained supply and take-up reels. The film cannot be completely unwound from the take-up reel and the cassette can be removed from the viewer at any time without rewinding. Patron film handling is virtually eliminated. The cassette format has proven very popular with British libraries where it has been used with satisfactory results in COM applications.[6]

Viewing Equipment

Success in format choice is contingent on the selection of appropriate viewing equipment. As Larkworthy and Brown point out, the best viewer for patron-use COM applications is one that can easily be operated by the least mechanically inclined person.[7] Fortunately, cassette viewers, while limited in number, tend to be very easy to operate. The viewer chosen for use with the *Union List of Serials*, the Memorex 1644 Autoviewer, features a simple control panel, fixed 24× reduction, easily operated focus and scan knobs, motorized film drive for high-speed searching, and a manual hand control for more precise image positioning. The screen measures eleven by fourteen inches in size, with sufficient brightness for comfortable ambient light viewing. Other cassette viewers examined, however satisfactory they might be in other respects, failed to meet the peculiar requirements of this particular application.

Discussion

Since its introduction in April 1974, the COM-generated *Union List of Serials in the Wayne State University Libraries* has enjoyed a satisfactory reception. Patrons have learned to consult the COM list with little difficulty. The selection of an appropriate microformat and easily operated viewing equipment have kept staff involvement in patron instruction to a minimum. There appears to be no reason for limiting potential library COM applications to those used primarily or solely by staff members. Given the severity of the current paper shortage, the consequent rise in paper prices and serious questions about the availability of paper at any price, COM merits serious consideration as an alternative output medium for the widest range of library automation applications.

References

1. Mary L. Fischer, "The Use of COM at the Los Angeles Public Library," *The Journal of Micrographics* 6:205-10 (May 1973).

2. Doris Bolef, "Computer-Output Microfilm," *Special Libraries* 65:169-75 (April 1974).

3. Howard A. Sullivan, "Metropolitan Detroit's Network: Wayne State University Library's Serials Automation Project," *Medical Library Association Bulletin* 56:269-71 (July 1968).

4. See, for example, *Auerbach on Computer Output Microfilm* (Princeton: Auerbach Publishers, 1972), pp. 1-10.

5. Hubbard W. Ballou, "Microform Technology," in Carlos Cuadra, ed., *Annual Review of Information Science and Technology*, v.8 (Washington, D.C.: American Society for Information Science, 1973), p.139.

6. D. R. G. Buckle and Thomas French, "The Application of Microform to Manual and Machine Readable Catalogues," *Program* 6:187-203 (July 1972).

7. Graham Larkworthy and Cyril Brown, "Library Catalogs on Microfilm," *Library Association Record* 73:231-32 (Dec. 1971).

COMPUTER OUTPUT MICROFILM EVALUATION

by Elizabeth Pan, *Computer Applications Section, New York State Library*

The Computer Output Microfilm experiment was undertaken to allow the Library to explore an alternate method of producing multiple copies of computer printout.

As a result of this experiment the library has concluded that:

1. Microfilm display met all the library's information requirements as successfully as conventional computer printout.
2. There was good user acceptance, and most users found microfilm superior in convenience and speed of retrieval.
3. There were no serious technical problems in the production or use of microfilm.
4. Use of COM resulted in a significant cost reduction ($5,973.00 in a 6-month period) over conventional computer printout.
5. COM has demonstrated potential as a format for distributing information about State Library serials holdings to other libraries.
6. Utilization of microfilm resulted in the projected reduction in the computer operations schedule and other related off-line operations.

Introduction

The purpose of this report is to make available the results of an evaluation of the Computer Output Microfilm experiment at the end of 4 months of a

Reprinted from Elizabeth Pan, "Computer Output Microfilm Evaluation," *New York State Library Automated Serials Control System* (1974), pp. 103-116.

proposed 6-month operation. Sufficient information has been gathered at this point for an evaluation which will enable the library to make recommendations as to the success of the use of COM before the contract expires. If favorable, it will be possible to continue operations without a break in service.

Problems

1. One of the stated objectives of the automated serials system is to make current information about State Library serials holdings available at a number of points in the library, resulting in savings in staff time and in improved reader service. It was also an objective of the system to produce this information in a form which could be distributed to the customers of the library elsewhere in the state. This information could update and replace serials holdings lists published by the State Library in 1953 and 1967. The library presently requires 10 copies of existing reports and approximately 1,000 will be needed for statewide distribution. It is this demand that necessitates the examination of alternate methods of producing multiple copies.

2. The library computer output requirements now exceed the 1 million page mark per year. This volume of output, coupled with the library's need for multiple copies (10) of existing reports places the Division of Electronic Data Processing in the position of being a producer of paper output at very high cost, which results in inefficiency of EDP operations. At the present time, the computer can only print five legible copies at one time, and the additional five copies require a separate print run. This causes several inefficiencies in operations, one of which is the use of a high speed computer for low speed output which in turn produces an extremely high cost per copy output.

Solutions

There are six generally used methods of producing multiple copies of computer generated reports:

1. High speed xeroxing of computer printout.
2. Repeated runs on computer printers using manifold forms (which is the existing method now being used).
3. Offset duplication from a master generated by computer printer.
4. Microfilming computer printout.
5. COM recording device to enlarger to offset duplication for paper copies.
6. COM recording device to microfilm.

The methods are listed in order of descending cost from the high of $3.50 per 10 copies of 100 pages each for the xeroxing method down to $.25 per 10 copies of 100 pages each for the COM microfilm. The difference in cost between the existing method now used and the COM microfilm is substantial, and, when taken into consideration with other factors such as availability of service, the length of time it takes to provide the service and convenience of use indicates that COM could possibly be the solution to the library's multi-copy problem.

Implementation

The following objectives of the study were established and reflect the intentions of the library and the Division of EDP:

Library:

1. Evaluation of a less expensive method (microfilm) for producing quantities of eye-readable output.
2. Gaining increased knowledge of problems of using library indexes and catalogs on microfilm, including an evaluation of the effectiveness of use by patrons and staff.
3. Identification of any need for improved techniques in microfilm indexing.
4. Establishment of acceptable standards of quality for COM reproduction and development of specification for microfilm readers that are best for COM use in libraries.
5. Evaluation of COM as a method for statewide dissemination of bibliographic information.

EDP:

1. Progress toward elimination of third shift operations. (Currently the Division of EDP is making a major effort in this direction.)
2. A more efficient computer operation, reducing the use of the computer solely as a printer.
3. Knowledge to be gained by programmers in preparing tapes for COM.
4. Experience with the potentials of COM for future consideration of COM devices in-house.

In order to realize immediate benefits from the experiment, it was decided to eliminate the extra print run that produced five copies of the information list and the retrospective holdings list. These were to be produced on microfilm and microfilm readers installed in those locations that would no longer receive computer printout. The areas decided upon were selected so that they represented a cross section of the entire library operation and had a high level of use of serials information. The locations were the General Reference Library, Interlibrary Loan, Legislative Reference Library, Periodical Section, and Cataloging.

Specifications describing the service to be performed and the number of microfilm readers required were sent to six COM service bureaus. The bids were reviewed and a contract awarded to FINSERV Computing Corporation. The contract called for the production of five copies of the serials information list for a period of 26 weeks, and five copies of the Retrospective Holdings List to be produced three times during the 26-week period. Also, five microfilm readers were to be provided. The operating schedule called for pickup by FINSERV on Wednesday morning at 9 a.m. and delivery by FINSERV on Thursday morning at 9 a.m. This has been maintained for four months with no problems whatsoever.

It was the responsibility of the Division of EDP to provide a magnetic tape that contained the serials information, and one that contained the retrospective holdings list. A problem of compatibility between the Education Department's CDC 3300 and FINSERV's IBM 360 Model 50 was encountered, resulting in the inability of the IBM 360 to read the magnetic tapes. This was resolved and no further problems concerning the technical aspects of the experiment developed.

One week prior to installation of the readers and microfilm, a general session for library staff was held to demonstrate the readers. The readers were installed the same time the first microfilm copies of the serials information list were distributed, and brief instructions on the operation of the reader were given to key personnel. The status of the experiment has not been altered since it began four months ago, and no changes are anticipated before conclusion two months from now.

Results

After four months of operation, the experiment has allowed the library and EDP to realize their goals with the exception of distributing the microfilm on a statewide basis. However, reels of microfilm containing the serials retrospective holdings list are available for distribution to interested libraries. The Division of Library Development has been alerted to this.

Observations

User Response

Response from the users in the selected sections has been extremely favorable. Interviews with operators and with section heads indicated that the microfilm reader was preferred over the computer printed list. The following comments pertaining to the comparison of the printout vs. the microfilm and reader are typical of those received:

1. Microfilm speeded activities considerably, cut time almost in half.
2. Microfilm is more convenient because cartridges can be handled easier than the heavier printouts.
3. Microfilm is much cleaner to use than printouts (no carbon mess).
4. Microfilm is physically easier to use than printouts (less fatigue from long batch searches).
5. Microfilm eliminates changing the binders each week.

A similar study by Yale University indicates that our responses parallel those reported in their findings.

Indexing

To facilitate searching, a simple method of indexing was devised. The computer tape generated for microfilming contains a series of 10 blank pages for every 100 pages of information. When advancing the microfilm in the viewer, the blank pages appear as a break in the pattern on the screen. A computer-generated index, which accompanies each microfilm cartridge, shows the numbered sections and the title that begins each section. This allows the operator to locate the section he is in and the number of the section that contains his title. The operator would then count the breaks in pattern until he arrives at the section containing his title. The operator would then scan at slower speeds. The index allows the operator to advance rapidly to a generalized area, and eliminates a stop-and-go search.

During the four months period, little or no use was made of the index. The majority of the users felt that the stop-and-go method coupled with a knowledge of approximately how long they would have to advance to a section was much faster than the index procedure. The Yale study previously mentioned also concluded that speed of retrieval of microfilm was comparable if not faster than the computer printed list. They further indicated that bar-coding was a successful method of indexing.

Readers

The evaluation of the Memorex readers was based on the criteria provided in "The Selection of a Microfilm Reader," *Library Technology Reports* (November 1968):

Size of format (16mm)	Acceptable
Compatibility between reduction ratio employed in making the film and the magnification of the reader (24:1 reduction - 24:1 magnification)	Acceptable
Size of reader screen (11'' × 14'')	Acceptable
Clarity on screen (sharp edge to edge)	Acceptable
Image rotation (fixed)	Acceptable

Generally speaking, the readers have performed well. Adjustments were required initially, but they have been infrequent and down-time insignificant. None of the readers has required major repairs. The ease of operation and their relatively low cost make them extremely attractive for library operations. The motorized are more popular because of the speed in advancing the film. The cartridges can be removed without rewinding the film, a very desirable feature, particularly if used with code line indexing. Inserting the cartridge turns it on and ejecting the cartridge turns it off. A limitation on the rotation restricts the reader to cine mode. Readers with rotation can accommodate both cine and comic modes.* This does not appear to be a critical factor at the present time.

The microfilm readers used during this experiment were two Memorex 1642 manual crank, and three Memorex 1643 motorized. Both models featured snaploading, no threading, no rewinding necessary for removing cassettes, and adjustable screen illumination. Listed below are some of the characteristics of the readers:

Screen	11" high - 14" wide, neutral tint, reversible glossy or matte finish.
Magnification	Fixed at 24x.
Lamp	Quartz halogen—for constant illumination during life of bulb. Fan for lamp and optical system coding.
Image	Full size (11" × 14") image on screen when viewing, 90 fixed image rotation.

---

*Cine mode - same as movie film: one frame below the other; comic mode - same as comic strip: frames are side by side

Film	Uses 16mm film in 100-foot roll or Memorex cassette form.
Film Drive	1642-manual; 1643-motorized.
Physical Dimensions	18″ × 16″ × 16″.

COM Recorders

The Memorex 1603 recorder utilizes fiber optics for converting digital signals to alphanumerics. Though cheaper and simpler than other methods such as electronic beam recording, it does not produce the sharpest image.

Microfilm Quality

The overall quality of the microfilm has been acceptable. At the beginning, it was felt that the characters were not as well defined as they could have been. Particularly, the right side of each frame was of poorer quality than the center of the left side. Improvements were made by adjusting the COM recording device and utilization of a better quality microfilm. At no time was the quality so poor that the films were not acceptable.

Advantages

1. Printing at computer tape speeds.
2. Retrieval coding placed on records as created to provide indexing.
3. Smaller records storage.
4. Reduced cost of supplies and materials.
5. Microfilm does not require decollating, bursting, or binding.

Disadvantages

1. Requires high cost COM device making in-house use not feasible at the present time (overcome by out-of-house COM).
2. Requires viewers to display information.
3. Use of printout affords random access capability while microfilm cartridges require sequential scanning of film.
4. Microfilm is "24 hours older" than the printouts. Production of microfilm requires processing after printout could have been produced.

Conclusions

1. The COM experiment has provided conclusive evidence that microfilm can be used as a realistic and less expensive method of disseminating information in the library.
2. Multiple copies on microfilm can be produced for considerably less money than other methods.
3. There is no significant objection by the user using the microfilm and reader instead of computer printouts.
4. Bar graph indexing might speed up the present search operation.
5. Simplicity in reader operation is a desirable feature for microfilm readers.
6. Distribution by mail is more practicable for microfilm than for the computer printout.

EXPERIMENTS WITH MICROFICHE IN AN ACADEMIC LIBRARY

by **Charles H. Stevens,** *Massachusetts Institute of Technology, Cambridge, Massachusetts.*

The M.I.T. Engineering Library has been designated as the model library for the experiments being carried out by Project Intrex (Information Transfer Experiments). The Intrex program, formulated at a conference in 1965, is directed toward the functional design of new library services and toward finding solutions to the pressing problems of large research libraries. User satisfaction with information services provided is central to the experimental program of the Project as it is carried on in the library.

Two major experiments are underway and work with users has begun. In the augmented catalog experiments library users interact through remote consoles with a computer-stored library catalog of papers, articles, reports, and books. Experiments deal with the feasibility of the system components, scaling problems, but chiefly with the usefulness of the search techniques and the results it provides to a variety of patrons. In the text access experiments, library users encounter microfiche in two ways.

Remote display terminals provide users with the opportunity to read the full text of any of the items cataloged in the augmented catalog. Over 10,000 items—mostly journal articles—have been filmed and stored in a pair of modified Houston-Fearless card retrievers. Page images selected remotely are transmitted over a coaxial cable link to the remote consoles. Selection and transmission time is less than ten seconds for the first page requested and less

Reprinted from National Micrographics Association, *Proceedings of the Annual Conference,* vol. 19 (1970), pp. 165-166, by permission of the National Micrographics Association. © 1970 by NMA.

than four seconds for sequential pages following the first. Image clarity is good and users may improve readability by selecting for display any of nine page segments desired. In another mode of operation users can select film copy of the material displayed. The film copy is generated and produced remotely through automatic equipment and the user receives a jacketed 35mm film strip for use. Users may obtain paper copies from the film copy or use the film in ordinary microfilm readers. Intrex experiments are measuring user preference for display copy, film copy, or hard copy.

In a separate but coordinate experiment library users are offered guaranteed access to a large collection of theses, government reports, and other materials on microfiche. Users request fiche at a service desk and copies are furnished for use and retention. Intrex is measuring user acceptance of film copies as a function of delivery time and expense.

Physical preparation of the Engineering Library space for the experiments has involved planning for both the traditional operations and for operations that utilize the new technology of computers, communications, microphotography, and reprography.

PRACTICAL ASPECTS OF OPERATING A MICROFICHE PROGRAM FOR REPORT LITERATURE

by Paul J. Nelson, *IBM Corporation, Armonk, New York*

The IBM Technical Information Retrieval Center (ITIRC) began operations in 1964 as a company-wide internal system for the dissemination and retrieval of technical literature, both internal and external. Its customers are the scientific and technical people everywhere in the corporation. It is based on a set of computer programs, called TEXT-PAC, that use a "normal text" searching technique.

One immediate result of any current awareness system is a demand for copies of the documents announced. When ITIRC was starting on a relatively small scale, this need was met adequately by the company's technical libraries. But as the user population grew into thousands the volume of input increased; the demand for hard copies became a serious problem, straining the available library resources.

A microfilm program had been in operation for some time, using 16mm cartridges and reels, and a substantial reference file of documents on film existed at the major IBM libraries. However, it was impossible to supply individuals with microfilm copies, and slow and costly to print hard copies on demand in the volume required. Since the basic need was for individual copies (reproducible unit records), we reasoned that documents on microfiche cards would be convenient units to handle—easy to mass-distribute and file, simple to reproduce on demand, and feasible to blow back on semi-automatic equip-

Reprinted from National Micrographics Association, *Proceedings of the Annual Conference,* vol. 19 (1970), pp. 165-166, by permission of the National Micrographics Association. © 1970 by NMA.

ment at reasonable cost. The acceptability of microforms to our users was an unknown factor, but we were encouraged by the success of other organizations.

Initial System Design

Filming one document per microfiche card preserved the unit record concept and made it easy to create computer listings that contained all the title information necessary for each document. Film production, distribution, and filing were based on the ITIRC accession number assigned to each item—a simple sequential number identifying year, data base, and order of receipt. The standard distribution for each batch of microfiche comprised over 40 sets to nearly all major IBM libraries, plus master files to ITIRC in Armonk and our European satellite at La Gaude, France for reproducing fiche and making printed copies. Our current awareness response cards were redesigned so the user could order either microfiche or full-size copy by simply punching out a Port-a-Punch chip and mailing back the card. For equipment, we selected a small diazo copying unit to reproduce microfiche on demand. Also, because we knew many users would not have viewers available, we needed a way to produce full-size copy on demand from the microfiche. We chose a semi-automatic step-and-repeat machine that can print up to 500-600 pages of dry silver copy per hour.

Early Activity

In the beginning we expected a heavy demand for printed copies, with a relatively light flow of microfiche requests. What actually happened was almost the reverse. In the first few months of operation (starting in late 1966), the ratio of microfiche to hard copy requests ran nearly 4 to 1, and it has remained near this ever since. Much of this surprising early acceptance was due to the fact that our users had already been exposed to other internal microfiche activities. A large volume of IBM System/360 documentation was being distributed on microfiche and used extensively at many locations.

User Acceptance

In three years over 150,000 microfiche requests were filled by ITIRC, compared to less than 40,000 requests received for printed copy. Of course, these figures do not include a considerable amount of activity in the IBM libraries—

references to the microfiche files, and document requests handled locally. Another measure of acceptance is that in 1969 nearly 3000 of the 4000 profiled users in the system requested microfiche copies during the year.

The 150,000 microfiche cards sent out are the equivalent of supplying over five million printed pages, reproduced *on demand, not* with economical mass printing techniques (the random nature of the requests would normally mean using office copiers). Also, our microfiche turn-around is much faster than that for hard copies. Add to this the difference between the cost of packaging and mailing 30 to 40 printed pages and that for a single film card, and the savings are impressive.

The Library Files

More than 43,000 technical documents are now in the ITIRC collection in microfiche form, with another 30,000 older items on 16mm film. Over 1000 new documents are being added each month. This entire collection is available for instant reference at all the major IBM technical libraries. The value of these files is increased by the fact that much of the IBM literature is informally published at a department or project level. Thus many of the libraries would have great difficulty in assembling the same collection in printed form on their own. As for space savings, the library microfilm file amounts to nearly three million pages of information. It's the equivalent of 130 five-drawer file cabinets stuffed with documents—but it's contained in less than three card files.

Program Refinements

When we decided that the users had grown accustomed to microforms and would accept small inconveniences, we began a cost reduction effort. Certain classes of documents were uniformly brief and could be grouped together. These we filmed five per card, one document per row, with only a code number to identify each one in the title area. Issues of various IBM journals were filmed as single units, run together, even though there are many articles on different subjects. The user could look up articles on the contents page, or browse through the issue. Lengthy symposia and proceedings were also filmed as single units, with articles separated by eye-legible target pages. The subject matter was quite homogeneous, and users were likely to look for more than one item on the card. These shortcuts met no significant use resistance, and we reduced filming and distribution costs substantially.

The Problem of User Resistance

Although overall acceptance has been good, we do have user complaints about microforms. Reports on microfiche cannot always be circulated to others readily. The user cannot make notes on or underline the text as he reads. Intensive study at a viewer is tedious to many. And most professionals do their technical reading at home. Although there are logical answers to these complaints, in terms of cost and availability, they constitute a problem area that we in the microform business should continue to attack.

Future Developments

It seems probable that new hardware and techniques plus growing acceptance of microforms will result in broader applications. ITIRC is a computer-based system and we distribute a large volume of computer print-out, so it appears inevitable that we will expand our use of COM techniques. The many thousands of abstracts printed on cards and sent to users each week amount to a sizeable bulk of printing and mailing. As the system grows, we will have to find an acceptable way to replace this method—with COM, or terminal access, or both. In another field, numerous publishing groups all over IBM write and issue many kinds of technical publications. Getting them involved with microfilm at the source would be a big job of coordination and persuasion, but could pay off in reduced printing costs and faster announcement and distribution.

Has It All Been Worthwhile?

The answer hinges on our concept of the "value of information." If we can say it is worthwhile to tell thousands of professional people about the existence of information pertinent and useful to them, then we can say that supplying the complete details on request is an absolute necessity. Hence the microfiche program has been worthwhile—first, because it has cost less than conventional means of distribution, and second, because without it we would not have been able to get the job done effectively.

A MICROFORM COOPERATIVE FOR ST. LOUIS AREA SECONDARY SCHOOLS AND PUBLIC LIBRARIES: (An ESEA Title III, P.L. 89-10, Planning Project)

by **Richard S. Halsey,** *Director of Learning Resources, School District of University City, Missouri*

In December 1966, the School District of University City, Missouri, was awarded a grant to plan a pilot *Secondary Schools-Public Libraries Microform Cooperative* for the storage, retrieval, and dissemination of a comprehensive collection of magazines, newspapers, pamphlets, dissertations, and other educational materials in microformats which would be maintained in a central depository. This paper will cover the following areas:

A. The origin of the cooperative idea and accomplishments of the initial planning year (May, 1966 - December, 1967).
B. The objectives and design of the three year operational prototype (May, 1968 - April, 1971).
C. The problem that we have encountered and still see ahead of'us.
D. Expectations of expansion (May, 1971 - 1980).

Project Origin

The Title III program of the Elementary and Secondary Education Act, called PACE (Projects to Advance Creativity in Education) is designed especially to

Reprinted from National Micrographics Association, *Proceedings of the Annual Conference,* vol. 17 (1968), pp. 21-30, by permission of the National Micrographics Association. © 1968 by NMA.

grant school districts an opportunity to look for imaginative solutions to educational problems. PACE seeks to (a) encourage the acceptance of innovations; (b) demonstrate worthwhile innovations in educational practice through exemplary programs; (c) supplement existing programs and facilities. The local school district is invited to step into a fresh region in order to better solve present problems. . . . We hope that this venture will provide an arena for the creative joining of technologists, educators, librarians, and administrators in common cause against a debilitating library shortcoming.

In the St. Louis area, secondary school and university libraries are having a difficult time hanging on to the curricular comet's tail. J. Lloyd Trump has stated that as soon as the student reaches high school he should be involved in depth studies for three-quarters of his time and the independent research in the classroom and/or schools' learning resource centers should take up approximately sixty percent of the school week. Contemporary libraries are being built to seat a minimum of thirty percent of their schools' student populations. Indeed, B. Frank Brown has had the temerity to insist that the library be made as large as the gym. This thrust is pressuring librarians to expand their collections and services so that they can accommodate active learner involvement, so that they can encourage unrestricted dialogues, discussion, interplay, and intrinsic motivation. The space, the philosophy, the technology are moving quickly; the collections and staffs are not. Lack of accessibility to twentieth century periodical literature has become a major concern of secondary school and public librarians. The content, contemporaneity, the informal appeal of the magazine as an information carrier are universally acknowledged. Today's superior library collections are well stocked with recent (less than five years old!) periodical literature. But the endemic and critical question persists—How can one house, maintain and circulate older issues of magazines and newspapers? Local school and public librarians have not been able to assume the necessary space, money and maintenance commitments contingent to investment in these highly desirable materials. Library support of the social sciences and humanities regions in secondary school curricula has been aborted because of the obstacles between students and this literature.

Pre-1962 social, political, scientific and cultural developments and happenings are most vitally reflected in the magazines and newspapers of the time. This literature is practically nonexistent in the local area secondary school and medium sized public libraries. In the School District of University City, the secondary school student cannot properly confront the exponentially expanding avalanche of serial and monographic publications. The superior teacher, respecting human and collection limitations, must assign students to an inadequate purview of prescribed monographic items. This exercise in stultification and spoon feeding is antithetical to the independent study emphasis endorsed by most sensitive educators. This project's primary aim will be the enrichment and extension of resource holdings and the minimization of information access delays.

Accomplishments of the Planning Year

During the planning year, four planning committees have coordinated in the creation of the operational proposal:

1. A librarians' advisory group (a) recommended the "starter," serials collection for the depository; (b) worked on interlibrary loan, distribution, availability policies; and (c) molded the proposal so that its objectives and realization should be consonant with and supportive of typical library practice.
2. An administrative liaison recommended political parameters for the overall structure, publicity approaches, individual member responsibilities, evaluation procedures.
3. A technical advisor, Robert N. Yeager (the project's associate director), considered facsimile and image transmission, storage, and retrieval devices, discrete components, total systems responsibility options proposed by industry.
4. A legal consultant interpreted copyright and patent laws as they might affect the project's structure and services.
5. Teachers, students, and local citizens generated ideas that helped us anticipate user modes and needs.

Three Year Operational Prototype Design

The prototype operation description that follows is the result of these five way deliberations. We agreed that the system should fulfill several basic requirements:

A. The collection should contain complete runs from 1964 going back to the beginning of publication of all serials selected by the librarians' advisory group.
B. Any title should be simultaneously accessible to all patrons.
C. The system should allow equally quick access to all patrons.
D. A patron should be able to browse any title in the collection and receive a hard or microfilm copy if needed.

In order to function in this manner, we sensed that the central depository should include (a) a file containing the collection in microformat, (b) a computer, (c) a file access mechanism, (d) image-scanning devices, and (e) image storage and transmission facilities. We recognized the computer would be a prime element, in that it would receive document requests, access the files, control image recovery and transmission, evalute system use patterns, and help us determine collection development and membership fee rates.

The retrieval or file access mechanism would select the requested article from the file, move it to an image-scanning device which would accept and suspend the information in buffer (or temporary) storage. The information bit would immediately revert to the file and be available for transmission to other patrons, giving the initial requester the illusion and convenience of unique access. Page movements, magnification and positional changes would occur at buffer storage and the information would be transmitted to the remote site user terminal via coaxial cable or similar means.

The user terminal would consist of a keyboard (voice telephone in the first stage of the project) for requests plus a television monitor for display. We anticipated that the terminal keyboard mechanism would later accept cards to identify the patron, his affiliation and privileges, the priority of his request, and record the transaction for evaluation purposes. The user would request and scan a projected, combined Wilson index (e.g. Education—Readers Guide— Social Sciences and Humanities Index) for author-title-subject coverages, identify desired citations, and request viewings after marking down the proper file address information. If he should need copies of displayed items, he could request a printout. At a central and supervised point in the remote site library or school building, facsimile transmission equipment would be activated. Unless copyright and/or patron privilege restrictions should apply, he could pick up his copy to use in the library or at home as a handy reference. Teachers and students might also have the facsimile transferred to an overhead transparency for classroom presentation. To facilitate convenience and ease the way for future developments, recent issues (1965-present) of large bulk, high demand items, e.g. *The New York Times* and *Congressional Record*, would be held in microformat, along with supportive readers and reader/printers, at this and the other satellite locations.

In summary, back in September of 1967, this was what we anticipated by May, 1971. In October, 1967, as a prospective ESEA Title III project applicant, we decided to recommend to the U.S. Office of Education a solution that would also conform to the following conditions:

A. The system or components suppliers should demonstrate an awareness of and rapport with secondary school and public library user modes and requirements.

B. Preference would be given to those bidders that could assume total system responsibility without compromising discrete component quality. The prospect of hovering over and harassing a herd of contractors did not appeal to us.

C. Because we were (1) dealing with service institutions that are directly responsible to, funded, and controlled by the public and (2) planning this project under the Title III aegis, we looked for the promise of maximum visibility in terms of student and public service at the earliest time possible. For example, combined image and facsimile transmission of requested serial articles (an unprecedented capability in the public schools) between our depository and only two remote sites by March of 1969 would constitute a dramatic, politically and educationally valuable first step.

D. We sought clear evidence of long-term thinking and anticipation of potential pitfalls in terms of faulty evolution of the project design. For example, the future input of other than serial literature should be considered and contingent provisions for its inclusion and retrieval anticipated. The system should remain flexible, capable of growth, able to evolve as membership and service demands would increase.

E. The hierarchy of system needs should be sensed and respected. The degree to which the initial collection requirements would be fulfilled would be a critical factor in our selection of a data base supplier. If we had to choose between (1) a vendor with a compatible, unitized format and ten percent of our title requirements already filmed, and (2) a vendor with an incompatible format and ninety percent of our initial collection on hand, we would be forced to prefer vendor (2), especially if format conversion seemed praticable. *Or* if we had to choose between a delivery delay or a compromise on image resolution requirements, we would prefer to wait. We did not want to get caught in a discovery—disappointment—disengagement cycle.

At the same time we considered the foregoing "ideal" system, we felt compelled to prepare an alternative perch further down the evolutionary ladder. In this "simple" system, monographic and serial publications in microfilm, microfiche, microfile, microprint, aperture card format would be jointly selected and centrally stored. Duplicate microforms plus enlargement prints could be prepared at the headquarters library and requested information distributed by traditional means such as the mail, vehicular transport, student motorcyclists, helicopters, or even carrier pigeons. These would replace facsimile transmission. Though admittedly not a dramatically innovative approach, the reduction of space, mutilation, weight, loss, duplicative purchasing, maintenance and circulation control costs would still be irrefutable advantages.

Administrative Design

Our administrative design would apply to both the sophisticated and simple solutions. Three associate directors would deal with *Technics, Content,* and *Function,* respectively. The *Content* development group would include subject literature specialists and teachers representing libraries and schools in the constituency. The *Function* group would be most important as it would propel, invigorate and promote the system. The public relations, statistics, research and development, teacher training experts would ensure realization of potential applications and constantly seek out new ways in which to utilize cooperative services. These people would not originate from within the prototype constituency, thereby ensuring the project directorship an input of relatively objective evaluations and recommendations. The *Technics* people would include independent and industrially based consultants. The three directors would be staff members of the applicant organization, the School District of University City.

Problems

During our planning year, our problems were fourfold. We had to carefully consider (a) local politics and personalities, (b) the relative flexibility and strength of the area schools' curricular designs, (c) the kinds of disenchantment with technology, and (d) the economics of future self-sufficiency.

We were lucky. In St. Louis County and especially within our prototype network of three public school districts, a parochial school, an independent private school, and a public library, we encountered a spirit of magnanimous and shared concern. This was in marked contrast to the bickering and internecine battling that had decimated similar cooperative attempts at the college and university level.

The similarities in curricular emphasis and library needs surfaced after we examined the two hundred title desiderata list that had been developed by our six network librarians. This core collection was derived from responses received from ninety-one school and public libraries in the St. Louis area. A massive dosage of 1,150 serial titles was quickly and democratically reduced to two-hundred premium quality, highly sought items. Also, the librarians were associated with schools that had adopted flexible scheduling and recently launched library expansion programs. The librarians were also conversant with and not fearful of the impending hardware.

We did encounter general disappointment with microform readers and reader-printers that confirmed William Hawken's* harsh critiques of currently

*See *Micrographics Equipment Review,* 1976 -   . (Westport, CT: Microform Review Inc.).

available equipment. And the welter of discarded computerized ventures, . . .that had faltered and fallen because of enemic, uninspired, and insufficient software, had led many recent converts to revert to "damn the machine" thinking. SDI systems, as applied to public education, were reputed to be ineffective instruments that had gagged clients with a disproportionately high ratio of misses, trash, and passes as against hits. The limits of human reading speed, available scanning times, and patience to sit it out, plus an unwieldy and unalluring literature have adversely affected this ratio. This is the prime reasons why we had emphasized that image *browsing*, not facsimile reception, should be the essential user mode in our project.

As we developed our proposal, we attempted to structure it so that its implementation would place a minimum financial burden upon the institutional participants.

We convinced the board of the public library that their service capability would be significantly upgraded. They could enrich their collection with vastly reduced parallel outlays of funds and space. Replacement monies could be diverted to other budget areas as the microtextual resources would be free from traditional wear, tear, and decay. Professional personnel and pages could be released for other functions than mending, fetching, and circulating periodicals. As the construction of the new public library in an urban renewal area had just been approved, their board was eager to participate in a design that could be emulated and copied in other metropolitan communities throughout the United States. Morever, because of its convenient location and collection strengths, this library had built up an excellent cross section of patronage, including the general public, Washington University and other academic faculty and students, plus resident secondary school students. Most important, this library had been designated as reference headquarters for a network of seven St. Louis County public libraries and the two cooperative arrangements would obviously benefit each other.

The secondary school libraries were all contemplating extended schedules into the evening, weekend, and summer. The parochial, private, and two of the three public secondary schools anticipated serving as local community summer research centers which would host students from other local jurisdictions whose libraries were not available.

The microform cooperative computer would be shared and used for various school district administrative chores such as fiscal accounting, purchasing control, central processing of instruction materials, and statistical evaluation of student progress.

Future Expectations

In the future, the participants foresaw an immense literature store that would be absorbed, analyzed, encoded, preserved, and made conveniently available. Manuscripts, rare books, patents, handbills, proclamations; curricular supportive packages in the investigative, appreciative, and social sciences literatures; administrative records, blueprints, student transcripts, locally and commercially produced materials could be integrated into the central holdings. The educational levels served would ultimately stretch from the elementary to university graduate school. Computer-assisted instruction, the development of repetitive curricular service packages, the enrichment of library collections could lead to an individualization of instruction that cannot today even be fully imagined. The school libraries could be used year-round, from early morning to late night, and homework, which actively discriminates against already disadvantaged kids that have unconducive home study environments, could be abolished.

By the late 1970's, the cooperative constituency would include most of the secondary schools and public libraries within one fourth mile radius of St. Louis. One sees beyond this to the utilization of lasers, the complete digital storage of all needed materials, and the development of increasingly complex and humanized questing—response—guidance capabilities. There is also the probability that patrons could have access to other than local university resources via cross-country networks. At this point, the library as the communications core of the school, would have fully metamorphosed from its traditional stance of inefficient passivity to its proper role as active and fully responsive catalyst, servant and informant.

APPENDIX

Excerpts from **A National Periodicals Center: Technical Development Plan**

Prepared by the **Council on Library Resources** at the request of the **Library of Congress**

Summary

In the fall of 1977, the Library of Congress (LC) asked the Council on Library Resources (CLR) to prepare a technical development plan for a U.S. national periodicals center (NPC). The need for such a facility was formalized by the National Commission on Libraries and Information Science in its 1977 document *Effective Access to Periodical Literature*, which recommended that the Library of Congress assume responsibility for developing, managing, and operating the center. LC and the Council agreed that the plan would be prepared in such a way that it could be used by the Library or any other agency prepared to assume responsibility for the creation of a major periodicals facility. Several foundations contributed to the cost of preparing the plan, which was completed in August 1978.

The goal of the National Periodicals Center is to improve access to periodical literature for libraries and thus to individuals using libraries. The intent of the plan is to assure that the NPC will accomplish this goal (1) by providing an efficient, reliable, and responsive document delivery system for periodical material, (2) by working effectively with the publishing community, and (3) by helping to shape a national library system through NPC operating policies and procedures.

Reprinted from *A National Periodicals Center: Technical Development Plan* (Washington, DC: 1978), pp. ix-xv, 32, 41-2, 51-3, 60-2, 79-84, 85-9 and 92-3.

The specific operating objectives of the NPC follow logically from this goal and are:

1. To provide a reliable method of access to a comprehensive collection of periodical literature.
2. To reduce the overall costs of acquiring periodical material by interlibrary loan (ILL).
3. To reduce the time required to obtain requested material.
4. To assure that for any document delivered through the NPC, all required copyright fees and obligations will have been paid.
5. To act, under appropriate conditions, as a distribution agent for publishers.
6. To provide libraries with additional options as they establish their own collection development and maintenance policies.
7. To promote the development of local and regional resource sharing.
8. To contribute to the preservation of periodical material.
9. To provide a base for the development of new and imaginative publication stategies.
10. To provide a working example of a national access service that might be extended to other categories of materials.

These operating objectives make it clear that the National Periodicals Center will link in new ways the collection and distribution functions of libaries with the distribution activities of at least some kinds of publishing. The center's governance must also be approached in a new, imaginative way, one that will assure close coordination between its operation and the development of other national programs (e.g., bibliographic control, communications, etc.) that together will constitute the foundation of a national library and information system. But the present library and information structure of the nation is composed of many discrete components. This fact, together with the complexity of library functions and the dispersion of library services, makes it unlikely that there will or should be a formal prescriptive centralized agency charged with operating a single hierarchical national library system.

What seems required, as the plan suggests, is a two-tier structure at the national level. This would involve the creation of a new organization with authority and funds to establish and coordinate the few fundamental programs that are best handled at the national level. The separate governing bodies of these programs would constitute the second tier. The first operating responsibility of a coordinating agency (a kind of national library board) would be to establish the periodicals center whose governing body would be responsible to the board through an executive director's office. This proposed governance structure, though an integral part of the plan, does not predetermine the specifications for the NPC itself.

As proposed in the plan, the National Periodicals Center will contain a centralized collection of periodical literature directly accessible to libraries throughout the nation. Initially projected at 36,000 titles, subscriptions for which would be generated as quickly as possible, the collection would continue to grow prospectively (adding more titles) and retrospectively (acquiring back files) according to an established strategy and in as timely a fashion as possible. All subject areas would be included with the initial exception of clinical medicine. Eventually the collection may number in excess of 60,000 current titles, but it will never contain all of the estimated 200,000 currently published periodicals. Though few of those not held by the NPC are likely to be in great demand, it is planned that the NPC would provide access to many of them through a system of referral libraries. The NPC will contract with referral libraries to provide service to requesting libraries that desire specific titles not in the NPC collection. All requests would be channeled through the NPC to assure uniformity of procedure and to provide the means to monitor system performance.

The NPC will develop and make available a finding tool to identify the titles and holdings to which the NPC can provide access. The finding tool will be organized by key title and International Standard Serial Number (ISSN) and will include titles available from both the NPC collection and the referral system libraries. For the first several years libraries will be required to request only material listed in the tool. Each order will have to include the ISSN or an NPC-generated substitute number and the key title.

The most important question for many librarians is which libraries will be able to go directly to the NPC. After a break-in period for the NPC and after the collection is well established, all libraries will have access. The decision to use the NPC or alternatives such as local, state, or regional resources should be based upon the actual dollar cost of the transaction and the reliability of access or delivery.

Several fiscal considerations will aid libraries in making these sorts of decisions. First, any library or consortium wishing to have access to the NPC will be required to establish a deposit account equal to the institution's expected request activity for one month, with some arbitrary minimum required. Second, a price schedule will be established that takes into account the copyright status of a particular item, its age, and the frequency with which it is requested. All NPC transactions will require the payment of a fee, part of which will be used to defray any legally required copyright fees or possible sales fees. Librarians using the NPC will be assured that for any item received from the center, the appropriate fees will have been paid. This will relieve libraries of some of the requirements established by the CONTU (National Commission on New Technological Uses of Copyrighted Works) guidelines.

Quite apart from the procedures to comply with the copyright legislation, it is imperative in the interest of effective scholarly communication that the NPC develop effective relationships with the publishing community. It is proposed that the NPC become a kind of service and fulfillment outlet for at least some publishers. Thus the NPC might provide a back-issue service (probably in microform), an article sales service (so long as the article remained protected by copyright), an outlet for on-demand publishing, and/or a source for the full text material published in synoptic form. All of these services would generate some income for publishers while providing the access to material that library users need. It is recognized that a relationship of this kind may tend to modify traditional information production and/or distribution functions. But each element of the information chain has a unique and valuable role to play in serving the needs of inquiring scholars, and each must be supportive of the other.

The internal structure of the NPC will be organized to achieve fast internal processing so that requests will be filled within twenty-four hours of receipt. Much of the most active collection will be stored in microfiche because this is the fastest request fulfillment mode of storage. Other less heavily used materials will be stored in their original form and retrieved for photoduplication. Most requests will be filled with paper photocopy; microfiche will also be available at an enticing discount.

Requests will be handled in as simple and direct a manner as possible. Libraries will be encouraged to transmit requests to the NPC in electronic form so they can be received, verified, and forwarded to the fill site by machine. For items not in the NPC collection, the machine system will batch and transmit requests on a scheduled basis to appropriate referral sites. ''Picking slips'' for requests to be filled at the NPC will be automatically generated and directed to the appropriate storage site for fulfillment. After copies are made they will be packaged – probably in a plastic wrapper with the picking slip now used as the address label. First-class mail will be used to send most requests. Other rapid transport systems (air freight/express) may be used to move mail into the U.S. Postal Service's one-day delivery zones. Some institutions with the capacity to receive materials via facsimile transmission may choose to pay the higher costs of this delivery mechanism.

A peripheral but nonetheless vital objective of the NPC is to participate in the national preservation program. Consequently, all materials received by the center will be handled in such a way as to assure access for as long as possible. The costs of preservation are high but must be assumed as part of the effort to provide effective access to periodical literature in perpetuity.

The cost of the NPC must eventually be covered by a combination of federal subsidy and user fees. However, the start-up costs must be fully subsidized for at least the first three years. First-year costs will be $3,750,000 and will cover the basic organization of the NPC and the first-year collection costs. Second-year costs rise to $4,850,000 and cover the costs of the second-year collection development effort as well as the costs of bringing all systems up to an operational level. Third-year costs rise to $5,450,000 and are only minimally offset by transaction receipts. This year is a break-in year for all operating systems and as such is expected to produce only marginal levels of activity and therefore income. Beyond the fourth year (basic operating cost $1,925,000) costs will become more directly related to the level of request fulfillment activity. However, in order to achieve full preservation microfilming, a $3,000,000 subsidy is required in year four. The annual subsidy should then decline as request fulfillment activity and income rise in each succeeding year.

The site of the NPC is dependent upon the quality of all relevant and available communications systems, availability of power and other utility services, and an adequate pool of manpower. The plan recommends new construction in order to avoid reducing the efficiency of NPC functions by forcing them into inappropriate spaces. The cost of construction for a building for the NPC should be $5.5 – 6.5 million for 130,000 net square feet. Construction funds should be available during the first year. Construction should proceed fairly rapidly since the building required is a simple modular warehouse facility. The most complicated features of the structure relate to the specific environmental requirements.

Upon acceptance of the technical development plan three separate kinds of activity should proceed simultaneously. The first involves the establishment of a legal basis and funding support for a national library board, the first operating responsibility of which would be the National Periodicals Center. Second, a senior executive with necessary secretarial and travel support should be charged with the responsibility of explaining the plan for an NPC to the library, publishing, and scholarly communities. This individual would provide a focus for the comments and suggestions that are bound to be generated by the circulation of the technical development plan. The third activity, which will require establishing a core of two or three permanent NPC staff, is to continue the detailed planning for the NPC, including identification of first-year titles, identification of appropriate back files, identification of any existing computer operating systems that might be appropriate for anticipated NPC activities, and the preparation of specifications for systems that will be required. These are important tasks that would accomplish two things: (1) provide a running start for the NPC operation and (2) demonstrate to the Congress that the library community is serious about and committed to a national periodicals center.

The creation of a national periodicals center will require the cooperative action and support of librarians, information scientists, publishers, politicians, foundation managers, and the eventual NPC staff itself. One thing is clear. Society has everything to gain from an improved capacity to retrieve and use the information generated by its members. A coherent national periodicals program should provide such an improvement. A national periodicals center is the first step.

Access to the NPC

The NPC collection and its bibliographic records will be organized by International Standard Serial Number (ISSN) and/or key titles and libraries will have to use the ISSN/key title in order to request material. The NPC will publish a finding tool containing this information for all titles under NPC control. Although other sources may also provide ISSNs and key titles, the NPC finding tool will list the most current information. It will be issued in microfiche and distributed as often as once per quarter, perhaps more frequently in the early years. When a library establishes a deposit account it will automatically receive a copy of the finding tool. To assure that the most current information is at hand, however, the library will probably want to subscribe to the tool on a continuing basis.

If a request is filled by a referral library it is likely to be filled with paper photocopy. If it is to be filled at the NPC, it can be filled either by paper photocopy or microfiche. As much of the NPC collection as is economically feasible will be kept on microfiche. Requests for material held in microfiche will be filled with a paper photocopy of the requested article unless the requesting library specifically wants a microfiche copy, for which a reduced fee will be charged. Requests for material that the NPC holds in paper form will be filled by paper photocopy for the normal charge. If a request is filled from the microfiche collection, the requesting library will get not only the requested material in paper photocopy but may receive a copy of the fiche as well, since this may be a by-product of the request fulfillment process.

NPC-Publishing Community Relationship

Operating Relationships: NPC and Micropublishers

As often as possible the NPC will attempt to acquire material in microfiche. The NPC will need to establish effective working relationships with the microfilm publishing community. The existence of a national periodicals center should not threaten the economic interests of micropublishers—it should instead actually contribute to micropublisher revenues. As with publishers, one way of assuring this is for the NPC to function as a sales agent for micropublishers.

As a sales agent for micropublishers the NPC will deal in the sale of small portions of published works. These "nuisance" sales are for less than a complete volume—a single article, for instance, or even single issues. In any case, unless specifically authorized by a micropublisher the NPC will avoid sales involving complete volumes or runs. The NPC will concentrate on its primary mission in the nation's emerging information system: to assist in the acquisition of specific pieces of information (usually single articles) for the inquiring library user.

The NPC will require access to materials for which certain micropublishers have exclusive rights granted by contracts with the original publisher. The NPC will honor these arrangements and will be prepared to pay for access to these materials. However, these payments should be based upon actual, and not anticipated, use. Especially during the early years of operation, data on anticipated use may not be reflective of actual future demand. Therefore, to protect the economic interests of the micropublishers as well as those of the NPC, payments must be based upon actual use and upon the fact the NPC may enhance the use of these materials.

Some micropublishers, viewing the NPC as one of its sales agents, may wish to give material to the NPC—or deposit it—in expectation of sales. Materials not covered by micropublisher-publisher contracts might also be given to the NPC in anticipation of sales. In all cases, when the micropublisher owns the copyright or has exclusive microrights to material, NPC transactions involving this material will result, when required, in payments in consideration of these rights.

Since all transactions involving the products of micropublishers will involve duplication, this activity will have to be authorized and considered a sale. For the most part such transactions will involve no more than one fiche. Charges should be developed on a per-fiche use basis.

Because each sale/transaction will carry the NPC processing fee plus a sales charge, it will not be rational for libraries to attempt to build fiche collections by purchasing them from the NPC—the micropublisher can sell the entire back file of a title for much less than the cost of acquiring it through the NPC. Thus the NPC cannot be viewed as a threat to the micropublishers' markets; if anything it is likely to enhance sales activity.

Collection Development

Fulfillment Capacity and Cost

Fulfillment capacity refers to the ability of the NPC to satisfy, based on its collection, a portion of all periodical requests generated in the United States, if most heavily used titles are available in microform, and these are concentrated in the most heavily used 5,000 titles.

Cost estimates suggest that in 1980:

1. Current subscriptions will average $43.00 per year (based on figures from periodical suppliers).
2. Back files in microform will average less than $25.00 per volume or year (based on analysis of microfilm publishers' catalogs).
3. Hard-copy back files will average about $40.00 per volume/year (based on analysis of out-of-print periodical dealer catalogs).

To project the costs of the back files, therefore, it is assumed that 80 percent of the heavily used titles will be available on the open market and that 80 percent of these are in microform. The average cost per volume or year of the back files (80 percent in microform, 20 percent in hard copy) will be $28.00. The total cost for 65,000 volumes or years of back files over five years will then be $1,820,000—or less than $375,000 per year. If back files are all within the first 2,000 titles, the NPC's overall fill capacity will be increased to more than 25 percent.

The cost of current subscriptions for 36,000 titles will be $1,548,000 per year, discounting annual inflation. The NPC will add new subscriptions at a rate of about 4,000 new titles each year. But some titles will cease to be published and by the second and third year the publisher-NPC agreements should begin to make available more nonsubscription material. It is therefore estimated that the NPC will require an average of $1,720,000 per year for the first five years for prospective collecting. When this figure is added to the $375,000 required per year for the purchase of back files, the estimated cost per year for acquisitions becomes $2,095,000.

With the above suggested acquisition rates a 90 percent request fill rate can be achieved if the NPC restricts requests to holdings that are published in a finding tool.

Retrospective Collection Development

As mentioned earlier, during the NPC's first five years there will be a significant attempt to acquire back files for the most heavily requested material. If the collection development budget for these five years averages $2,095,000 per year, as much as $375,000 of it should be allocated for the purchase of back files. Once the NPC is able to fill half of the potential traffic it might receive, the emphasis can be shifted from back files to current subscriptions and the all requests were directed to the NPC. It is not anticipated that all requests will be sent to the NPC. Even so, it is a useful concept since the NPC will be used as a backup for local resources and therefore must collect those titles heavily used in local libraries. To collect prospectively means to obtain new material by subscription or other arrangement as it is published. Retrospective collecting, on the other hand, refers to the acquisition of back files. To assure that the NPC will eventually have the capacity to fill a high percentage of all ILL requests, it must receive on a current basis a broad spectrum of titles. To be most useful to libraries, it must be able to fill at least 50 percent of all ILL requests by the fifth year of operation.

It is proposed that the NPC prospectively collect at least 36,000 titles. Even though after 25 to 30 years the NPC would be able to fill over 90 percent of ILL requests, after five years of such prospective collecting it would have less than a 30 percent fulfillment capacity. To increase its capacity to the desired 50 percent, the NPC must collect retrospectively as well. Obviously the back files of titles most heavily in demand should be collected first to raise the fulfillment capacity as quickly as possible.

Raising the fulfillment capacity quickly in the early years is important to the acceptance of the NPC by the library community. Acceptance will depend not only on the NPC's performance in delivering what it promises within acceptable cost and time parameters but on its overall usefulness as well. That is, how often can a library expect to use the NPC to fill its requests as opposed to other resources? If the NPC collects exclusively in a prospective manner, its fill-rate capacity will be limited to only 7 percent after one year. This is unlikely to stimulate a demand for its services among libraries, which could not use the NPC as often as they might desire. Thus retrospective collecting in the NPC's early years for heavily used items is necessary to increase its overall usefulness to libraries and their users.

For the purpose of producing cost estimates, this plan assumes that the NPC will obtain most periodicals through purchase of subscriptions and back files. While back files of many of the heavily used titles may be available as donations from libraries, especially from those that maintain multiple subscriptions, the NPC cannot count on this initially, nor can it rely on donations from publishers as discussed earlier.

It is estimated that the NPC must collect at least 65,000 volumes of back files in the most heavily used 2,000 titles. If for some reason back files for these titles are not available, the NPC will have to concentrate on the next 3,000-10,000 titles. This latter group of back files will have less impact on the NPC's capacity to fill requests. Further, collecting these back files will increase costs since they are less heavily used and thus more likely to be available only in a more expensive hard-copy form. It is estimated that only half of the 10,000

NPC can then concentrate on expanding its depth of coverage in terms of numbers of titles.

Selection

The emphasis of the retrospective collection development activities must be on the most heavily used titles in order to increase the capacity of the NPC to fill requests. Cost is also a factor. To acquire back files other than those having a relatively heavy demand is expensive since the majority of those titles would probably not be available in the less costly microformats.

Acquisition

There are a number of ways in which back files can be acquired. Among them are:

1. *Donations/Deposits.* While the NPC will purchase the most heavily used titles, it is possible that some of them will be available from libraries holding multiple copies. Early acceptance of the NPC as a reliable institution may increase the amount of material received from this source. If libraries know that they have a reliable source for specific periodicals at a reasonable cost and with a rapid response time, they may be less apprehensive about weeding their collections in order to make room for material with a higher probability of local use. The donation or deposit of back files will contribute to the comprehensive nature of the NPC's collection and thus the capacity of the NPC to respond to ILL requests.

   In the early years before the NPC has assumed a more permanent stature, it will be necessary to create a deposit mechanism that will encourage libraries to donate periodical material to the NPC. This deposit mechanism would assure that, should the NPC fail for whatever reason, the donated titles would be returned to the original donor. The NPC would have the option of converting the material to any other format for its own purposes and would not be under obligation to preserve the original format. It would also have to be agreed that the NPC would be held blameless from any loss resulting from circumstances beyond the control of prudent management practices. Such arrangements might be expected to lead to the donation of substantial amounts of material from libraries all over the country.

It is possible that entire collections may be donated to the NPC. A case in point is the periodical collection of the Center for Research Libraries. In other cases where a university eliminates a department or an entire school closes, collections supporting that activity might also become available. There are other potential sources of collections. Abstracting and indexing services such as Chemical Abstracts have back files of serials that could be added to the NPC. The size and impact of these collections would have to be evaluated.

2. *Publisher Agent.* As mentioned earlier, the NPC will ask cooperating publishers to furnish a single copy of their back files, which the NPC will microfilm, giving one copy of the film to the publishers. The NPC will then provide copies of individual issues to libraries on demand, charging a sales fee, a portion of which would be paid to the publisher. Since many publishers (particularly academic presses) are not normally responsive to back file requests, this might be a useful service for them and a potential source of additional income. The cost of the back files to the NPC would basically be the cost of filming the issues.

3. *Universal Serials and Book Exchange (USBE).* The existence of the NPC will have an impact on the serials operation of the USBE. USBE obtains a significant portion of its issues from the LC discard file. The NPC may absorb a portion of these titles directly from LC. But USBE has other sources and may be extremely useful for filling gaps and for providing limited back files, particularly in the early stages of the development of the NPC collection. Referral libraries may also find USBE useful for completing back files for which they accept referral responsibility.

Preservation

In order to assure continuing availability of periodical literature, it will be necessary for the NPC to provide long-term preservation of that literature against deterioration and damage from all causes including use, abuse, environmental factors, biological agents, fire, flooding, and other disasters. Given such a preservation commitment and because the NPC collection can be expected to grow in breadth and depth as well as, possibly, in type of publication (e.g. monographs), it would be appropriate and logical for the NPC to become a major element of the developing national preservation program.

Materials acquired by the NPC will, from the preservation standpoint, be of two types: those to be retained permanently (or at least for a very long time) and those that are expendable because they can be replaced easily or because they are to be converted to microfiche in the near term. Some materials will be acquired as individual issues, either current or retrospective. Others will be acquired as bound volumes of retrospective issues or in microformat, primarily microfiche. All material will be processed according to type.

Preservation will be accomplished largely through converting to microform those periodicals not originally purchased in that format. However, the capability of converting all hard-copy acquisitions may not exist at the NPC in the early years. By relying on the referral system libraries to preserve those titles that they have agreed to service, the NPC will be relieved initially of the need to collect a high proportion of *all* periodicals and can concentrate instead on collecting those having heavy or moderate use. The referral system will aid the NPC in preserving periodical literature as well as in improving access to it. But as funds become available through a stable subsidy and processing fees from a steadily rising demand, the NPC itself will mount an effort to microfiche every title received.

Material Acquired in Hard Copy

Each hard-copy item will be examined after technical processing to determine whether:

1. It is to be converted to microfiche. Generally this will be done only for current high-demand titles, for oversized materials (over 11¾ inches tall*), or for material that is too deteriorated or fragile to withstand shelving and subsequent handling. Many, but not all, of the items microfilmed will be discarded immediately after filming or relatively shortly thereafter; they will not, therefore, require deacidification.
2. It would suffer significant damage from deacidification treatment.
3. It should be fumigated. This is relatively unlikely except for a limited number of shipments of older retrospective materials.

Each item will be marked to indicate its classification with regard to conversion to microfiche, fumigation, deacidification, and retention period. Those hard-copy items requiring fumigation will be treated in a standard Vacudyne processor with carboxide or an equivalent fumigant before being deacidified. Those items that do not need fumigation will go directly to a deacidification

---

*By limiting the paper copy collection to materials no taller than 11¾ inches, shelving in the NPC stacks can be uniformly spaced with no requirement to adjust them in order to accommodate the taller materials. The savings will be in operations that require relocation of material.

unit, provided that they have not been marked to indicate either susceptibility to damage from processing or that they do not require deacidification because they are not to be retained for an extended period.

After fumigation and/or deacidification, hard-copy materials will be marked to indicate that they have been processed and then will be shelved as explained in the chapter on storage and retrieval. Titles to be retained in paper will not be bound by volume but may be bound as individual issues when demand warrants such treatment.

The storage area for hard-copy materials will meet the following specifications:

1. The temperature will be kept between 55 and 65 degrees Fahrenheit. The temperature will not vary more than five degrees Fahrenheit in a 24-hour period.
2. The relative humidity will be kept between 45 and 55 percent and will not vary by more than 6 percent within a 24-hour period.
3. The air will be dry filtered to eliminate 95 percent of particulate matter, washed with water having a pH of 8.5-9.0, and charcoal filtered to remove oxidants.
4. The lighting will be controlled so as to hold radiation in the ultraviolet portion of the spectrum to a minimum. In those stack areas containing little used materials, lights will be turned off except when employees are actually working there.
5. An automatic fire suppressant system such as Halon 1301 will be incorporated.
6. The NPC site will be selected and the building designed or modified so as to minimize danger of flooding.
7. Stringent good housekeeping procedures will be enforced to preclude damage from dust, spillage, animals, and insects.

Periodically a carefully selected sample of materials in the stacks and microform storage areas will be checked to determine the effectiveness of the preservation techniques in use. A replacement copy will be sought for any item that is badly worn or deteriorated. If replacement is not possible, a film or paper copy will be made of the item.

As funds become available, all materials received by the NPC will be microfilmed in order to assure continuing access to the material. During the early years of the NPC, funds are not likely to be available for total microfilming and so choices must be made. It has been calculated that filling requests from the microfiche file costs less than filling requests from papercopy storage. There is an algorithm based on the frequency of demand and cost of fulfillment that determines when a title should be filmed and when it should be stored as paper copy. Since the decision point is a function of demand, titles should be filmed according to the list, ordered by demand, of titles requested. Filming for purposes of efficiency of response to requests should not be considered a preservation cost but should be attributed to operation. The cost of filming all other titles, though facilitating response times to a degree, should be considered a preservation cost.

Those hard-copy items that are to be filmed rather than stored in their original format should be separated after they are checked in from those items to be stored. After filming, each original will be marked to indicate that it has been filmed. The camera negative will be duplicated by roll-to-roll duplication to produce two printing masters of each fiche. These masters will be cut into separate fiche and retained at the NPC. One will be kept in the active file to be used for generation of hard-copy or distribution fiche as described in the following chapter on reprographics, and the other will be stored locally in a backup file so that it may replace the active file copy if the latter is lost or becomes too worn to make good copies. The backup file will be stored in the same environmentally controlled area as the hard-copy documents. The rolls of camera negatives will be cut into individual microfiche and stored off site in accordance with the then current ANSI (American National Standards Institute) standard for archival storage of silver halide film. Thus camera negatives will be available for making new printing masters if necessary.

Material Acquired in Microform

Microforms acquired by the NPC (as opposed to those produced by it) will be handled and stored in accordance with the future availability of replacement copies, the type of microform (roll film or fiche), the quality of image, and the type of microfilm (silver, diazo, or vesicular). While every effort will be made to acquire only high-quality silver halide microfiche, it is quite likely that some microform acquisitions will be in roll-film format on nonsilver stock. It is also likely that some will be of limited resolution and contrast and of nonarchival quality. Specifically, microform acquisitions will be processed as follows:

1. Silver film, whether camera film or subsequent generation, that has sufficiently good resolution and contrast and is of archival quality will be treated as if it were camera film produced by the NPC (see above).
2. If feasible in terms of image quality and economics, roll-film acquisitions will be photo-optically converted to standard 98-image silver microfiche of archival quality. These fiche will be treated as if they were NPC-produced camera film. Roll film that is not to be converted to

microfiche will be stored in closed containers in an area where the temperature and humidity are moderate and do not fluctuate more than a few degrees or a few percent from day to day.

3. Microform acquisitions for which there is no clear way of obtaining replacements should be duplicated onto silver film regardless of the image quality. The copies will be used for making distribution copies and the original acquisitions will be archivally stored off site.

Reprographics

Without modern reprographic technology, an NPC as projected would not be possible. The majority of articles furnished by the NPC will be in either microfiche or paper photocopy form. The paper photocopy will be produced by office copying machines. Whenever possible material for the NPC collection will be acquired in microfiche. The microfiche will be of the best quality available so that one or more subsequent generations of duplication will be practical.

The following description of the reprographic activities of the NPC briefly touches on the closely allied functions of preservation and of storage and retrieval. These functions are discussed in detail in other chapters of the plan.

Microfiche is the preferred medium for storage, retrieval, and duplication at the NPC because:

1. Microfiche require a minimum of storage space, a compaction of about 95 percent being a commonly accepted index of advantage over paper copy.
2. Properly manufactured, processed, and stored, silver halide microfiche can be expected to have an effective life of hundreds of years.
3. Microfiche can be quickly and inexpensively duplicated or converted to paper form for delivery to requesters.
4. The standard dimensions and small size of microfiche make them relatively easy to store, retrieve, and refile.
5. Duplicate microfiche can be easily and quickly packaged and inexpensively mailed; several hundred pages can be mailed for the minimum first-class postal fee.

Despite these advantages, it may not be possible to use microfiche as the storage format for all NPC materials because it may not be economically feasible to convert little used titles to that medium. Further, some material, such as maps and other scaled items, may not be amenable to reduction. In addition, some retrospective materials may be available only on roll film, which may not be technically or economically feasible to convert to microfiche of good image quality.

For a variety of reasons all items will be available to requesters in paper photocopy form. However, to encourage the use of microfiche and in recognition of its cost advantages, there will be a discount for all materials supplied from the NPC collection on microfiche. In a small percentage of instances it may be necessary to arrange to lend an original periodical issue rather than to make a film or paper copy. This may happen, for example, when color, texture, or some other "noncopiable" characteristic of an original is essential to the user's purpose. If a situation like this can be predicted at the time of acquisition, it will be desirable to acquire two copies of the item and thereby protect the integrity of the collection against the possibility of loss of the item while it is away from the NPC. When it can be determined that an issue or title falls into this special category, it should be so marked during technical processing. An alternative to lending these special items from the NPC collection itself would be to use the referral libraries. The NPC might purchase such items and place them for access purposes in a designated referral library. The NPC would not then have to devise a special circulation system for a small number of items. This approach does not solve the "lost in transit" problem, however.

It is also possible that certain popular or relatively popular titles should be acquired or recorded on color film and either duplicated on color film or fiche or reproduced in color on photographic paper. Alternatively, these special items might be copied from the original using an office copier with color capability, but this is an unlikely possibility. Again, the referral library system might assist in providing access to these special-condition materials, perhaps by lending originals in some instances.

While these special copying services need to be planned, their implementation should proceed in accordance with demand; they should not be made available during the first years of operation.

In-house Production of Microforms

After it has been checked in, all material to be converted to microfiche will be prepared for filming by checking pagination, removing such extraneous matter as staples, cutting the pages apart, smoothing pages, inserting filming targets, and so on. Every batch of material to be filmed will be accompanied by a punched paper tape bearing microfiche header information for each issue in the batch. The tape will be prepared as a part of the check-in process and will be mounted on a reader built into (or electronically linked to) the microfilm camera. Alternatively, header information may be recorded on magnetic tape or disk and be transmitted to the camera from a remote computer site or read in by a unit that is part of the camera. One such improved header generator is expected to be available this year. It will significantly increase the effective speed of the camera for which it has been designed. In a few years it may be possible for the camera operator to initiate the recording of a header on film by means of a mechanism such as a bar code reader, which acts on a label placed on the document during the check-in process. Besides increasing throughput speed, this would increase accuracy and thereby reduce the volume of re-filming.

The cameras used for in-house filming would be of the high-speed automatic, step-and-repeat variety. With the Documate II, for example, a single operator can record more than 2,000 pages an hour by using a variety of automatic page-handling features.

The product of these cameras is silver halide microfiche in continuous rolls. In most instances a periodical issue will be complete on one or two microfiche. There will never be more than one issue on any one fiche. This technique will facilitate storage, retrieval, and duplication. The rolls of exposed film will be processed and then duplicated on silver halide stock using roll-to-roll duplicators. The original roll and one copy will be archivally stored at separate external sites. A second duplicate roll will be cut into separate fiche, which will be put in envelopes and stored at the NPC for quick retrieval. This set will be used for making fiche distribution copies. Fiche-to-fiche duplicators, such as the Datagraphix Model 76, will be used. Paper copies will be made by means of high-speed fiche-to-hard-copy printers, such as the Xerox 970 which is capable of turning out up to 2,000 pages an hour.

If a sales relationship can be developed between the NPC and the publishers of heavily requested titles, multiple copies of the issues of those titles can be made initially and inventoried for quick retrieval and distribution on demand. This will reduce the cost of and the time required for producing a duplicate.

Distribution fiche will be put into fiche envelopes and automatically wrapped along with an address form. Paper copies will be wrapped in the same way and both types of packages dispatched by first class-mail.

Copying from Paper Originals

Much of the NPC collection will be acquired in its original printed form, preferably as individual issues but in some instances as bound volumes. Copies of articles in these periodicals will be made by copying machine. In most instances it will be possible to record two original pages on each sheet of copier paper by utilizing copiers having large platens and lenses that reduce the image by a factor of about .25; that is, the dimensions of the copy are about three-fourths the dimensions of the original. This technique almost halves the cost of copying and greatly reduces postage costs for many items. Further reduction in postage may result if special lightweight paper is used for copying, although at this time such paper causes more jams in copiers than does heavier paper. Two-sided copying will also reduce postage and paper costs.

Some issues and volumes with tight bindings and/or narrow gutters will have to be copied one page at a time using a copier having a book-copying platen. Some volumes in poor physical condition may also have to be copied in this way in order to reduce the risk of damage to the volume. It may even be necessary to copy from especially fragile volumes by microfilming, since repeatedly turning such a volume face down on a copying machine can do much damage, particularly if it is a heavy book. However, because most fragile volumes are relatively old, it is unlikely that there will be much demand for copies from them. Also, because of the NPC's preservation function, these seriously deteriorated items should be converted to microfiche as soon as possible anyway.

Each article photocopied will be physically associated with the requester's address information on the "picking slip" so that the copy, with address on top, can be passed through a packaging machine in preparation for mailing.

Collection Storage and Retrieval

Storage of Microforms

The compaction afforded by the standard dimensions of microfiche makes it possible to store a large collection in a single room of modest dimensions. For example, a year's cumulation of 10,000 periodical titles on fiche can be stored in three to four fiche cabinets, each having approximately the same dimensions as a standard four-drawer filing cabinet. But, for reasons of efficient access, all microfiche printing masters should be kept in powered, rotary storage cabinets arranged so as to be convenient to fiche duplicators located in the same room.

Each fiche will be marked with a unique number and will be filed sequentially according to that number. A diagonal stripe will be marked across the tops of the fiche in each drawer to assist in the prevention of misfiling.

When an issue is recorded on two or more fiche, each will bear the same unique number and an issue sequence designation, e.g., "2 of 3 pp. 96-193." All the fiche making up an issue will be kept in a single envelope.

The retrieval and refiling operation for microfiche will proceed as follows. Using a computer-sequenced list of fiche numbers corresponding to requests addressed to the NPC, a searcher will remove the associated fiche sets and their envelopes from the file, leaving a marker of contrasting color in place of each set. The fiche sets will be carried by the searcher to the operator of a fiche duplicator or fiche-to-paper copier depending on the character of the request. After the item has been copied, the searcher will pick up the masters—still in filing sequence and in their envelopes—and proceed to refile them and remove the markers. When searchers pick up the masters that have been duplicated, they will also deposit for duplication the next batch of fiche that they have pulled in the interim.

If it is feasible in terms of arrangements with the appropriate publishers to make multiple fiche copies of the more popular titles in anticipation of demand, production costs and request fulfillment time will be greatly reduced. At the same time the space requirement for fiche storage will be increased. Should this approach be possible, the printing masters will be stored in rotary files, as detailed above, but the duplicates will be kept in batches, possibly in a pigeonhole arrangement with the unique number marked below each batch. Each fiche set (one issue) will be kept in an envelope in order to keep individual sets together. As an indication of the space required, it is worth noting that pigeonhole storage for fifty copies of eleven issues (one year) of 5,000 titles could be set up in a room about fifty feet square.

It is possible that a small percentage of the working collection will be on role microfilm. This file should be kept on reels in microfilm cabinets in the same area as the microfiche collection. An appropriate number of reader-printers equipped with quick threading take-up reels should be nearby so that plain paper printouts can be made rapidly. No effort will be made to provide film copies of materials held in roll microfilm. Because of the exceptional nature of the procedures required to handle roll microfilm, as little material as possible will be acquired in this format.

CONSER File on COM

CLR has awarded a grant of $23,000 to the National Library of Canada (NLC) to enable NLC to publish bibliographic records produced in the CONSER (Conversion of Serials) project in computer output microfiche (COM). The Library of Congress will undertake the U.S. distribution of the list, known as CONSER/COM.

The CONSER project is a cooperative file-building effort initiated five years ago to develop a national data base of serials records. CLR funded and managed the project using the resources of the 14 North American libraries and the on-line computer facilities of OCLC, Inc. NLC and LC also act as centers of responsibility to authenticate the records contributed by the other participants, thereby ensuring the bibliographic quality of the data base. Although LC has planned to assume CONSER management, fiscal constraints intervened. It was recently announced that the project will remain at OCLC with that organizaton assuming the management role.

Up to now, only those libraries that are part of the OCLC network have had access to the records contained in the CONSER file. With the publication of CONSER/COM, all libraries will have access to the authenticated records, now in excess of 74,000 titles. Pricing policies have as yet to be determined, however.

Reprinted from *CLR Recent Developments*, vol. 6, no. 2 (November 1978).

INDEX

INDEX